CW01461145

READ ME HERE
AND LEAVE ME
FOR
OTHERS TO ENJOY

H.

EX LIBRIS

HECKFIELD
PLACE

Jane Austen: Daddy's Girl

Jane Austen: Daddy's Girl

The Life and Influence of
The Revd George Austen

Zöe Wheddon

Zöe Wheddon

PEN & SWORD
HISTORY

First published in Great Britain in 2024 by
Pen & Sword History
An imprint of Pen & Sword Books Limited
Yorkshire – Philadelphia

Copyright © Zöe Wheddon 2024

ISBN 978 1 39907 112 3

The right of Zöe Wheddon to be identified as
Author of this Work has been asserted by her in accordance
with the Copyright, Designs and Patents Act 1988.

A CIP catalogue record for this book is
available from the British Library

All rights reserved. No part of this book may be reproduced or
transmitted in any form or by any means, electronic or mechanical
including photocopying, recording or by any information storage and
retrieval system, without permission from the Publisher in writing.

Typeset by Mac Style
Printed in the UK by CPI Group (UK) Ltd, Croydon, CR0 4YY.

MIX
Paper | Supporting
responsible forestry
FSC
www.fsc.org
FSC® C013604

Pen & Sword Books Limited incorporates the imprints of After
the Battle, Atlas, Archaeology, Aviation, Discovery, Family History,
Fiction, History, Maritime, Military, Military Classics, Politics,
Select, Transport, True Crime, Air World, Frontline Publishing, Leo
Cooper, Remember When, Seaforth Publishing, The Praetorian Press,
Wharncliffe Local History, Wharncliffe Transport, Wharncliffe True
Crime and White Owl.

For a complete list of Pen & Sword titles please contact

PEN & SWORD BOOKS LIMITED
47 Church Street, Barnsley, South Yorkshire, S70 2AS, England
E-mail: enquiries@pen-and-sword.co.uk
Website: www.pen-and-sword.co.uk
or
PEN AND SWORD BOOKS
1950 Lawrence Rd, Havertown, PA 19083, USA
E-mail: uspen-and-sword@casematepublishers.com
Website: www.penandswordbooks.com

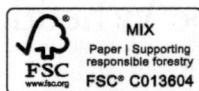

For Mr W – the best Daddy anyone could ever have.

Contents

Foreword

We owe George Austen a debt of gratitude. At a time when only two out of five women were literate, George valued education for his daughters as much as his sons. Jane was educated at home by George, an Oxford graduate who ran a small school from the Steventon rectory, and on two occasions away from home at boarding schools. George encouraged Jane to read, giving her access to his own extensive library of 500 volumes of both classical books and novels. Unlike academics and more traditional readers of the day, novels were of great enjoyment in the Austen family and from a young age, Jane was encouraged to be intellectually curious and creative.

George actively supported Jane's ambition to be a writer. Jane started writing at the age of 12 and read her short and humour-filled stories aloud to the delight of her friends and family. Jane's sister Cassandra recalls her reading excerpts from early iterations of *Sense & Sensibility*, then called *Elinor & Marianne*, when the family lived in Steventon, and of Jane's most famous novel *Pride & Prejudice*, then called *First Impressions*, which was a particular favourite for her listening audience. It was George who, in November 1797, submitted Jane's completed manuscript of *First Impressions* to publisher Thomas Cadell, an act that shows the support George had for his daughter's talent and her dream of becoming an author.

The Watsons was the only unfinished work Jane did not continue to revise or seek to publish when she moved to Chawton. Jane was writing *The Watsons*, the story of a widowed clergyman and his children, when George died from an illness in 1805, and it is thought that the pain of his death prevented her from ever revisiting this work.

As a daddy's girl myself, I know first-hand the importance of a father-daughter relationship and how empowering it is for a girl to know that her father believes in her. As head of the household, George held Jane's fate in his hands. There is no doubt that Jane was born with unrivalled literary talent, but talent alone was not enough for a woman born in the 18th century. Jane's education, the love and encouragement of her father, support of her family, access to books and the provision of paper, quill, and ink, laid the foundations for the course of Jane's life, both literary and personal.

Jane had the courage to refuse an advantageous offer of marriage from Harris Bigg-Wither, whom she did not love; the confidence and skill to rebut a request from the Prince Regent's librarian regarding her next novel; and the tenacity to pursue her literary ambition in earnest. Without George, we wouldn't have the great works of Jane Austen.

This thoughtfully written book gives us a unique insight into the extraordinary life of George Austen, Jane Austen's father (and my fifth great-grandfather), the man who shaped a literary icon.

Caroline Jane Knight
Jane Austen's fifth great-niece
Founder & Chair, Jane Austen Literacy Foundation

Acknowledgements

I
t takes a team to bring a dream to fruition and writing this book has been
a testament to that truth. I am so grateful for the help and support of so
many people in bringing this book into being.

Firstly, I want to thank Catherine Curzon for contacting me on a mission
to 'pay it forward'; her initial belief and encouragement were the beginning of
this journey.

I am so grateful to Jon, Michelle, Laura and all the team at Pen and Sword,
who offered me this opportunity and were always on hand to answer my
questions. Their constant support gave me confidence to continue exploring
and writing.

Thank you to all at Jane Austen's House for their support and kind welcome
every time I visited, including Lizzie Dunford and especially Sophie Reynolds
who helped me so often and in such a friendly way. A huge heartfelt thank
you to the team at Chawton House, Chawton, especially Clio O'Sullivan, Kim
Simpson and Emma Yandle.

I am so grateful to the many experts who gave me their time and expertise,
and provided some very special, once-in-a-lifetime moments along the
way. They include the Reverend Michael Kenning, Rector of St Nicholas'
Church, Steventon (1992–2000), with whom I have had the most interesting
conversations; C Hoare & Co archive, especially Pamela Hunter, Archivist,
who brought out heavy ledgers by the score (I am still in awe of the history
and beautiful surroundings at the bank); Beverley Matthews, School Archivist
at Tonbridge School, who made me feel so welcome and offered every support
– including delicious homemade cakes; and Alexander Lock at the British
Library who showed me Jane Austen's *Juvenilia* notebooks. I had to pinch
myself to believe it was all true.

Thank you to David Rymill and the team at Hampshire Archives for all
the work that they do and the kind interest they took in this project. Thank
you too, to the teams at the Guildhall Library and the National Maritime
Museum Greenwich for all their assistance.

My special thanks to the President and Fellows of St John's College Oxford
and Archivists Michael Riordan and Georgy Kantor. Michael especially has
been endlessly patient, answering all my queries with grace and friendly support.

Thank you to all the individuals and organisations who helped with permissions to use photographs and documents, and all the interesting conversations that we had along the way.

Thank you to the world of Janeites online for their encouraging enthusiasm, especially Rose and Natalie.

Thank you to my colleagues who asked me about what I was doing and didn't wane in their interest despite me talking about it – a lot.

My special thanks to Karrie Brown for her beautiful illustration; she has truly captured the essence of George and Jane's special bond. Also, to Caroline Jane Knight, Jane Austen's fifth great-niece via the line of Edward Knight who is ever poignant to me. I am so honoured to have her write the foreword for this book.

And finally thank you to my own family, Matt, Josh, Becca and Tom for their loving support and patience, and for sharing their academic and technological expertise.

I wanted to tell George's story so much – he is truly an unsung hero, as are all these kind souls and all those who helped me over the finishing line. I will be eternally grateful.

Please note: I have retained the original spellings in all quotations, and I have opted for the eighteenth-century spelling of Tunbridge that Jane Austen would have known. The spelling was changed to Tonbridge in the nineteenth century.

Introduction

No one who had ever seen George Austen in his infancy would have supposed him born to be a hero.[1] Yet the life of Jane Austen's father could well have been the stuff of legend. As they say life is often stranger than fiction and may even imitate art, and so it was for George. His own life's journey had the necessary three distinct parts of the oral folklore or fairy tale of the past. His 'character arc' followed the traditional and celebrated path of the mythological quest.[2] In other words he travelled from zero to hero, from a blighted life as a lowly orphan, through his own forest of challenges and tests, taking on the metaphoric brambles of his life as schoolboy, clergyman, farmer and schoolteacher. His life provides many plot twists to entertain and surprise us along the way. Having cut through these obstacles with the trusty sword of his personal truth – his character and integrity – George arrived in a clearing speckled with sunlight. Against all odds he emerged triumphant, victorious in the last act. A true diamond in the rough, resplendent as a father of his own treasures, his eight happy, positive and cheerful children, gleaming and glittering in his hands. This surgeon's son left a legacy to the world that included, amongst others, eminent clergy, the landed gentry, an admiral and vice-admiral of the Royal Navy and a beloved and celebrated author.

An intriguing man, from the very beginning Jane Austen's father, his history, personality and purpose in life, became the subject of his daughter's acute observational powers. George was someone whom Jane was able to observe up close in every aspect of his daily life and it is his outline I aim to trace further as it seeped into her personality, and at the edges of her stories too. Jane was too conscientious a creator to copy people and events directly into her works; however, as her own brother Francis-William (known in the family as Frank) was happy to point out to an adoring American fan, he did believe he saw traces of himself in the carpentry skills of the talented Captain Hardwick (*Persuasion*).[3] In the same way I believe that Jane etched elements of her father's world and their friendship into her work too. In this book I intend to examine these examples, to turn them over in our hands like a collection of precious coins in a nineteenth-century gentleman's library, to study them more mindfully and to ponder them in more depth. In Jane's writing we see George in fleeting wisps and moments. We catch the sight, sound and scent of him, his roles, his character traits, his tastes, his foibles and his opinions. As well as their shared jokes and experiences, their conversations, contentions and conflicts. In this book we will follow the trail and attempt to catch hold of his coat-tails as he passes us by.

Fathers feature throughout Jane's writing, from her earliest scribblings and 'scraps', as she called them, to her fully-fledged novels.[4] Fathers and, significantly, the consequences of their actions, behaviours and personalities became main characters in many of her hero and heroines' lives, such as in the cases of Mr Bennet (*Pride and Prejudice*), Sir Bertram (*Mansfield Park*), Mr Woodhouse (*Emma*), General Tilney (*Northanger Abbey*) and Sir Elliot (*Persuasion*). They were also sometimes hidden in the wings, performing just slightly off the stage, such as Mr Dashwood (*Sense and Sensibility*), Mr Darcy senior, Mr Lucas and Mr Gardiner (*Pride and Prejudice*), Mr Price (*Mansfield Park*), Mr Weston and Mr John Knightley (*Emma*), Mr Morland (*Northanger Abbey*) and Mr Musgrove (*Persuasion*). Some were even missing from the scene all together, yet their presence was still felt very strongly in the influence they exerted upon the lives of their children, such as the Misters Wickham and Collins (*Pride and Prejudice*), Crawford (*Mansfield Park*), and Hawkins (*Emma*).

Jane's life and novels offer us many routes through which we can trace a little more of her life with the benefit of getting to know her better and gaining a deeper understanding of her work. Fans enjoy exploring the myriad of ways in which we might continue to empathise with her characters, her plots and her narrative voice. I believe that the life of George Austen and his relationship with his youngest daughter is an important one, of great interest and worth to every Jane Austen fan. Her life at home at George's Steventon rectory has often been passed over in one slick stroke of a pen or sweep of a brush, as indeed has her father and the deeper implications of his role in her life. Jane's life in the parsonage from babyhood to age 25 was not that of a 'snow white' shuttered away in the woods or a 'sleeping beauty' held undetected in the forest. It was bright and vibrant, almost magical, and her father as far as can be from the image of a stuffy, sober, dusty and distant cleric.

In this book *Jane Austen: Daddy's Girl*, I wish to debunk the assumptions and myths that have surrounded the Reverend George Austen. I seek to go beyond the rough sketches of a man painted into the shadows of his daughter's life. I dig deeper into the layers and nuances of his experiences in order to provide a true likeness, a portrait. My aim is for us to be able to sit a while and look deeper into his hazel eyes in order to really get to know him.[5] I hope that this will be just as compelling and revealing as it was for Elizabeth Bennet (*Pride and Prejudice*) *that* day at Pemberley when she stood and focused on Mr

Darcy's likeness and at last heard the reliable truth reported of him for the very first time.[6] In following in the footsteps of George's life, I hope to redefine and redraw him in order to introduce him properly to the scene as an important protagonist in Jane's life and not just a one-dimensional figure hiding away in insignificance in the background for an early chapter or two. In drawing a much more representative and detailed picture of a faithful yet fallible father, my aim is to cement a new relationship between him and fans of Jane's work. In turn I hope to draw us closer to Jane Austen and her novels, the very genre that her father loved, and to bring our friendship with her into clearer and dearer focus too.

To write only about the three or four families in a village or place that one knew well was Jane Austen's mantra.[7] She believed sincerely in the need for authenticity in writing and that for an author to be respected and taken seriously, they should write within the realms of what they truly knew. She wanted to depict life in all its layers and chose to do so from her own observational standpoint as a point of principle and personal confidence. From a specifically chosen moment and place in time, Jane set about showing her readers a world they recognised in a way they had never seen it realised before. Jane put her characters and readers at the centre of all the action and reflected thoughts and events from the inside out. What better place to start with the heart of the matter than in the home, a home one might have known, or perhaps only dreamed about or seen in the headlines staring out from the newspaper stand. As the figurehead of that home, the heroine's father was a topic Jane loved to mine again and again, and it was her greatest delight to applaud others who did the same.[8]

Fathers ruled the roost back in the long eighteenth century. Fitting into the patriarchal model provided by Christianity, most families adopted the framework of father as head of the household. As such *he* was secured in an unquestionable position of power and privilege. No matter what the socio-economic background of a family, it was the father who was in control, his wishes that held sway, his opinions that were permitted to dominate – at least in the outside order of things. He had hold of the purse strings and the final word in any decisions made. For better or worse the family followed the direction of his lead. Their fortunes were tied to the integrity, capability and empathy of the father they had inherited. If he had an open or closed mind, was filled with ambition or lethargy, adhered to healthy or unhealthy habits, the fate of the family was still irrevocably in his hands. The father was considered responsible for providing shelter and food for his family and, depending on which social class the household belonged to, dowry or wedding clothes for his daughters and an apprenticeship to a trade for his sons. Subsistence was the minimal expectation but in reality, any type of lifestyle achieved was entirely at the whim, discretion, work ethic and prior wealth of each father. How you fared depended upon the fatherhood lottery ticket of life that you were allotted.

We still see this social model and the frustrations that can arise from it around the world today. Recently global movements and activism have highlighted in more detail the difficulties experienced by different groups of society, held back by the privilege of others. People have begun to educate themselves, and to align with values that protect and assert the rights of these hitherto largely ignored and often actively oppressed sections of society. In all that I have learnt about him, I am struck by how much George Austen was at the same time part of his social system and also set apart from it, by his circumstances and by his own choices. I have found his attitude and practice in educating and supporting his own daughters refreshing and inspirational for the times. In his image I was reminded of Malala Yousafzai's father, Ziauddin, a Pakistani education activist who never faltered or altered the path his own values directed in regard to educating girls and boys, even though the risk to himself and his loved ones was so high. George did not have to face any threat of violence and there was a form of schooling available to girls in the late eighteenth century, but he shared and enacted the same values by extending the opportunities available to all his children, regardless of their gender. He championed his daughters' talents through his attitude and his efforts as equally as he did for his sons at a time when this was not the social norm and neither was there any expectation of it, yet in doing so, he altered their life paths.

In Jane's fiction we see her carefully crafted characters interact with their own fathers, or the memory of them, and see how her pen lingers over the qualities, the essence and, above all, the power of this pivotal relationship in their own life journeys. Here, too, then we shall stop and pause a while and mull over the messages and mysteries of her inclusion of these interactions. Jane evolved each of her characters internally as their own particular, private world revolved around their father's public orbit. The fathers in her writings act as a force, both pushing and pulling at her protagonists, and the significance of these aspects and their outcomes merits further examination. Jane never included anything in her writing by accident and she clearly had a lot to say about both the advantages and disadvantages that one's father could bring into one's life during this period.

Jane's frustrations with a patriarchal society bubble to the surface in her works, and this angle cannot be ignored when reflecting upon the influence of her own father on her life. Like Cervantes' Don Quixote, we saw Catherine Morland in *Northanger Abbey* read too many novels of her preferred genre and suffer in living under such strong influences. She too ended up mixing the unreal with real life in a way that distanced her from reality. She was led, as was Quixote, into a delusion, an 'engaño', and Jane channelled this same spirit into her thoughts about family life and happy ever afters, questioning if they really were compatible with 'modern' life or if they had become a way of living simply forced upon and assumed by women. There are clear elements in her stories of a generational gap, a difference in viewpoint, a 'desengaño' or disillusionment felt by her younger generation, a new realisation and awakening in regard to their reality. We see reflected in her heroines' lives an examination of society's dictation of a woman's lot, and of what her father's generation had decided adult happiness should look like for them. Clearly, Jane felt at odds with her father's and his generation's world view of some topics.

George played a unique role in Jane's story, firstly in regard to the power of the patriarchal position that society had allotted to him and the degree to which this prompted both frustration and bliss in her life. However, this book is also an account of his personal response to life and the approach he developed as an individual to leading his family. Above all this is a fan's eye view, a biography which seeks to illuminate the significance of George's own relationship with himself and his daughter as a catalyst for her imagination and her personal expression of herself through her writing. In this book I seek to examine who George Austen really was, to take the many different facets of his identity, those he claimed as his own and those which others have attributed to him both at the time and ever since. Together we will observe the facts and unravel the fictions about him in order to observe him anew in the context of his role in Jane's life.

As you pull this book down from the shelf and open its pages, may it conjure up a quiet corner of George Austen's Steventon study and may you linger there a while with him and Jane in their happy place.

Chapter One

In the Beginning

We begin our story, and an 'epic' story this truly shall be, in the year 1739. It is February, one of the coldest on record so far. We have to pick our steps gingerly as we make our way through the thick snow and treacherous ice that covers the streets of London. There are not many people in sight as we continue right into the commercial heart of the capital's publishing industry, St Paul's Churchyard. Souls have perished at the hands of these freezing temperatures, and most people are hungry as supplies cannot be brought up the frozen River Thames.[1] It has been this way for many weeks now.

We are following directly in the footsteps of Shakespeare and the early printed editions of his works, treading the same paths that he trod, albeit it 150 years later. We take a turn down Newgate Street. Here, jostling amongst other businesses touting their wares hangs the sign of The Angel and Bible.

Outside, the streets are teaming with the wealthy, well-to-do and well known, fresh from their rambles through Cheapside and on the hunt for the perfect glove, a pair of spectacles, cape cloth and petticoats. Inside, weaving his way amongst the lined shelves, a young 8-year-old boy helps his uncle. Scrabbling in, out, behind and under the counter, he ducks here and there tidying away pamphlets and manuscripts with his small yet nimble hands. In the movement of a moment, he can be seen shimmying up and down the ladder to fetch customer orders before heading out the back to sweep up. The boy's name is George. The hero of this story. Yes, one might even reflect, an unlikely hero. One just like Jane Austen liked to imagine, when she was writing about Catherine Morland or Fanny Price.

George's life so far had not had many happy chapters, and tragedy had recently touched his life once again. He was born over 30 long miles away, in the small market town of Tunbridge, Kent, in the early part of 1731 to his surgeon father, William Austen, and his mother, Rebecca Hampson. The pair had married in the drier, warmer days of 1727. Rebecca, already a widow with a 5-year-old son, William-Hampson Walter, had moved to Tunbridge following her physician husband's death to start a new life near her family, or at least to survive the sadness and loss she had already known.[2] There she had met and married her William.

William had returned to Tunbridge on completion of his indentureship to William Ellis of Woolwich, where he had been learning his craft as an apprentice since 1718; watching and assisting Ellis as he cared, for example, for injured sailors enrolled in the navy.[3] Surgeons often practised the skills of their trade on board a ship, just like the courteous Mr Campbell, (*Mansfield Park*) who served on *The Thrush* which came into dock at Portsmouth just in time for him to visit Fanny Price's brother, another respectable William.[4] However, the quality of training and surgical standards varied greatly between practitioners. There was, as yet, no formal, separate guild for surgeons as there would be by the turn of the new century. Instead, the 'barber-surgeons' were at this time a collective whose very name came to define the delineation of the two ends of the professional spectrum. With a distinction emerging between the two trades as the century progressed, by 1745, the separation of the two types of practitioner acknowledged a universally agreed truth that barbers were to be excluded from undertaking acts of surgery as part of their wares, and vice versa.[5] Surgery was still developing in terms of its understanding and use of scientific knowledge and best practice, although it is to be hoped that William had a little more professional prowess on his side than the inimitable Lady Williams in Jane's youthful writings who attacked her unsuspecting patient with little more than a high degree of enthusiasm and a pocketful of luck.[6]

Both sets of skills were an important consideration in regard to the amenities that a growing town could offer its community, and as such were gaining a footing in the consciousness of the populace. It was obvious to Jane Austen's Mr Parker, travelling en route to Sanditon, that any town worth its salt would have a surgeon. One whom might even have a reputation and accommodation equal to that of a gentleman and who, being located in the same part of the world as William Austen, might even advertise in the *Kentish Gazette*.[7] However, surgery had yet to evolve into the profession of today; Jane was careful to point out to her niece Anna that in those times a surgeon would have been considered socially on a par with those of a 'trade'. He would have been looked down upon as much as looked up to, and William would most definitely not have moved in the upper circles of society nor would he have been *invited* to mix socially with any men of particular standing or 'rank'.[8] Due to this status he would not even have been thought much of a catch in the marriage market.

So, William himself must have been quite something to attract the hand of a baronet's daughter such as Rebecca. Alongside his abilities, he must also have exuded a necessary air of goodness and his face must not yet have looked too drawn or too lined with any undue wrinkles as was often assumed to be the case by families who believed that surgeons learnt their skills out at sea in all weathers. Therefore, they gained a reputation for having seafaring faces seen most detrimentally by some, a sure sign to put them off a match for their noble daughters. This being the case, they were often looked down upon as less eligible, as Jane observed was sadly true for her poor young Mr Sam Watson (*The Watsons*).[9]

In reflecting upon Rebecca and William's match, one is put in mind of the adoration and admiration, albeit of the sibling kind, with which Fanny Price prized her own William.[10] Perhaps the attraction of George's father was that he possessed the hard-working nature of a William Larkins, estate manager to one Mr Knightley (*Emma*), or that he was one such as the aforementioned seaman, surgeon Mr Campbell, whose talents, manners, skill and integrity had secured him his position in life.[11]

In any event, the pull of his Austen family roots had been enough to see William return to his hometown and was proof of his 'attachment' to the area and his own liking for Kent.[12] He set up his practice there in the High Street, just a few doors down from his apothecary brother Thomas and around the corner from his sister Betty. This move had also happily drawn him into Rebecca's orbit. William may well have collaborated with Thomas in business matters, as apothecaries sometimes took part in surgeries as part of their training, and it is possible that clients were shared between the two with Thomas preparing and prescribing medications and treatments for post-surgical recovery.

The profession of surgeon, as has been noted, was not as high-ranking and wealth providing as it might be considered nowadays, and there would soon be considerable demands and constraints upon William and Rebecca to provide for their growing family. In the year following their marriage, they welcomed a daughter, Hampson, but two years later, only weeks before the arrival of their second daughter, little Hampson died. Philadelphia was born in May 1730, swiftly followed by George and the following year by another daughter, Leonora. Yet in February 1732, only a matter of weeks after Leonora's birth, Rebecca herself died – she was 36 years old.[13]

Overall, it was just as well that William had returned to Tunbridge, not only for support in his livelihood, but also for personal reasons. In the months and years following Rebecca's sudden death, his family were the very people on whom he relied. On call would have been his brother Thomas, and his sister Betty who had recently married and was living close by. His brother Francis had remained in Sevenoaks and was now practising as a solicitor. His youngest brother Stephen had settled successfully into his business and career in London. Like William, although respectably employed, the brothers were still not quite the rank considered beyond offence by certain prejudiced gentlemen to whom anyone proceeding from such a family might yet evoke 'strong objections'.[14]

However, the children were now facing life without a mother, just like Emma Woodhouse (*Emma*) and Anne Elliot (*Persuasion*). William would need to remain strong for them, and time alone would tell how they would all fare.

William's situation was difficult; not only did he have his grief to live through but with William-Hampson, Philadelphia, George and Leonora to take care of alongside his work, he sorely needed the practical help and support of his family around him as well as their emotional encouragement and love. But his family harboured griefs of its own and held a bittersweet truth at its heart. Scars of abandonment ran deep and raw memories of previous family struggles were all around them. The ghosts of loved ones lost and family betrayal, the scent of wealth and poverty, and tales of both good and ill-gotten gains hung in the air. In the reality of the Austen family's day-to-day living, previous experiences of close family members haunted them still. Years after they occurred, the pains of the recent past were still palpable enough to rub salt into the wounds of the struggling and distressed Austens of the present.

At 31 years old William was already familiar with the pangs of loss that followed death and the reality of the consequences to be survived by the living. An orphan by the time he was 20, his father John had died when he was only a toddler, and his mother Elizabeth Weller had been left with his father's debts, his six sons, one daughter and very little else. She had fought daily battles against injustice after injustice served upon her by her husband's family, most notably his father, John Austen III, a relation of the 'grey coats': the wealthy clothier Austen dynasty of the village of Horsmonden in Kent. Elizabeth had prevailed against many economic hardships that her father-in-law had not only failed to mitigate but had added to in his cruel reversal of his promises to his only son, made as he had lain terminally ill.[15] This was an act considered profoundly unkind, unethical and unfair to the point of immorality in the later literary world of Jane's characters. It was a rejection and a sentencing to poverty that grated so hard upon the soul in the situation of the Dashwood step-siblings (*Sense and Sensibility*) and seemed a near unforgivable mark against Mr Darcy (*Pride and Prejudice*) when Mr Wickham poured out his orphaned heart to Elizabeth Bennet.[16] Elizabeth Weller had fought these forces of financial evil and had paid off the debts by selling her own household goods and relying on her own wits and capabilities.

When John III himself died just a few spite-filled months after his son's death, William's elder brother, John V, known as Jack Austen, had become the only real beneficiary. The wealthy deceased's final jibe had been fired off in his last will and testament. It was a miserly move, seemingly intentionally and personally unkind and cruelly specific. Granting only £40 for an apprenticeship that would normally cost hundreds of pounds for the other brothers, and a

'£200 as a stake in life' when they came of age would seem callous enough, but worse was yet to come.[17] This John was not of the benevolent kind like Sir John Middleton who comes to the Dashwood women's aid in *Sense and Sensibility*; he was not minded to provide for his relation. No, in his case, his bequests as laid out in his will relied on the twisted demand that the widowed Elizabeth's eldest son John be deliberately and irrevocably taken away from his mother and raised separately under the guardianship of two uncles, chosen not by her but by the deceased. Elizabeth had been forced to accept this crucial demand, or the money for her other children would have been forfeited and all her family would have been left destitute. She must have felt dazed and confused, yet unsurprised having experienced her father-in-law's harsh moods and whims before. With her Jack now living under the complete care and custody of his Uncle Stringer, Elizabeth's economic struggle on behalf of her other children, undoubtedly compounded by an extra serving of grief in separation from her son, was set to continue.

It was Elizabeth who was going to have to battle on alone, to find an income for food, for clothing, for healthcare and for a roof over their heads. Without the support of a resourceful and sensible 'Elinor' in her life, she would have to step forth herself and utilise a great deal of imagination in her problem-solving. Her character was steely and resilient and she possessed great foresight and creativity in her thinking. In an imaginative sidestep, she made a brave and decisive choice, not only in favour of survival but in the hope of a better, more ambitious future for her children. Elizabeth was herself the daughter of a gentleman of Tunbridge, and she had lived all her life in the town. Leaving behind her own ancestral roots and striking out for pastures new, she moved the whole family to Sevenoaks. In doing so she was uprooting herself from all her familiar surroundings that might have offered her personal comfort, confidence and security at this difficult time, but it was the future of her children that she was firmly focused on. Taking up the reins of their lives she volunteered herself as the breadwinner and took on a paid position, the role of housekeeper-cum-housemistress for the unmarried headmaster of Sevenoaks School and his pupils.[18]

This was a move that, in addition to the income from caring for the boarding pupils, would ensure an education for her own sons in due course. This was not lost on Elizabeth but it was at the heart of all that she and her deceased husband believed in. Her hope and faith were firmly tied to the mast of education.[19] This would be the ship that sailed her family into calmer waters. She would work tirelessly, taking meticulous care with her finances, with a clear focus on providing as stable a future start in life for her remaining children as possible.

By the time Elizabeth died in 1721, her vision had largely come true. William and his male siblings had indeed benefited from the lessons and learning at Sevenoaks School. He, alongside three of his other brothers, had all secured an apprenticeship each, confirmed at considerable expense to their mother. His elder sister Elizabeth had married well to a Tunbridge attorney. His younger brother Robert, the only one who did not take up an apprenticeship or stay local to Tunbridge in the longer term, succumbed to smallpox at the age of 26. The 'blessed' son, John V, died in the September following Robert's death, leaving his fortune to his own offspring, under the auspices of his male heir.[20]

In May 1736, four years after Rebecca's death, William Austen married again, and the children had the happy prospect of a mother figure re-entering their lives in the form of his new wife, Susanna Kelk. Susanna was a local woman, over a decade older than William. Not much is known about how they met other than their proximity to one another as they moved in the same vicinity. Maybe they met at a ball in the town just as Jane would imagine when conjuring up other rendezvous. It would be romantic to imagine that they might be a match of a similar nature to that of Jane's Mr Weston and Miss Taylor in *Emma* with Susanna's maturity of mind and spirit echoing the fictional bride's. Susanna might bring great advantage to her younger husband through her greater experience of the world, just as one might expect Mr Knightley to share with his Emma in due course. Thus, William's new wife might be able to assist in providing a secure upbringing for the children, who had long missed the touch of a mother's presence. However, their love story, whatever it may have looked like, was destined to be a short one as sadly their married life did not last long. In December the following year, William Austen died.

His death must have been a huge shock to all of his siblings, but even more so to his young family. William's last will and testament had been made a few years earlier in the aftermath of Rebecca's death but it had lain unamended ever since.[21] Being relatively young, fit, strong and in love, the practicalities of paperwork must have been the last thing on his mind, but so too would have been the prospect of his new wife turning her back on his children in his absence – but that she did. Under the law at the time, Susanna, as stepmother, had no formal parental responsibility for the children; there was no legally binding expectation upon her to provide for, help or care for them in any way following her husband's death, just as there was no requirement for any financial responsibility from William towards his stepson. Nevertheless, knowing all that the little children had suffered in recent years, it was still a shock when on inheriting all of William's property and worldly goods, she shut the door on 15-year-old William-Hampson Walter, 7-year-old Philadelphia, 6-year-old George and 5-year-old Leonora for good.

This unfair demise, this desperate and destitute state of affairs experienced by his three offspring could not have been further from William's dreams and desires for them. No doubt inspired by his mother's legacy and the values that she had founded within his heart, he had made it plain in his will that all of his money and wealth should be used to provide for the education of his son *and* also, as outlined most clearly and specifically, for his two daughters. William was a father ahead of his time, one who knew his own mind on these matters. Other men of the period would neither have been expected, nor perhaps even thought it necessary, to provide in writing ahead of their deaths for their daughters. They might perhaps have expected future husbands to have taken care of them and thought it quite appropriate for an elder brother to have the fortune left to him to decide for himself how much to bestow upon his sisters as custodian of the family wealth. This again speaks to the huge influence that William's strong, independently minded, role-model mother had on him, for even beyond the grave her hand can be seen in the arrangements that he intended for his children. A desire for the honourable care of each one of his children, for an equality of opportunity, demonstrated by his high regard for the provision for the female members of his family, was the best way of stewarding a child's future wellbeing.

William had made sure that neither age, birth order nor gender would be a decider in the division of his wealth. No, William wanted his children to be treated alike, firstborn and last to receive the same, and his son George to share in his father's provision equally with his sisters Philadelphia and Leonora. So, William had it written into his will that all his assets, his messuages and buildings be sold prior to being divided between them and that the money be given transparently and proportionately, equally, and even-handedly to each of his individual children.[22] But all that of course was only on the death of his widow. There could be no claim on any of the property left by their father whatsoever until then: an event that seemed as far off as could ever be imagined. In the meantime, this real-life drama, mirrored rather hauntingly in the echoes of Jane's early story of *Catharine, or the Bower*, was to sting the heart. The children, just like the Misses Wynne in this little tale, were at the mercy of their need and entirely dependent on their kin.[23] The poignancy of Jane's words of woe and want, whittled from her father's world, is such that we cannot but feel the plight of the young siblings. It must have been a tale of stark realities told with feeling, even down the tunnel of years past.

With Christmas approaching in December 1737 and the children now rejected by their stepmother, William's executors and named guardians – his wealthier brothers Francis and Stephen – had to make plans to step into the breach. Francis was as yet unmarried, but Stephen was. He already had a son the same age as Leonora living with him and his wife Elizabeth in London, and he was doing very well in his publishing business. Perhaps it was this provision of a mother figure that clinched the deal and was the decisive factor in the children being sent there, for under the care of their father's youngest brother they duly came. That is William's three biological children, for a grieving William-Hampson Walter, ten years older than George and now a strapping 15-year-old some way into his further education, was not to follow his siblings. The thought of the three very young, recently bereaved children travelling in a state of bewilderment and confusion forbears us to pause and take stock. Would they find themselves the beneficiaries of a happy home as the Crawford orphans of *Mansfield Park* had done? Their journey from the relative countryside of Tunbridge (although some, like Edmund Bertram [*Mansfield Park*], of course, might not have called Tunbridge the country[24]), a settlement which boasted a population of under 1,000, was a place laced with woodland walks and uncultivated heaths, punctuated by springs, rivers and streams. Leaving Tunbridge meant leaving behind not only a natural environment but a homespun community of agricultural artisans, one where everyone would have known everyone else.

Perhaps the three children were snuggled up, hands clasped together, accompanied by their Aunt Betty, or perhaps they gazed out of the windows of their carriage in silent wonder whilst their Uncle Stephen read on or perhaps lectured them in the ways of his household. What about their mode of transport too? Were they settled into a carriage sent by their Uncle Francis or packed into a public post-chaise as they made their way? What a marked change of landscape was awaiting them upon their arrival in central London. The city may have now recovered from the decimation caused by plague and fire, but views of an unhygienic and densely populated city, a city filled with more people than they had ever seen before or even imagined possible, around 600 times the number of people they were used to, would have caused a similar level of shock. For these children, an old world had passed away; their former lives destroyed just as completely as this area had experienced in the not-so-distant past. And just as this part of London was slowly coming to terms with the colossal changes and reconstructions that had characterised its recent history, the three young siblings would have to embark upon and familiarise themselves with entirely new lives.

As they jostled their way, squeezing through the thronged streets and nipping into spaces between other carriages, the huge dome of Sir Christopher Wren's 'new' St Paul's Cathedral would have loomed into view. The assault on the senses, on the eyes, nose and ears must have been the equivalent of arriving in a foreign land. If they arrived at night, then illuminated shop windows would have welcomed them; if during the day, then the chimes of the cathedral bells, chatter from the coffee houses and the crazy calling of the shopkeepers would have greeted them. The very air that they breathed would have been something totally new to experience, thickened by smoke from the surrounding chimneys and the scents wafting towards them from the Newgate meat market. It is a scene which evokes compassion and sympathy and might even bring young Fanny Price to mind in a reversal of her journey from Portsmouth's city smog to Northamptonshire's rural harmony.[25]

Yet family legend has it that just like the aforementioned orphaned Misses Wynne found themselves entirely at the mercy of their need and their family's willingness, or not, to meet it, the children's struggle for subsistence and quest for compassion was not met with unrestrained kindness. Uncle Stephen was not particularly pleased to have to take on the care of the three children. In fact, we are told quite clearly that he made the trio's arrival a less than welcoming one.[26] Perhaps having to cope with such a change to his own family circumstances all at once seemed a bit of an imposition. However, the coolness of his uncle's manner was something that the young George picked up on at the time, a painful frosty reception that lodged itself in his heart and memory so clearly that younger generations not present could still recall his memories of that day years later.

Perhaps we can sense a little frisson of this disgruntled tension still percolating under the surface in the words Stephen chose in his own will, made some eight years later. In it he signed over all his property and legacies to his wife, despite having what he called 'great respect' for others to whom he was related. His words and choices were laced with effusions of emotive regret that he could not help, and great importance, deference and store were put upon his spousal duty to his wife.[27] Reading them nowadays might perhaps remind readers of the thoughts colliding in John Dashwood's mind (*Sense and Sensibility*) as he considered his commitments and expenses when providing for Elinor, Marianne and their mother after the death of their father.

At the time of the children's arrival, Stephen, aged 34, was focused on building up his business's reputation and success in his 'respectable line of trade' as Jane might have put it.[28] He was ambitious and having completed his apprenticeship with William Innys, publisher, bookseller and stationer in the same locality, he was now intent on establishing himself in his own right. He had begun networking with the community of booksellers and publishers scattered in relative proximity to one another surrounding St Paul's Churchyard. Being on the northern side of the cathedral grounds, The Angel and Bible directly reflected his wares quite aptly, located as he was in the geographical area traditionally more closely associated with publishers of sacred and classical texts.[29] It would seem that Stephen was an astute businessman who was interested in maximising his sales, selling what the marketplace wanted as well as worthy titles. He worked at publishing and co-publishing a range of educational books and articles, historical works and treatises as well as sacred texts including sermons. Indeed, he was becoming a settled feature amongst the local bookselling trade, albeit that he was a shining light in a profession which Jane would disdainfully poke fun at in her *Juvenilia* as being of a low social level on a par with a grocer.[30] Nonetheless he would certainly have been useful to anyone who might be looking to spend some money on books should they come into a little spare wealth as Edward Ferrars (*Sense and Sensibility*) once teasingly imagined of the Dashwood sisters. 'What magnificent orders would travel from this family to London,' Edward had said. 'What a happy day for booksellers, music-sellers, and print-shops!'[31] Stephen would have only been too happy to help.

Like other successful publishers in his social and professional circle, those who exemplified the more seriously business-minded at this time, Stephen was diligent in protecting his rights to the publication of different works and would pursue anyone trying to evade the copyright laws enshrined in 1710. He was unafraid of taking on even publishers of renown. In 1739 he was hot on the tail of the entrepreneurial Edward Cave, founder of *The Gentleman's Magazine*. Alongside fellow local booksellers Gulliver and Clark, Stephen took his case to court to stop Cave from publishing further extracts of a work that he himself held the licence to publish. Cave had many clever arguments for wriggling out of copyright clashes and often argued that he was doing everyone a favour by publicising books to potential buyers, but the publishers in question did not view it that way.[32] The fact that Stephen was part of a group of booksellers who could, and would, zealously fight a copyright case proves his status and standing within the society of fellow stationers at this time. It was not every publisher that was in a sufficiently strong position financially to do so; indeed, not every publisher held lucrative copyright contracts to defend in the first place.

Stephen was also actively involved in sitting on juries in local legal cases, including the nearby Old Bailey, and had established himself at the heart of local community and political matters, becoming an elected Common Councilman of the Castle Barnard district of London.[33] Interestingly records show that Stephen moved from his family's home above the bookshop to this area just across the churchyard, at around the same time as the three young Austens arrived on his doorstep.[34] It is possible that Francis and the Austen family made some sort of financial provision to help him out with accommodating the three little orphans prior to them arriving. Perhaps the conditions above the bookshop, where many proprietors kept their living quarters, quickly became too cramped for comfortable living.

In view of his geographical location and with all his social climbing, it is interesting to conjecture if Stephen ever climbed the steps up onto the roof of St Paul's Cathedral for a view of the city skyline and the river. It gives pause for thought to envisage him standing up there near the dome as tourists were wont to do. Did a young George accompany him? Did they both scratch their initials into the lead roofing as many were in the habit of doing?[35] It is a wonderfully evocative image. Yet for all his moving up in the world, Stephen had also never quite forgotten his family connections with Tunbridge, his home town, and from as early as 1729 he had signed himself up as a sponsor alongside other subscribers to raise money to supply books for a school there.[36] With his eye on the growing trend for making books available for children and for learning, it has to be wondered if Stephen ever took George and his son to one of the newly established libraries in the area for them to choose a book to read.[37]

It was a very busy Uncle Stephen who was there for the children when it counted; he, alongside his wife, gave them shelter and care at a time when they needed the very clothes on their backs and food in their mouths. They took them into their family life and fashioned for them some form of normality and routine in an alien and unnavigated new world. It is into his world that we stepped at the start of this chapter, as the weather spread its icicled and frosted fingers around George and his siblings. But whether the children's stay in London was always considered a temporary measure or whether Stephen had finally decided that the arrangement no longer suited him and his family, as the decade ticked over into the 1740s, change was already under way. Leonora was still residing with Stephen and Elizabeth, and it is thought that she had particular needs, perhaps even some form of damage to her brain following the circumstances surrounding her birth, the very same that had affected Rebecca so tragically.[38] But George's older sister Philadelphia was not. She had been separated and removed from her brother and sister and sent to live amongst her mother's sister's relations, the Freeman family in Tunbridge. Effectively the children's happy home life had been fractured further after all. With a chill wind behind him, in the late spring George too was now to be sent away, forced into leaving Leonora alone and into facing the future not as one of four, but by himself. He was going back to live with his Aunt Betty, just a stone's throw from his former home. But back to what? What type of memories would greet him there as he stepped foot once again into Tunbridge as a 9-year-old, nearly two and a half years after he had left? When would this season of cold, harsh conditions finally abate? Would there be a better welcome awaiting him on the other side? In separating him from his sole remaining sibling, would this decision bode well or ill? In future years might this choice hint of kindness or of cruelty?[39]

Chapter Two

Schooldays

As luck would have it, young George now landed safely and securely under the care and protection of his Uncle Francis. Elizabeth's second child, now in his forties, was established as a solicitor in Sevenoaks and lived at a grand residence known as The Red House. He acted as attorney for many of the family's connections over the years and, although as Jane would teasingly put it, he was employed in 'the law line', he had established himself in the higher echelons of local society acting as the political agent for the Duke of Dorset, MP.[1] Francis had made the most of his talents, having experienced the same shared difficult circumstances at the start of life as his siblings – beginnings that later generations were all acutely aware of and full of admiration for. He had most definitely proved that *he* had talent enough 'to rise', and that he possessed ability and intelligence that might even impress someone with the high standards of a Miss Emma Woodhouse (*Emma*).[2] Yes, as family members would later reflect, Francis had come a long way with his '£800 and... bundle of pens'.[3] As we know from the fortunes of Mrs Bennet's father – an attorney who could leave her the huge sum of £4,000 upon his death – it was a profession that could pay well although it too could still be called into question when status was to be considered.[4] Jane chose this profession for the husband of the raucous Mrs Philips (*Pride and Prejudice*), so it was not always a guarantee of taste and gentleman-like qualities; indeed, Mr Wickham's father (*Pride and Prejudice*) was in the same profession and gave it all up to oversee Mr Darcy senior's estates.

Uncle Francis' outlook was much more open and he turned generously to his nephew, much in the manner that many of us may have wished some hitherto unknown rich uncle would turn up and take care of us. But for George, just like for little Eliza in *Sense and Sensibility*, with 'no family, no home', it quite unexpectedly did happen. Francis, with a generous touch foreshadowing that of Colonel Brandon, took George under his wing financially with a parent-like level of kindliness.[5] This is the type which is thought of longingly and with a wistful air of loss and regret by the grieving Emma Watson (*The Watsons*) who, in a reversal of George's situation, was returned to her family home on the death of her uncle and remarriage of her aunt.[6]

Taking full responsibility for his care, Francis paid for George to attend Tunbridge School. There were charity schools in the vicinity of St Paul's Churchyard, so the decision to send George to school in what was his birth town seems quite intentional, whether on the part of Stephen who did not want to continue to oversee George's upkeep and education, or on the part of Francis, who most definitely did. With the school fees coming in at between £20 and £30 per annum, paying for George's education was a financial commitment but the familial touch was also part of the deal. George had not quite been 'banished from home', as Jane Austen's Emma might have seen it, in having to enrol at the school because he began to attend firstly as a day pupil.[7] At around 9 years old, he was perhaps still on the younger side of life when he was sent, as her Lady Susan might say 'to one of the best private schools in town'.[8]

Tunbridge School had opened by way of Royal Charter in 1553 by Sir Andrew Judde, a native of the town and a venerated member of the Skinners' Company, who rose up from amongst their ranks to become master of the guild as well as the Lord Mayor of London.

At the heart of the school lay its commitment to Protestant Christianity and a classical education. The school was a grammar school in the most literal sense, the teaching of grammar strictly according to the royally approved schema of the time. Latin language and literature were taught first and foremost, with some Greek too and, rather surprisingly for modern learners, general conversation in Latin was also encouraged. Known as a 'dead' language, spoken Latin is not generally taught in the way that Modern Languages are now taught with a focus on listening and speaking skills in equal measure to written translations and reading comprehensions. In fact, when George arrived at the school, there would have been an extra charge for French just as there was for dancing, along with writing and accounts – seen as expensive optional extras at the time. Written reports and summaries would have been taught and penmanship honed, but original composition was not high on the agenda and Science barely featured in the curriculum. The school statutes, in all their sombre sincerity, were hopefully not in the same category as those which Jane Austen chastised as 'long sentences of refined nonsense'.[9] They prescribed a carefully constructed routine designed to honour and uphold the principal aim of the school: that of 'bringing up the youth in virtue and learning.'[10] The youth referred to were mostly the kin of local gentry from Kent and Sussex, or pupils of wealthy fathers from the West Indies, and usually numbered about forty boarders and ten day boys.[11] Even by the time George arrived, just over ninety years after the foundation of the school, the statutes that governed its ethos and culture were still embraced whole-heartedly in principle and were still fairly strictly adhered to in practice, though that would later change. However, that said, in order to meet the entry requirements, pupils were expected to be able to read and write to a creditable standard in English and Latin. George may very well not have been able to meet this criterion, as in reality it has since been widely accepted that many could not. But ages of entry varied and at the very least we can expect that George must have been bright for his age, already showing signs of his intelligence, literacy and eloquence: firstly, in order to impress his Uncle Francis enough to recommend him and, secondly, for the school to accept him. According to Austen scholar Le Faye's perusal of family manuscripts, certainly the family believed that George personified someone 'blessed with a bright & hopeful disposition.'[12] This was the very nature that Jane Austen imbued young Emma Watson with, in order that she might survive the opposite of George's current experience, being forced back into the bosom of her nuclear family after living a most refined and blessed life with her educated and generous uncle and his wife.[13]

On his very first day of admission to the school, George would perhaps have entered to the sound of the bell being rung from the bell tower that stood in those days, up on the roof of the schoolroom. He would very probably still have had to deposit his sixpence into the common box. The funds from this were used for providing books as deemed necessary by the headmaster for the common good of all the scholars, the very fund his Uncle Stephen had supported in the preceding decades.[14]

Routines were carefully considered, in line with the original wishes of Sir Andrew Judde as enshrined in his statutes. The pupils' school day was planned out to the hour, with prayers upon their knees at 7 o'clock in the morning in the rectangular-shaped schoolroom. They were led by the headmaster or usher who would have seamlessly stepped from their own residences that effectively book-ended the approximately 13-metre-long and nearly 7-metre-wide schoolroom, or as measured by the Skinners' Company during routine maintenance, 44 foot six inches by 22 ft 6 wide.[15] There was no scrambling themselves into a little education for these boys as there might be for Jane Austen's characters later.[16]

We learn a lot about the schoolroom itself from the annual bills presented to the Skinners' Company by the Reverend James Cawthorn, headmaster of the school from 1743. There were requests for repairs and refurbishments made to the oak floor, walls, workstations and various parts of the room, with bills for carpentry, painting and glazing. This area saw a lot of activity and it took its toll on the classroom with a regular need for whitewashing and replastering.[17] Cawthorn really did take pride in the appearance of the room, showing vision for how it should look with a keen eye on quality standards and calling for prompt attention to maintenance wherever it was due. Although the Company was thrifty and prompt to give advice and directions on reusing and recycling materials and prioritising work, it did also want everything to work well and look good, insisting, for example, that the oak wainscot not be painted.[18] It was supportive of protecting past investments in the school, not stinting on the regular upkeep and improvement of them.

All of the pupils studied in the schoolroom together. In a classroom layout fashionable at the time, the desks were arranged facing inwards from both of the long rectangular sides of the building. The older boys stood at the tall wooden benches of dark wainscot, making them look a little like draughtsmen or accounts clerks at their desks. One cannot imagine that the boys stood all of the time and there were long benches that backed onto the outside wall behind them. In front of the older boys were four more desks described as being on fixed 'columns' for the use of the younger boys, and in front of those, in turn, there were also two smaller bench seats for the newest members of the school. The whole feel strikes one as based upon a Greek amphitheatre-style effect, with the two last benches being spoken of as being at the bottom of the classroom.[19] One wonders if the smallest boys sat working on small slates upon their laps. At the end of the room to the right-hand side (if one were stood outside looking at the front door), on a raised platform that backed onto the second master's house, sat some further pupils and probably the master in charge; the rope belonging to the school bell, recast at the end of 1758, hung down amongst them.[20]

At 11 am there was a break for lunch when George could have slipped back home to eat at his aunt's house, returning ready to start his lessons again promptly at 1 pm (although there is as yet no evidence that he did so). Classes continued for all ages until around 6 pm in the evening, the headmaster and his deputy taking different parts of the same schoolroom to teach different age groups of boys, before the day finished as it had begun, in prayer. As a teacher myself I can only imagine that, especially in the dark evenings of the winter months, some of the younger boys must have been nearly asleep and some of the eldest ready to make a break for a bit of fresh air and freedom after such a long school day. Initially even holidays were extremely controlled with not a day off given in a fortnight, but this was tempered as the years went on and the boys were generously allowed their 'remedy' or time off once a week. There were not many scheduled breaks or time set aside for running around outside or playing games up and down any of the grounds, unlike in Mrs Goddard's happy school in *Emma*.[21] Each hour was carefully planned with its purpose allotted and strictly adhered to. Even if a respected visitor of rank awarded a little break to the boys, this could not happen twice in a week without consequences.[22]

Jane herself never really did have much time for masters and the airs and graces that they seemingly gave themselves, nor the power over others that society assigned to them. No, indeed, the thought of one of her heroines marrying the writing-master's son was laughingly scoffed at by the honourable Mr Knightley (*Emma*) and portrayed by her pen as scraping the very bottom of the marriage-market barrel.[23] Jane's honourable women vowed that becoming a teacher was the worst professional post imaginable, only marginally better than marrying a man one did not love. It was something to be seen as very much a last resort in the battle for one's own economic survival.[24] The reach, the power and the jurisdiction of these teachers, particularly that of a headmaster, in regard to the boys' time, was something never lost on Jane in the future. Scornful of their autocratic yet idiosyncratic ways, she found them an easy target for her wrath and wit, her scoffing and her scrutiny. They certainly got her hackles rising. Their total freedom to control the lives of those in their care, this unimpeachable yet, at times, dubious jurisdiction over the everyday lives of their pupils left them a subject to be lampooned in Jane's eyes. In her opinion, they weaved a web completely full of contradictions. She found ways to shine a light on their ridiculous flaws and their follies, their desire to make and create their own rules and at the same time be a law unto themselves. For example, to be able to approve or disapprove a family's request for leave of absence for a pupil and yet blatantly reserve the right to demonstrate their own willingness to part with a pupil as soon as final exams were over, even if that was weeks before the end of term, just because it suited them best.[25] Jane liked to imagine that pupils rebelled and snuck out on the odd occasion, making a bolt for freedom to a tavern in the city where they might lose their minds and their money whilst escaping from the expectations and the rules for a while.[26]

But that was not likely to have happened at all at Tunbridge School and it goes without saying that the pupils were expected to be at church promptly for the Sunday service or they would face a dressing-down from the master and a fine on Monday morning.[27] Such was the attention to detail and the importance placed upon prioritising one's time for the instruction of oneself through a strict observance of studious and conscientious details, such as punctuality and being found to be doing the right thing at the right time. Tunbridge pupils were raised to study and to adhere to the rules, which it was believed would then draw all forth into following the call into a higher way of living and consciousness; that of mastering oneself. The school held lofty aims and guided each pupil to aspire to attain a higher standard through the acquisition of knowledge and the thorough training of one's body, soul and mind. High expectations for anyone to aspire to, it would have been easy for new boy George, one amongst approximately forty-three mostly more experienced pupils, to have felt overwhelmed.[28] Yet he would have been aware that he was following in the footsteps of his own beloved stepbrother and he had a role model in the form of the head boy, Henry, his cousin, son of his Uncle Thomas, the apothecary. Even so, with a formally arranged set-up of nine classes grouped in order of age and seated in order of aptitude and achievement, with the most able sat nearest the master, it must have been quite intimidating.[29] One would have been conscious of the pecking order and the self-awareness brought about from being moved up or down the seating plan would have been enough to keep every learner, let alone a new pupil, on their toes. In the end, happily, George, living up to his personality and character and the faith placed in him by his Uncle Francis, was regularly placed at the top of his age group.[30]

This culture and ethos, which still permeated the way of life at Tunbridge School when George was a pupil there, was about to gain a new lease of life. Under the Reverend Richard Spencer, the headmaster at the time George was admitted, the numbers on roll had until recently swelled to record numbers and the reputation of the school had spread. Now that he had resigned, it was with some trepidation that a new headmaster was appointed, for who could follow in the Reverend Richard Spencer's shoes? It would take quite a character to have the confidence to step into them. At first, parents were not sure what to make of the Reverend James Cawthorn, a Yorkshireman, fresh from his most recent experience of teaching at the Soho School in London.[31] A keen reader who also loved art and music, he appeared to think nothing of taking a long ride off on his horse to attend a concert or visit an exhibition (although there is no evidence that he ever rode away to London for a haircut, unlike Frank Churchill! [Emma]).[32] In a strange twist of coincidences, it has also been proposed by a more recent relative of his that James was a frequent visitor to St Paul's Churchyard as he was very close friends with a Mr C. Hitch, a publisher there.[33] This was the very same Mr Hitch who was a collaborating partner with Stephen Austen. Had George already come face to face with his new headmaster back in Newgate Street? How would they now get along?

The Reverend James Cawthorn was a complex, very human character. On the one hand he was in touch with his sensitivities to such an extent as to appreciate the exquisite sense of awe encapsulated in a piece of music or a painting, and he wrote poetry prolifically. He lauded his pupils for their oratory skills and would love nothing more than to throw out a question and get the boys to debate it there and then, testing their disputation skills to the limit and revealing some diamonds in the rough amongst his pupils.[34] On the other hand, he was remembered as a strict disciplinarian, someone who every pupil revered and no one wanted to cross.[35] Cawthorn was vigilant and demanding, ever alert to the smallest infringement of any of the statutes and school rules, and he was very happy to hand out fines to pupils for each and every misdemeanour, funds which he siphoned off for the explicit purchase of books for the school. For many years a story circulated, a very harsh rumour that cast him as the fateful protagonist and a long shadow over his reputation. It is a story that puts us in mind of the imaginations of one Catherine Morland (*Northanger Abbey*) and the sensibilities of the readers of those 'horrid' Gothic novels.[36] It was variously alleged that on disciplining a pupil, Cawthorn had him shut up in a cupboard or perhaps in the attic of the school, and then on setting out for one of his excursions he had forgotten about the boy who had then subsequently perished.[37] The stories of Cawthorn's ghost roaming the school's corridors and dormitories lamenting the loss of the child's life was fuel enough to fascinate and entertain boys for many decades, making pupils who had never even met him shudder in fear.[38] But despite the memories of his exasperatingly strict expectations, pupils remembered him fondly and even left him legacies and sponsored the posthumous publication of his poems.

Every year at the beginning of May, the Skinners' Company would send a delegation or 'visitation' to the school for two days, to scrutinise the performance of the pupils and the masters, and to make general checks to ensure that the statutes of the school were being adhered to and upheld. 'Skinners' day', a mixture of a board of governors' school inspection, pupils' end of year examinations and a celebratory speech day, like all the other days in the Tunbridge School calendar had an itinerary that was strictly prescribed and included a great deal of ceremony.

The original visit was, in fact, for two days and although there was some adaptation to the order of events as the years passed, certain elements remained firmly fixed traditions. The delegation would arrive and be fed and watered with a picnic out on the common at Sevenoaks. Traditionally the High Street of Tunbridge was lined with birch in their honour and banks of local people craned their necks to welcome the visitors.[39] The Skinners must have made an impressive sight as they proceeded to the school on horseback, dressed in the luxury robes their Company was so famous for. They were welcomed on arrival by the head boy who greeted them in Latin before they retired to a local inn for the night.

On the first of these occasions under the new headmaster, the next day began with a divine service at Tunbridge Church (the school would not boast its own chapel until 1859). The Company's representatives made gifts of cloth to the poor of the local parishes before they returned to the school and took a tour of the grounds with the headmaster. The group reviewed the state of all the buildings and saw for themselves the need for certain repairs as Cawthorn brought them all to their notice. Next they proceeded to the schoolroom to hear a public reading of the school's revered and prized statutes. Then, in the company of this great assembly in the presence of the Reverend Mr Nicholas Fayting, an examiner of many years' experience and connection with the school, the scholars were examined. That year the visitors reported back their delighted impressions of the headmaster, and the students, who even under all that scrutiny 'by their ready and proper answers to the several questions proposed to them by the said examiner did sufficiently testify the great diligence and application as well as ability of the said schoolmaster.'[40]

In fact, one of Cawthorn's greatest teaching talents lay in instructing the boys in 'rhetoric'; in teaching pupils to speak persuasively. Tunbridge pupils were schooled in how to argue a point, to influence an audience by the use of effective and artful reasoning, and in such a way that revealed a deep understanding of logic. Pupils would have to do this in English and in Latin, and Cawthorn was notorious for spontaneously 'downing tools' at the drop of a hat and laying down a gauntlet, putting a pupil on the spot with a question thrown at them out of the blue.[41] The chosen boy would be expected to stand and hold forth with an excellent answer and an impressive piece of speech. Once, as a punishment, Cawthorn set an extract of Homer as homework for a pupil, expecting him to memorise and perform a portion the next day. William 'Memory' Woodfall, as he became known, went above and beyond, learning the whole speech by heart and moving the headmaster to tears in the process.[42] Reading aloud was an ability that Fanny Price (*Mansfield Park*) would go on to appreciate in well-educated men, and through her experience we see how Jane Austen both lauded and laughed at this venerated skill. She valued it as being a weighty matter of social importance and a skill sorely regretted if neglected (even if she herself might also make mention of it with a little tongue stuck firmly in her cheek). Being able to dramatise a reading and to speak well was a trait most strongly attributed to the aims of the master and of the school, something that the Edmund Bertram and Henry Crawford (*Mansfield Park*) of the future would have truly appreciated.[43]

After lunch the honoured guests gathered again to be entertained as disputations, or debates, as well as various other oral exercises and tasks were undertaken by six of the very finest pupils in the school. This was an activity that the boys practised regularly in class to exercise their logic skills but being adjudicated by such a fine panel would have been a different level altogether. With the boys handpicked to answer questions previously laid out by the headmaster, this was a real honour, for they were not only carrying their own reputations but also those of the school itself upon their shoulders.

When all the boys had had ample time to display their wits and debating skills, the master, or, in this case the examiner, from All Saints College at Oxford University would pick a winner. It is unclear if Tunbridge indulged in the practice in place elsewhere whereby the victor got to thwack the loser with a wooden stick, and no doubt the questions would have been on loftier matters too than offering 'the best defence' of Marianne Dashwood's (*Sense and Sensibility*) 'favourite maxim, that no one can ever be in love more than once in their life.'[44] Certainly, the young men would have been very adept at wielding phrases and ideas like small swords and would have been 'abundant in quotations and allusions', which Jane Austen would herself associate from her father's experience with the sort of education becoming of the finest of men and not of the sort unfortunately ever experienced or destined for women in general, or herself in particular.[45] When she would write years later to the Prince Regent's librarian, James Stanier Clarke, on these matters, following his urging for her to write about the life of a clergyman not dissimilar in nature to himself, it would not have been lost on her as she gave her witty rebuff that he had experienced the same Tunbridge education as her father and would have been schooled in the oratory arts and sparred with the spoken word there himself.

Prestigious prizes of special silver gilt pens, as decreed by Sir Andrew Judde in his original statutes and then expanded from his original three to six by the 'Company's own tradition', were then awarded.[46] Rather than scratching forever more on a 'little piece of ivory' as Jane did, the boys would surely have treasured these prizes and taken particular care with the words that would proceed from them in the future – if they could bring themselves to use such a valuable object. With an inscription on the stem and a huge amount of detailing on the 'feather' quill, these objects were beautiful and are still highly sought after today.

As part of the celebration of the school's artistic taste and talent, the boys also performed a play – the actors having to pay a fine for the privilege that went once more, under the auspices of the headmaster, to the provision of books.[47] The whole school then processed through the streets to the church for a service of thanksgiving. The lucky prize-winners got to travel at the back of the queue with the master and headmaster, with a 'garland' on their heads: at times, a simple laurel wreath and at others, a 'conical' hat. It probably gave the teenage boys as much embarrassment then as it would now, if the school had not discontinued the practice in its original guise. The day finally ended with a celebratory meal with the masters and the head boy.

In Cawthorn's very first year at the school, he picked 13-year-old George as one of the six boys to take part in the disputations. It was a huge honour, a measure not only of the esteem in which he was held by the headmaster but also of his reputation as a scholar within the school community. His intelligence and skill must have already been a cut above the rest as there were other older boys from which to choose. The gentlemen Skinners certainly recognised that the speakers did themselves and the school proud, performing 'with great reputation and credit' and George was duly awarded one of the precious pens.[48]

George was also picked the following year, no doubt exhibiting greater skill and ability and perhaps a little more confidence as he faced the examiner. However, he still had not done enough to win the unqualified praise of his Uncle Stephen who, in a letter written the same year as his will, commented thus:

'My nephew, George Austen shows away before the Skinners I understand, they praise the boy too much as indeed they did my nephew Harry, it gives them a wrong turn of mind and makes them ridiculous conceited.'[49]

The following year Cawthorn penned his inaugural traditional Skinners' day 'pen-winner's' poem; as one of the most senior boys in the school it is very likely that George Austen was chosen to read it.[50]

As the years progressed the new headmaster was praised and thanked, granted an annual gratuity of 30 guineas 'for his good behaviour' over the course of each passing year in the role, and admired for his preaching of excellent sermons.[51] He was deemed to be taking very good care of the school, both in regard to its physical and academic state, and the Skinners' Company approved his repairs and bills, holding his opinion in high regard and trust. The benevolence of the headmaster, who made sure that George, now in his final summer term at the school, had his chance to shine in front of the Skinners' Company, meant a lot. Thanks to his master's nurturing notice, George had now been dazzling them all for the past four years.

Cawthorn had achieved all this despite personal heartache and grief on a major scale, with the death of twin daughters the year before and a third baby girl and his wife that same year. The fact that he remained so open and generous towards George under these circumstances seems even more poignant. James Cawthorn himself had had a humble background and knew what it was like to be academically able but poor. His own scholarship to Cambridge had entailed upon him the role of waiter to his peers, having to serve his fellow students at every mealtime.[52] As headmaster he would have been well aware of the details of George's situation. Perhaps he recognised himself in George and empathised with the challenges he faced.

Alongside the prizes given for oratory elocution and prowess, the Skinners' Company also had it in their power to award exhibitions – prizes of monetary value – supported by an endowment made by the grandson of Sir Andrew, Sir Thomas Smythe, for pupils moving on to study divinity who showed promise and whose family background meant that assistance was both appropriate and useful.[53] In addition, the founder of St John's College at Oxford, Sir Thomas Whyte, who had been a friend and supporter of Sir Andrew Judde, had, out of admiration and respect for him, also bestowed a rare and highly prized fellowship to the university college, upon Tunbridge School, reserving it for one of their esteemed pupils.

On that Skinners' day in 1747, it so transpired that this fellowship, perhaps the most coveted prize in the gift of the Skinners' Company as it was bestowed for life, or until the holder resigned their position, had recently become available. That day, the now very familiar face and celebrated star of all of Cawthorn's previous visitations, George Austen, was awarded the St John's College Thomas Whyte Fellowship. One cannot help but feel the poignancy of the moment and envisage the hand of his father on his one shoulder and his grandmother on the other. What a long way George had come in his six years at the school. Uncle Francis' generosity had been amply rewarded. Education had been like a lifeboat for the young orphan.

George's time at the school had, on many levels, been a success; top of his form for the first three years of study he had climbed steadily up the ranks, helped out a little by the fall in pupil numbers perhaps, and although he never quite made it to head boy, he had held steady at the end in third position in what must have felt a little like a league table.[54] He left the school with pride in his achievements, but whether he loved the Latin language enough to wear it on his clothing as Jane would later joke about Lady Jane Grey (*History of England*) on her way to the scaffold was perhaps a step too far for him.[55] His understanding of the determination necessary for mastery of the language would remain with him throughout his life. His reverence and respect for anyone showing such skills would not be lost on his future connections. Yet his daughter would go on to tease the pretentiousness and arrogance of some proceeding from this insular scholarly world.

Boarding school life too was a culture that George would have needed to internalise and respond to in order to acclimatise and thrive there. In all his years at Tunbridge he would have learnt more from his education than mere lessons could teach. His tendency to lean towards the positive, and his wit and intelligence surely enabled him to overcome the difficulties of being just a 'raw schoolboy' among many boys, as Jane would later say, and to have grown not just physically but also within.[56] He would have needed all his strength of character to come to terms at such a young age with having to make friends and avoid enemies, to learn how to socialise, how to comfort oneself against any home sickness, loneliness and perhaps even lingering grief. He would have learnt how to support others, how to lead and how to follow, how to be courteous and respectful at all times with those who naturally inspired gratitude and those who simply demanded it. We can hope that George made the most of his education and all of the opportunities to grow well, that he made lifelong friendships and strong social bonds that helped him endure and that might continue to do so into the future.

Now, as he set sail once again for pastures new at university, he was not only leaving behind this little community, but he was also still separated from his stepbrother and sisters. Leonora was living with Stephen and his wife in London. Philadelphia had been moved on from her residence with her Aunt Catherine's family and had returned to the capital, to take up an apprenticeship to a milliner in Covent Garden.[57] London was a place rife with a range of lifestyles and entertainments and where a young woman could be vulnerable to all sorts of influences and intentions. It was no easy atmosphere to make one's home or living in. How would she progress and how would George now fare? He had certainly been given plenty to learn and benefit from, but would he be 'as well fitted to mix in the world' as confidently as a Robert Ferrars (*Sense and Sensibility*)?[58] Would he be able to prove himself worthy amongst the other 'future Heroes, Legislators, Fools & Vilains [*sic*]' as Jane once named pupils, now they were all released from the confines of their school to embark on the next stage of their education.[59] How would he cope in the big wide world of university at the tender age of 16? His metal was about to be tested in a whole new way and it was now to be seen if his literacy and scholarly knowledge would be enough to see him through into his next challenge, to see if he was yet to be praised or to be pitied. Had George's time in the safety of school life awakened in him, as his grandmother would have wished, a belief in education as a way forward, a way of improving the future lot of both himself and also therefore his siblings? In the Elizabeth Weller school of thought, being educated was a means for providing for oneself, and yet the highest moral ground belonged to those who kept promises and provided from their abundance for their family too.[60] These were sentiments wholeheartedly agreed with by Jane's Miss Crawford (*Mansfield Park*) in her scathing observations of her own brother-in-law Dr Grant.[61] Either way, George was moving away from his Tunbridge roots once again and heading for the hallowed halls of St John's College, Oxford. It was time for him to stand on his own two feet, to make the most of all his talents and abilities, and all the opportunities that the fruits of his labours and those of his supporters had afforded him.

Chapter Three

Student Life

Truth be told, Jane never was to come to a universal acceptance of the worthiness of either the education offered or the scholarliness of a large proportion of students who reached the giddy heights of university. George, however, had an inner motivation that rose above common reasons for study. In learning Latin, he had been prepared and destined for a future in either the law or holy orders, and it was the latter vocation that formed the basis of his study at St John's. Whilst there the distance imposed upon him and his siblings grew wider still. Uncle Stephen died in 1750 but Leonora, now 18 years old, continued to live with his widow Elizabeth. When she remarried a member of the local bookseller and publishing community, Leonora moved with her and her new husband to Paternoster Row, an area in the vicinity of St Paul's Churchyard.

Philadelphia, however, moved even further away. She was shipped off to India, on a route commonly experienced by young women of the time, who were being sent away in order to find husbands and thus financial security for their futures which would not rely on or incur further expense to their families. Aged only 20 and possessing, it has been said, a degree of beauty, Philadelphia had no doubt a great deal of youthful energy and vitality. Judging by her later letters, she too had the same bright, positive personality traits of her brother, along with her own share of engaging intelligence and sociability. It has been remarked upon how quickly she was matched with Tysoe Saul Hancock. He, like her father, was a surgeon, and was working for the East India Company. He was seven years older than her. Within three years of Philadelphia's arrival, they were married. Although this must have brought some layer of comfort to George, years later it was a scenario Jane could not help but question, and with some feeling. Had this really been a marriage made of love or had it been a more pragmatic and practical arrangement? Had it even been her idea in the first place, or had the family urged it upon her? The story of Philadelphia's fate would have been well known to Jane, and the facts are available to us too, but the insight into the emotional upheaval she picked up on seems to have come from her insider view of conversations after the event. The discomfort and danger of the boat journey out of England and across the ocean to a brand-new world, and the negative aspects of the whole affair with its undertone of imposition and implied lack of choice or voice, impassioned a young Jane's imagination in her short story *Catharine, or the Bower,* in a way that could only happen to someone living in the light of a family's discussions and influence. Jane's view of the relationship and how it could have panned out paints it as an unhappy affair, yet Philadelphia would make friends there too, including the influential Warren Hastings.

As George grew into young adulthood, he stood tall and alert with a striking countenance and an equally bright intelligence to match. It would seem that just like in Edmund Bertram's (*Mansfield Park*) case, the move from school to university did not dint his personality or his ability to demonstrate kindness or attract friends.[1] In fact, it gave him another opportunity to double down, increase his learning and prove himself useful and obliging to his masters. There was also the added benefit of having the associated accommodation. For a young man who had known no real home of his own, he must have stood in awe as he gazed around the room allocated to him, with its little supply of furniture, whitewashed and perhaps wainscoted walls. In his situation many declared that, like the Englishman of old, they had come home to their very own castle. For George, this was the first place to feel like his own particular home and it must have felt enormously exciting and reassuring. He hit the ground running and bounced buoyantly from what he saw as blessing to blessing and challenge to challenge.

The Buttery Books, account books from his time in college, reveal that he was actually there about a week before his official matriculation date, at the end of June.[2] Looking into the accounts is very interesting as we glean a little insight into his early days as a 16-year-old living away from his relatives and fending for himself out in this new world. In his first few years he spent his money on a modest range of extras to supplement the food and drink that he was apportioned via his 'commons' allowance. Many payments were made each week to the sub-promus, or underbutler, for what was most likely to have been beer, the water being somewhat undrinkable in those times. Many private schools of the era also served beer, often home brewed on site to staff and students as a safer way of hydrating them. Something quite difficult to imagine nowadays, although the concoctions would have been fairly weak in terms of alcoholic strength. Like most teenagers George must have needed some extra snacks to supplement his dinner as quite a lot of his expenditure went to the pocket of the coquus, or cook, and there were payments for what seems to be a steady supply of cheese. About every three months George submitted his beautiful hair to the hands of the visiting college tonsor, or barber. He also made donations to the College's chosen charity school with equal frequency. There are also payments made to the janitor in order to keep his rooms clean.

However, perhaps the most interesting note is the frequency of payments for the postage of letters. George wrote weekly, a habit one hopes he also had at Tunbridge. We do not know to whom or where the letters were directed, but with his sisters spread quite literally abroad, and his uncles and aunt back in Kent, it is most probable that he was keeping in touch with them. It is most notable that unlike some other scholars he does not make any payments at all to the saddler, so he did not have his own horse, or transport, therefore making the need for a different method of communication all the more necessary and important to him. Keeping in touch with his family was a clear priority and with such a frequency, those letters must have been communicating a lot of detail about the events of his day-to-day life. He might have been said to have always had a letter on the go, a journal of sorts giving an up-to-date account of his world and sharing news as it happened.

George made immediate progress in his studies at university, making the most of the trust and financial support that had been invested in him by both his Uncle Francis and the legacy from Tunbridge School. He went on to successfully achieve his BA in the summer of 1751. Having been forced by circumstances to grow up quickly and at a much earlier age than many of his contemporaries, George had developed a keen awareness of the need to secure financial support. At university he demonstrated an ability for seeking out further such opportunities, which as a fellow he would have been expected to do. He not only showed great leadership and initiative in coming across exhibitions and grants that were available, but he also kept a sharp eye on when they were up for renewal or there was a vacancy. George was tenacious at working hard and therefore giving himself the best chance of being noticed. He was successful in communicating not only his knowledge but also his congenial and well-mannered nature. His attitude to learning and his application to his studies, coupled with his courteous and timely responses to his masters, married well with the other criteria he fulfilled such as his length of time in college and his family's financial background. He began inspiring confidence in his potential for patronage through his natural abilities, diligence to his studies and congenial ways. As Jane would later joke, with a touch of bitterness, there was no guarantee that luck would tip support in his favour. A vice chancellor or a benefactor, or in George's case, his masters and college leaders might vote the other way and choose another candidate.[3] However, through his own efforts and personality, he demonstrated his suitability for them and surged ahead in the stakes, securing financial help for himself as he went.

And so it was that, in November 1751, George received an exhibition, an extra small sum of money on top of his fellowship stipend, this time under a bequest from Sir William Paddy. An ancient and revered early St John's scholar, Sir William had gone on to a distinguished career as a respected physician to King James I who was to bestow his prestigious title upon him.[4] The exhibition was intended for a Batchelor of the Arts, which George now was, or someone at the beginning of their college career particularly for a scholar who was considered poor and lacking economic security.[5] At one point the exhibition stipend paid £5 a year. Only four fellows were selected for it and, by tradition and statute, they had to be approved by the college physician as well as by the president and the deans. It would seem most clear then that George was considered a worthy candidate by the powers that be. He most definitely did not fall into the category of charming idler that certain leading men in Jane's novels belonged to during their time at Oxford.[6] He was not of the sort as some 'gentleman-commoners' were, who attended solely for the necessary terms, dipping back home whenever they had the chance. This was partly down to his more elevated position as one of the fifty fellows of the college, quite simply he was expected to be in residence. However, it was also due to cost for at a subsistence level, the academic setting offered security as it had done at boarding school. George truly did have a love of learning, but his residency, although not without periods of absence, was also because he did not carry a great sense of home as being linked to a particular place. His siblings were so scattered that he did not need to return to a central hub, and in any case he had no base in particular to which he could return even if he had wanted to.

George's commitment and continued presence demonstrated that he did not have the luxury of resting on his laurels, in his case the care and generous compassion of his Uncle Francis. He had to take on college roles to make ends meet. In pursuit of a gentleman's education, George kept a keen eye on any salaried positions that might be available to add to his stipend and commons allowances. As he moved up through the ranks of experience and qualifications, simultaneously rising through the pecking order, as shown by the college accounts books from untitled undergraduate to the status of 'sir' and a graduate, he was chosen to take on some of the college roles and positions. In the year following the completion of his first degree, he had the honour of fulfilling the post of assistant logic reader, teaching or 'reading' logic to other undergraduates. This brought not only financial reward (about £2 per term) but also the chance to gain vital experience in teaching and professional academic life, and thus the hope of aligning himself with any future employment opportunities.[7]

George, now aged 21, had continued but also elevated his academic ambitions by embarking on an MA. Having graduated, his fellowship stipend increased, and, in the spring of 1752, he now gained himself further support in the form of another year-long exhibition valued at £5, this time following a bequest of Mrs Frances Barker.[8] This was a benefaction made available for four of the younger fellows who had spent fewer than six years at the college. Fellows could only be nominated under certain criteria, but they would also have needed to have met once again with the approval of the two deans of arts and the president of the college in order to be awarded the exhibition. In this case the chances of success also narrowed as under the terms and conditions of the award, preference was given to any fellows from Reading, in Berkshire, from whence Mrs Barker had hailed. George must have proved himself worthy to clinch an exhibition for himself. His success in gaining awards demonstrates his determination to succeed for himself, to match his academic abilities and his outstanding character with bona fide practical and financial support. George had his uncle's backing but he was also keenly aware of the necessity of a sustainable income in order not just to survive but to thrive.

George developed an admiration for those scholarly achievers around him, showing a real respect and deference for anyone with Latin and classics training throughout his life. Long into the future his own children would remember this quality in their father and how much of an appreciation he had for hard-working and gifted scholars who made their way in his part of the world of academia. His children's words in regard to any family news of a relation of theirs beginning to learn Latin, or as in George's future nephew's case, of triumphs in their studies, reveal just how much of an affinity George felt with this period of his life spent studying.[9] To his sons he always held aloft his sister's friend Warren Hastings, who, of a similar age and mentality to George, had been educated at Westminster School and would go on to become Governor-General of Bengal. George was struck by his scholarly abilities and would be forever urging his son Henry to follow his standards and aspire to be as proficient as Hastings.[10] These future feelings show just how well George bonded with and fitted in to the academic lifestyle and how much it spoke to his own inner man. Here he was once again nurtured into being and given a sense of purpose and confidence. This period of his life was one that he would always feel a connection with. It was here that he discovered a real sense of self after all the years of feeling lost as a child.

In the second year of his MA, George took an extended leave from summer into November, thus ruling himself out of the chance of taking an officership in college. However, he had good reason as he used the time to prepare himself to apply for and successfully secure the valuable Skinners' Company Sir Thomas Smythe exhibition.[11] This gift payment, bestowed by an endowment from no less than the founder's grandson, was granted following a petition by a candidate who could also provide a referee. The Company was duty bound to consider not only a candidate's ability and school record, but also the financial poverty of their parents.[12] Reported to have been worth £10 per annum for the length of seven years, it was explicitly and exclusively to support a Tonbridgian, an old boy of Tunbridge School in his studies at Oxford who specifically had their sights set on ordination.[13] George was clearly now looking ahead to his adult future, and a vision of what that might be was coming into view at last. Based upon the community expectations of his college and its founder, George himself was now also developing a sense of vocation. Here was a clear career path with the accompanying salary and provisions that would be attached to it. In the final year of his MA, to accompany his new-found sense of self, George successfully secured the Sir William Paddy exhibition for a second time, enabling him to continue his studies and fend for himself.

With his MA now completed, George was ordained a deacon at Oxford. In the college account books his status changed from 'Sir' to 'Mr' and he received a greater share of the 'fines', a charge on any tenant renewing or agreeing a rental of college property, a dividend that along with any other abundance or windfall bonuses to college funds would be distributed throughout the ranks of the fellows. Alongside his fellowship stipend, a termly allowance for clothing and other roles he performed in the college, he would now have received another payment called 'Pro-Presbyterio', specifically for clergy as an encouragement to continue and progress in their holy orders. This all enabled George to stay on at college and achieve an increasingly greater sense of financial stability.

Meanwhile, back at Tunbridge School, George's headmaster, James Cawthorn, was going through a period of great personal difficulty. His father and brother had recently died and his usher, his deputy master who had worked with him for the past seven years, had resigned. On the one hand, James's bereavement left him with an inheritance and financial capital, including shares in a lead mine (adapted as an idea by Jane for her distinguished ancient Willmot family in an early story called *Edgar and Emma*).[14] On the other hand, it left a vital supporting role vacant. James finally had money of his own to fulfil a long-held wish for the school, but he had no right-hand man, no one with whom he could forge ahead.

That George had reached such an advanced stage in his college career was perfect timing. In Cawthorn's mind, George Austen, his favourite pupil and protégé, was the perfect man for the job. There was one stumbling block. In order to retain the votes and favours pertaining to his role at the university and to continue to hold down all of his stipends and income, George had to occupy his rooms at St John's for a minimum amount of time per year; he also had to keep up a certain number of payments to the college to secure his fellowship and voting rights. However, with the school academic year being what it was, this was doable. In fact, it was an opportunity that George could, and did, take with both hands. He was returning not only to a school which he knew well from his personal experience, but also to a man who had shaped him, believed in him and from whom he could continue to learn. The nostalgic pull of this familiar setting, relationship and community, coupled with the guarantee of an income and of career experience, must have pushed so many buttons for George. Not only that, but it provided him with the opportunity to return to Tunbridge itself and to his family's heartland. In the light of all this, the decision cannot have been hard to make and, as one was permitted to take an extended break from the university of up to five years, the deal was sealed, at least in the minds of James and George.

To become an usher at Tunbridge School, however, was no small matter. Not only would George need to be a Latin scholar and a teacher of sufficiently high standards to impress the Skinners' Company, the headmaster and the parents, but there was also the small matter of Sir Andrew Judde's statutes too. In issuing his solemn promise to fulfil the role to the best of his ability and with the respect that it deserved, George would be commiting himself to nurturing the young people in his care 'in virtue and learning.'[15] As such there was a strict code placed upon him, just like any aspiring usher. He would have to be a role model of the highest order, for if the expectations of the founder were high in regard to the pupils, they were even higher in respect of the adults into whose hands the boys and the school's reputation were to be placed. This post would be perfect training for anyone aspiring to hold themselves up in the community as their rector or religious example and would be a good grounding in perceiving and fulfilling the needs of his young community. The statutes called for the usher, just like the headmaster, through a mix of their own personal integrity, faith and scholarly attributes, to 'stir and move' scholars in their religious knowledge and faith leading them upward and onward into goodness and in their Christian experience.[16] Education at Judde's school was intended as guidance and nurturing for life, and a cultured, respectable life at that. A life where one might fulfil one's duty to God and one's fellow man with a layer of taste and good sense within with which to stir one another up.

The statutes were very clear about the personal qualities expected of the second master, and his private life was scrutinised as much as his professional public one. With a clear call for modest behaviour in regard to speech, conduct and morals, the incumbent also had to demonstrate that as well as being an upstanding defender of the Protestant faith and Latin grammar, he possessed a clear regard for taste and decency. They were specifically not permitted to 'haunt taverns' or to gamble for, in line with society's expectations, it was the rule that outward shows of character duly reflected the quality of the inner life.[17] The usher, therefore, also had to demonstrate modesty of dress and as one certain Miss Crawford (*Mansfield Park*) might observe, they may *not* 'set the ton.'[18] They could not look overly ostentatious or show any leanings towards the dubious qualities of a flaneur, gandering about in layers of attention-seeking garb, a little like those whom George would have noticed frequenting the streets and the shops surrounding St Paul's Churchyard in his early childhood. No, they should not be slaves to fashion in any way. Equally they could not court any sort of flamboyant lifestyle, especially publicly, as the reputation of the school and the example they were setting to the boys in their care must be uppermost in their minds at all times. They had to be the consummate example of taste and decency of the age.

As well as his teaching duties in the schoolroom, the usher was also offered the role of housemaster and could take up to eight boarders into his home.[19] Ushers were allowed to be married but as George was single, much of the care of the boys would have fallen to him. No doubt he had some support in terms of laundry and perhaps feeding them, but he would have spent the evenings with them and as such would have been a guiding and nurturing influence on all aspects of their lives. Just as others hoping to offer board to pupils, he was guided by a strict code of conduct written into the statutes that insisted upon the boys' time being occupied in virtuous ways, with a real watch that they were not gambling or involved in any unbecoming or morally suspect behaviour.[20]

According to the statutes, George was not allowed to be absent from the school without a very good reason and in any case for no more than twenty days in any school year (and preferably not even that). Through his sheer presence alone, he was an anchor for many of his charges, offering the boys a sense of routine and dignity as he consoled those who felt homesick. Through his household routines and atmosphere, he created a whole world away from home. In charge of the boys at church on a Sunday too, he would have been a large presence in every aspect of their day-to-day experience of life and, as such, he exerted influence on them all.

George lived rent-free in accommodation on site, received sickness pay and not only the 40 shillings of old as decreed by the founder, but a much larger salary of £12 in addition to the stipends that he held. Once a year both the headmaster and the usher were also awarded a gratuity, a bonus payment for their 'good behaviour' and performance in the role for the previous twelve months. From the Skinners' records we know that George received a very welcome 10 guineas.[21] He was able to simultaneously earn and learn, taking up the curacy of nearby Shipbourne Church. This post was only recently vacated by the previous usher at Tunbridge, Johnson Towers, who had taken over for a short while from George's cousin Henry: the very same cousin who had previously been head boy at Tunbridge School and was moving on to take up a rectorship in a Hampshire village called Steventon under the advowson of the husband of a distant Horsmonden Austen relation, Thomas Knight senior. George was the lucky recipient of this timely vacancy at Shipbourne Church. Not only did it enable him to gain valuable experience in the run-up to being ordained as a priest the following year, but also it rather happily increased his income once again.

When George was finally chosen and approved, James Cawthorn must have been delighted. He not only had an usher who intrinsically understood, believed in and expounded the values of the school, through professional adult judgement, but also these very same values had personally influenced and shaped George to such a high degree as a pupil.

As eminent Austen scholar Brian Southam concurs, Cawthorn now had a deputy who was acclimatised to his exacting personality and, as such, would have been able to walk the fine line through his moods, traits and foibles.[22] George had already learnt by experience just how to push or not push his new boss's buttons. He had already been trained in his expectations and knew how to impress him. George understood what Cawthorn's values were and in which order he prioritised them. He had already learnt how to be guided by him and also knew just the right words, timing and diplomacy needed if he disagreed with him on something.

In fact, Cawthorn's leadership was not yet done with George because even as an adult his mentor still had more to teach him. With certain traits of stubbornness, determination and the courage to fight for his vision, Cawthorn's truth was to rub off on George and become ingrained in him too. In the next few years watching him operate up close, George's own instinct for dealing with the outside world and the powers that be would become finely honed. His integrity and truth was taking root deep within him like words through a stick of rock.

Cawthorn had always harboured the dream of creating a bespoke library for the school. When he arrived, there were relatively few actual books in the schoolroom, all of which were housed on just a couple of shelves. However, as the printing process evolved and books became cheaper, the dream came tantalisingly closer and at last seemed within reach. Sponsorship was sought at every given turn, either from wealthy subscribers or via sanctions of the boys' misdemeanours. Cawthorn became quite zealous about it, handing out punishment fines on his walks about the school with regularity and rigour, leaving one to ponder if his reputation for discipline and high standards was directed by his teaching aspirations or his determination to supply the boys with more books. As a result, more and more purchases were made and the number of books that the school owned and used now rapidly swelled. This valuable addition to the school's assets caused difficulty going forward for the members of the Skinners' Company tasked with the annual stocktake. And so it was that when Cawthorn's father died and he inherited a substantial sum including shares in a lead mine, he finally felt able to approach the Skinners' with his plan and request for a fully-fledged, purpose-built library building.

He shared his vision closely with George and after months of preparing and poring over the plans, compiling submissions of estimates and expounding explanations of the vision he had in mind, in January 1756, Cawthorn wrote his letter to the Skinners' Company to ask for their agreement. The court of assistants convened at the end of that month duly considered the request and granted it on the condition that they would not pay a penny over £60. Cawthorn would have to send them invoices and receipts to prove that all the work had been done.[23] This was a huge undertaking and commitment from the Company, both financially and in terms of trust in their headmaster. However, the caveat of the limits to cost was a definite line in the sand too. The Skinners' Company agreed but for them this was an investment in the education of the boys and in their building; there were limits to the imagination and romanticism that they were prepared to indulge.

The old headmaster's study on the southern end of the building next to his accommodation could now be demolished and a brand-new purpose-built library could indeed be built. Its architectural design was inspired by images of Roman and Greek facades with huge pillars and columns on the outside reminiscent of the Acropolis. For a school which focused on the pursuit of all things classical this was perfect. It exuded scholarly taste, and matched the mission of the school perfectly. Cawthorn was clear about what he wanted and, buoyed by the knowledge that he could afford to contribute should the Skinners' Company complain about any costs arising, he stood firm for the building that he wanted. The Cawthorn library was completed by October 1756 and the Skinners' Company records confirm that the £60 worth of bills were all honoured.

Demonstrating the formidable strength of character for which he was well known, others have commented on the personal characteristics that George must have possessed in order to work alongside such a forthright colleague, and this must have been especially true at this time. As anyone who has ever undertaken a building project can attest, the bumps in the road and the unexpected costs and changes can take their toll on any relationship. In this case that was true in regard to Cawthorn and the Skinners' Company. However, time would prove that this had been a formative experience for George. More than a library had been built during this time. In the future, one would see that more than a little of Cawthorn's relentless persistence in the face of resistance had rubbed off on his deputy.

George had watched as the headmaster had held out for what he felt was the exact fulfilment of his vision for the school library. The Skinners' records for summer 1756 see them scrabbling to prove the authentic wording of two Acts of Parliament established in the reign of Queen Elizabeth I in relation to a portion of land that was held by them, but in trust for the school, at Sandhills, in London.[24] The Skinners' Company had been approached to sell the land for a fine sum to the Foundling Hospital, which was seeking to build upon it. However, this was a legally protected source of income for the school. In the meeting in which the funds were approved for the library, the Company decided not to dispose of its Sandhills estates, which would have brought a significant boost to the school's coffers.[25] Requesting such a large sum of funding from the Skinners' Company for the library (£60) at this particular moment in time is something which Martin Cawthorne, in his biography of James Cawthorn, also acknowledges put a strain on the relationship between the headmaster and the school's owners.[26] This left both Cawthorn's and George's leadership exposed.

Whatever the case, records show that, in February 1757, the Skinners' Company wrote about their 'apprehension' to Cawthorn and required him to check whether or not George was still living within the terms of the will of Sir Thomas Smythe and, as such, if he were therefore still eligible to receive the said exhibition that they were paying him. Within the month they had ascertained that George was not residing at Oxford as the terms of the donor's will desired. His exhibition was voided by the Company and its withdrawal was confirmed a second time the following May.[27] The exhibition was not taken up by another petitioner and would go on to lay vacant for a number of years, but the Company's point had been duly made. From that summer onwards, the Company began to require estimates in advance for any repairs to the school building. They had other financial interests and the scrutiny of their accounts began to take on a tone not experienced thus far by their worthy and previously so esteemed headmaster. In any event, by the following summer, accounts show that the annual bonus payment was now to be shared between George and a brand-new usher *and* that the master of the Company would join with the headmaster in overseeing in what proportion this annuity might be divided up.[28] George's days at Tunbridge School had come to an end. One enigma and possibly an anomaly remains, however; the accounts books for the Skinners' Company appear to show the salary paid to George for the position of usher continued until 1763 and that even the payments on the Smythe exhibition were paid out until 1762.[29]

Chapter Four
University Life

In any event the university also desired George's presence. He was either recalled or intuited the need to return and pay much more attention to his responsibility for his studies, his status as a more senior fellow, and his stipends back at St John's College. He resigned the Shipbourne Church curacy and threw himself into preparing for his degree in divinity. Within a year George was impressing his college once again. In just twelve months he was appointed assistant chaplain to St John's Chapel, a role that in the past had been offered to one who was able to sing along competently and tunefully with the choir, as well as fulfilling the condition of being a fellow of the College, an MA and also in priest's orders.[1] This was a position nominated and elected directly at the discretion of the college president and it paid a salary of £20 as bequeathed by a previous president, Dr Holmes.[2] A payment which must have been a welcome thought if George was standing in and reading out the prayers at six o'clock in the morning, one whole hour earlier than his Tunbridge usher days!

In addition, the month previously, George had secured an important position of responsibility as junior dean of the arts, another position paid for by the legacy of Dr Holmes.[3] The £5, to be added to the £2 usually given, was to be an extra encouragement to the duo of deans to give their very best in the role and to model exemplary attendance as a permanent presence and faithful fixture at morning and night prayers in chapel.[4] The renumeration was intended to support the deans in giving their fullest commitment to ensure the highest standards of discipline and good behaviour at the college. Together with the senior dean, George was now jointly responsible for overseeing the teaching and learning of all the arts undergraduates, which constituted more or less the whole of the student body at St John's. At the time there was an incident going on in the kitchens with one cook serving out his notice with his replacement working alongside him for more than half a term.[5] This was a difficult situation which must have made for a charged atmosphere on occasion. George's role, however, was more that of a senior tutor and included responsibility solely for the monitoring and guidance and, if necessary, the discipline of the students' behaviour, nobody else's. If they did not show up at services or lectures, or did not heed the curfews or gate times, it was the dean team to whom they were answerable. Maintaining the college's standards in regard to student behaviour was their reason for being. Disciplining of the youngest students in the past had even meant punishment by the rod, rendering a dean equally feared and admired, and commanding respect.

George was also now called upon by the college to witness decisions made by the president and officers, including appointments to posts and expenditure, and his signature now appeared in the college register alongside those of the most senior colleagues. George's awareness of the responsibilities of his status now that he was a more senior fellow brought with it the knowledge that he was now in a position to be nominated for other benefices reserved for them within the college. And so it was that his devotion to his work, his innate abilities and his good character secured him another £5, this time in the form of a three-year exhibition paid for by the gift of Hugh Hindley.[6]

In the summer of 1759, as George approached the final year of his divinity degree, he was elected to a role not by his college but by the university itself, the position of junior proctor.[7] This was a time from which he was first hailed and acclaimed as the 'Handsome Proctor'.[8] Very tall, and according to strangers and family alike, extremely good-looking, he had a face that drew one in with its charms. His cultured conversation and manner, and his eyes, not dark but a vibrant hazel, endeared him to his listener.

This role included supporting the vice chancellor in hearing disputations and conferring degrees. However, as well as this administrative role in support of the leadership, George would also have worked with the student body at large to ensure that students were adhering to the codes of conduct and behaviour. This could often mean that George might have to go and round up the undergraduates from the local taverns and streets, and keep these wealthy yet perhaps not that motivated and focused young students in check. When we hear Edmund Bertram (*Mansfield Park*) reference having to prop up a man 'for the length of a street' at Oxford, one can just picture the young George in the same role.[9] Perhaps one of the undergraduates in their first term away, such as James Langford Nibbs, might have equally admired and appreciated this guidance as well as having the urge to rebel against it a little, for some kept in touch with George even many years after their time at the university had come to an end. When we get to eavesdrop on the conversation between Catherine Morland and Mr Thorpe (*Northanger Abbey*) and the comic, almost tongue-in-cheek dialogue that Jane pens in regard to the amount of alcohol drunk at Oxford University, we soon catch the drift of our heroine's heartfelt understanding that there was indeed a good deal drunk there.[10] We might spare a thought at this point for our unfortunate proctor. As we, the reader, raise an eye at Thorpe's quick explanation of partaking in a paltry 'four pints' and his knowledge of the qualities of a good wine versus a bad, we can imagine the reality of George's role on any given night.

From his office and preferments, we know George to have been a sober and well-behaved young man himself or he would not have been entrusted with the roles he had, but he must have seen more than his fair share of students' excesses, enough to have more than a few stories to tell on the matter. It may well have even sparked some material for his own sermons, preaching and teaching. George was now to put all the values of his own education and those he had been instilling as a teacher at Tunbridge to good use. His experience of working with a mixed age group of boys, along with his memories of Cawthorn's strict disciplinary methods and the Skinners' Company values embodied in Sir Andrew Judde's school, must have been ringing in his ears as he rounded up his charges on a Saturday night or knelt in church with them at the start and end of his day.

It was perhaps, though, not only George's physical countenance that struck those who met him and led to the spread of his goodly reputation at this time. For this was also a period when George had to draw deeply upon his own character and convictions. He had to find the strength to express his own particular point of view and reveal the true 'complexion' of his inner man.

His role as junior proctor meant that he was expected to support the vice chancellor in the smooth running of the university. This meant attending ceremonies and taking a leading role in the logistics of academia, particularly at busy times of the year such as in examination season or graduation, which was often a ceremony reminiscent of the Tunbridge School visitation days, full of verse and prose, disputations and prizes, examinations and honours.

It was at the very beginning of his year-long experience in this role that he was to be most sorely tested. George, along with the second junior proctor, William Wright of Merton College, were called to an important meeting or convocation of the university's leadership body. The university had been trying for some time to wrestle back its authority and control over its own affairs. A meeting had been called to discuss and to ratify by vote two statutes that the vice chancellor had proposed that would give the university more power and control over its own voting processes, which was so key at times of appointing sensitive positions of power such as that of chancellor. The university leadership wished to distance itself from the control of the statutes known as Archbishop Laud's code, drawn up and ratified by royalty way back in 1636.

The proposal had been under consideration by different factions of the university's leadership team for some time previously. However, George and William were very new in their posts and later claimed that they had not been brought up to speed or properly briefed upon their appointment. Importantly, they had both also aligned themselves on the opposite side to many of the powers that be. These included the vice chancellor, the formidable legal mind of William Blackstone, and the Tories, who represented the old order but wanted to lay a claim to the university's right to its own autonomy. George and William were the figureheads for those who disagreed with exerting the right to change the statutes independently. In reality this meant that they were supporters of those who desired a new order politically, the Whigs, who were intent on resisting giving more power to the Tories and their plans. Before the convocation, the junior proctors had both sent out a joint paper stating their case and their opposition to any change. George was later to write up a report on how the two proctors were treated at that convocation on 12 July, which was to say the least, very roughly. George and William had walked into a lion's den.

The vice chancellor's proposal had already met with some resistance as it was aiming to assert the university's right to independence over its own affairs, but so far that opposition had proved disorganised and disjointed. So it was that on the day of the meeting, the vice chancellor, 57-year-old Thomas Randolph, was spoiling for a fight with 28-year-old George. Tensions were running high, with Randolph determined to get his own way and to exercise what he saw as his right to lead. In his view this included making any amendments to the statutes, the laws governing the policies that underpinned the university, as he saw fit. However, this was not the view of some of the others, including the two new proctors. They believed that the statutes could only be changed by seeking Royal licence and could only, as a matter of absolute principle, be altered or laid down at the express approval of the king himself. George and William told them all so.

The whole of the meeting in front of the convocation of assembled university leaders and clergy was carried out in spoken Latin. The vice chancellor began by reading out the newly proposed statutes. He had just called for them to be read again, which would have effectively been moving them along to be voted upon and signed off. However, it was at this point that the junior proctors rejected a second reading and refused to take a vote. The vice chancellor took up his argument, beginning by ridiculing the position of the paper sent out by the proctors. He put them both on the spot, separately asking them if the paper that he had received contained all their reasons. The proctors then had to stand back as the vice chancellor challenged their claims as false, distorted and misrepresenting the truth. George and William bravely asked him to point out the errors in their paper. He told them that the statutes had been under consideration for many months and that they had only just written to him on 15 June. This was, in fact, true, but the proctors were very new in their posts and had had to quickly verse themselves in all the details of the case immediately upon their appointments.

The vice chancellor then turned upon them with much 'Earnestness and warmth' in calling upon them to justify having *their* own point of view on the matter of the university's right to alter a Royal Statute.[11] In his agitated state the vice chancellor denounced the proctors for their suggestion that the university approach the king for his approval on the matter. George and William were quick to point out in their written self-defence that this was, indeed, a suggestion they made, and that they felt it to be a most reasonable solution to the situation and the disagreements amongst the governing body.

The meeting disintegrated into a mostly one-sided debate with the vice chancellor becoming increasingly agitated; he pointed to himself as being at the very heart, the very centre, of the seat of power at the university, and therefore the one best able to advocate for any changes and best placed to make alterations to statutes as the university had always done. But the proctors firmly believed that although that might be the case, where no statute had been confirmed by the Crown, it was definitely inappropriate and a dishonourable contravention of the rules to change a confirmed statute without permission. They ventured that if the university had fallen into this error, then they should cease that way of behaving and turn back to the honourable way.

It was the tone and caustic mockery of the proctors, who in their eyes were seeking to do right by the university in their position as scrutineers in exercising a veto, which prompted George and William to write a report in answer to the objections made against them, especially in regard to their conduct in the meeting.[12] The proctors were very clear that, despite all of the opposition in the meeting, they believed that they had behaved with dignity and had sought to uphold the truth in this situation as was very much in keeping with the role they had been appointed to. However, they were aggrieved enough by the treatment that they received in the meeting that they felt compelled to put it all in writing. They were still convinced that they behaved correctly yet aghast at the raucous behaviour of the members of the convocation, which sounded reminiscent of the partisan yelling and booing often witnessed in the Houses of Parliament during a modern-day debate or speech. They were shocked that the vice chancellor had rounded upon them and with such vehemence, and they were appalled by the behaviour of men who they considered should know better on account of their education and upbringing.

The two proctors wrote so eloquently (in Latin!) in response to their treatment, standing on the side of what they saw to be truth with dignity and calm. They had acted, they believed, with a real feeling of integrity and right being on their side. They considered themselves worthy in regard to how they had behaved and approached their duty. It was their true wish in setting out their response to how they were treated in the meeting that hearts and minds, once cooled from the passion of debate, would see that the proctors had acted appropriately and in good faith. They hoped that perhaps the convocation members would speak out against the unjustified and wholly undignified way that they were treated on the day.

George had always sought in his life to date to work with people and to be helpful, to learn and seek knowledge diligently and to be useful. It may not have been his politics which led him to the conclusions he drew and upheld in the convocation, but rather for him this had been a matter of principle. George had been asked to fulfil a role as proctor and in seeking to carry out that role with integrity and purpose, he had perhaps been more driven by his own values in standing on a point of legal principle, rather than involving himself in the political nitty-gritty of the day. However, his allegiance to the opposition of the proposals had allied him with the 'New Interest'. As L.S. Sutherland points out, it was not after all the detail of the statutes being put forward but rather the legality of attempting to change a statute that was the foundation of the proctors' opposing arguments.[13]

In reality, however, the leadership simply waited it out. Once a new set of proctors were in place the following year, their proposed statutes were indeed approved and the whole nature of the university and how it was to be organised changed forever. The legal stance that the two junior proctors had taken found support many years later in the nineteenth century, but by then so much more water had passed under the bridge and the time for questioning such matters really seemed to have passed. One of the heads of house who also sided with the new political viewpoint and was opposed to the altering or 'explaining' of the university statutes was the president of St John's College, Thomas Fry. So George's foray into the political machinations of the university would not have wrought harm upon his own career in college. Another was the esteemed master of Balliol, Theophilus Leigh.[14]

At the end of March 1760, in the run-up to taking his divinity degree, George resigned his position as assistant chaplain. Later that year he was promoted to the role of senior dean of the arts, transitioning as he did so to a higher position within the college as would have been expected of a senior fellow.[15] Cawthorn would no doubt have been very proud of George, the pupil he had celebrated and supported for so many years. Unfortunately, however, his opportunity to enjoy a visit and partake in any revelling in George's success was cruelly cut short. In spring 1761, just a few months before George was to begin work as a lecturer in Greek (for the regular associated fee, of course, about £1 5 shillings per term) something that would most definitely have called to mind his days learning and teaching back at Tunbridge School, the worst happened to Cawthorn.[16] Whilst out riding his horse, something that he was notoriously bad at, he stopped to let the steed drink at a local Tunbridge pond. However, the animal unfortunately lost its footing and threw its rider. Cawthorn suffered a broken leg and a few days later he died of his injuries.

It had been believed that the year of Cawthorn's death marked the final year of payments from the Skinners' Company and Tunbridge School, however, as we have previously seen, the Company's accounts seem to show that George was still receiving money under the exhibition for another two years under the Thomas Smythe fund and also by the gift left by Sir Andrew Judde. The true legacy of all that George had inherited from his time at Tunbridge School with his mentor – his scholarly studies and his teaching and leadership experience – now stood him in good stead as he merged his vocation and fresh new qualifications into a stimulating, purposeful and useful combination. George had achieved great things with his education and was now ranked among a highly-educated elite, many of whom, unlike George, had a great number of useful family connections. George had used his own talents and wiles to build upon the opportunities and inspiration that had come his way from his own more modest patrons. He had exceeded many people's expectations for someone starting at the point he had. Perhaps not, however, the hopes and expectations that his grandmother Elizabeth Weller might have wished for him.

In a timely turn of events, as George's mentor and advocate Cawthorn died, a new benefactor helpfully stepped into George's life. Mr Thomas Brodnax (now Knight) of Godmersham was married to a distant relative, a cousin, Jane, of the Kent family line. Mrs Thomas Knight was a descendant of George's Uncle John V's in-laws and, as such, the granddaughter of Stephen Stringer, the uncle whom John V had been sent to under the terrible terms of John III's will. This was the very person who had most likely broken Elizabeth Weller's heart when he denied her a second chance to care for her son when at Sevenoaks School. Here now, once again following in the footsteps of his cousin Henry, five years his senior, just as he had at Shipbourne, in November Thomas Knight granted George the living of rector at Steventon, a parish in North Hampshire. He was presented the promotion just as Henry moved on to a more desirable position in West Wickham in Kent. Thomas Knight made an application to the Bishop of Winchester on George's behalf, one which was witnessed by Thomas Austen, George's apothecary uncle from Tunbridge, the vacating Henry's father.[17] The Bishop of Winchester then added his own mandate and sent it on to Thomas Balgny, the Archdeacon of Winchester, to induct George into the rectory of Steventon.[18]

George had one more step to go in his application and his college did him proud. He received the blessing of St John's College in their written reference, a glowing testimonial in support of his application. Written entirely in Latin, the language of the Church, they vouched for his suitability in regard to his character and knowledge, his vocation in the Anglican tradition, and his upstanding moral behaviour. They confirmed his honesty and sobriety as well as his industrious endeavours in giving due attention to his studies. It is poignant to see the signatures of his president Thomas Fry and the colleague whom he used to assist as logic reader, Mr Hitchcock, sitting at the bottom of the page.[19] George now had a living of around £100 a year to add to his income. As was common practice amongst parsons at the time, he initially decided to remain in Oxford and rely upon his curate, Thomas Bathurst, to run the day-to-day operations in situ. Could this have been a relative of Richard Bathurst, who took centre stage along with George on Skinners' Day back in his Tunbridge schooldays?[20]

The pull to leave St John's must still have seeped in at times. Separated from his siblings there was still a family life that he might have lived, just out of reach outside the university's walls. His sisters continued along their own life journeys away from him. Leonora, now approaching 30, was living a stone's throw from their Uncle Stephen's old bookshop with Elizabeth Austen, now Hinton, and her husband, a fellow member of Stephen's publishing community. Philadelphia was still so very far away in India. How George must have desired to visit her when in December 1761 she gave birth to her long-awaited first child. Married now for eight years, her daughter Elizabeth was a surprising addition to some, leading to some speculation about Philadelphia's friendship with her husband's business partner and friend, Warren Hastings. Hastings' baby daughter of the same name had died at just two months old in 1758 and his wife had died the following summer. Hastings was named godfather of Philadelphia's child, inflaming the rumour mill even further. How Philadelphia must have longed for a visit from her own kith and kin and not just to have received George's warm and conversational letters. Perhaps in some way Philadelphia's friendship with Hastings flourished because he had so many of her brother's corresponding characteristics. Warren Hastings, was, like George, fostered by his uncle and had also succeeded in his school life at Westminster School. The two men shared a similar outlook on life, including excelling in Latin. Hastings was even a contemporary of Cowper, one of George's favourite poets. The two men did have a lot to draw them to each other as friends, and Philadelphia's report of the reputation of each would certainly have incited reciprocal confidence.

In view of all the tragedy in his life, it could well have been this friendship which finally convinced Warren Hastings to send his 4-year-old son George to England for a better life, perhaps in regard to the boy's health and perhaps with a longer-term view and an eye on his future education. How it came to pass is unclear, but Austen family accounts confirm that young George was eventually sent into the care of George Austen. It would have been impossible for George to have housed a little child at the college, so if he was under George's direct supervision, he must have either lodged outside with him or had the child boarded out. However, what seems far more plausible, and is also a belief confirmed amongst some biographers, is that the child did not come into George's care for a little while longer and was actually fostered by another family, going by the name of Leigh, in Harpsden, who had friendship ties with the Hastings family, which for generations held estates located close by at Daylesford and Churchill.

In the meantime, George remained at the university, aware that normally this would have been a prerequisite of keeping his fellowship and his associated voting rights. If he had moved out to accept a college living, he would have had a 'grace year' in which to continue to enjoy the benefits of his university membership, but for now there was more than one compelling reason to stay. As he moved into the next academic year, clocking up another at the college, George redoubled his efforts and expanded his repertoire of roles. In line with the new status conferred upon him with the Steventon living, he was appointed college preacher: preaching to the congregation of undergraduates, commoners and fellows in chapel. In the same period, he celebrated becoming the natural philosophy reader, reading to the students and lecturing them, to the extent which it was understood in those times, on the equivalent of our science curriculum. In return, he received a small fee of approximately £1 5 shillings per term.

At this time there existed a tradition of fellows making a payment to the college library upon their promotion instead of spending that money on a 'treat', a practice that traditionally accompanied their moving tables in the dining hall to a 'higher' table.[21] Such movement and payments may have chimed with George's memory of old Cawthorn and his ways. A poignant and perhaps nostalgic reminder of his educational journey, his roots and his life to date. Perhaps in some way these traditions became echoes of comfort to George, enabling him to feel at home and increasingly settled by the routines, and rhythms of his academic way of life. Visits to the library, where books in the past had often been chained to stop them from being removed, would have been a privilege to be enjoyed, with borrowing a practice that was regulated and had in the past been paused altogether. Only people of respected seniority within the college were allowed to take a book back to their rooms.[22] The value and esteem in which a library should be held was brought home to him once again as it had been back in his Tunbridge schooldays with Cawthorn.

George was also to undertake another officership in line with his status, that of Waple lecturer. An endowment proffered to senior fellows to enable them to improve their preaching dexterity, this award was made by a venerable predecessor of George's at the college, Edward Waple. Buried in the college chapel where George had served as assistant chaplain, and now forever looking down from his portrait in college, Waple would have been a familiar feature of the university to George. In his career at St John's, George had also undertaken some of the same roles that Waple had performed before carving out his own career which culminated with his appointment as the canon of Winchester. Waple had become renowned for his sermons, publishing in his lifetime an annotated account of the Book of Revelation and had given money for an annual series of lectureships at the college in his name. Once again, four fellows were elected by the senior leadership team at the college and were to preach these special lectures for a fee of approximately £3 a term. They were specified to be upon the following topics: The Covenant of Grace (the baptismal vow), The Creed, The Ten Commandments and The Catechism. The Waple lecturers also led the two sacraments on the last Wednesday of the month.[23] Taking on this role was another indicator of George's rising seniority within the college community, which meant he was also getting older. Now 30 and having spent more than ten years at the university, his founder and his contemporaries would have been expecting him to take the next step into full-time life as a member of the clergy. The president was usually the only member of the community in his forties and the only one permitted to live as a married fellow. George may well have been feeling some expectation upon him to move on; however, on the other hand, he may have envisaged staying until one of the college's more lucrative livings came his way.

The college at this time is now remembered as a place full of calm and leisurely learning. Purposeful and active pursuit of knowledge and understanding seems to have been the order of the day for scholars and masters alike, but at a pace that has been described as 'gentlemanly.'[24] An atmosphere which must have seemed most conducive to George to whom living in an educational establishment was something he was quite used to. He had taken on the powers that be in the name of truth and honour, and had managed to survive any fallout, progressing his career and making friends and acquaintances that would follow him into his future. There was no doubt that for him at this time, life was good and looked set to continue in that way. For many who had grown and flown up through the ranks of the college as he had, the next steps were to move on to a doctorate in divinity, which would have been costly, and then perhaps to a position on the inner senior leadership team. In any event, despite some looks from some quarters, there was no real hurry to leave as long as he was progressing. As well as his fellowship stipend, the fees for the roles he was carrying out, and the award of annual exhibitions, George would also have enjoyed income from his share of any dividends from windfalls such as fines, new legacies and surplus funds from rents. This was all shared out amongst the fellows and the more senior he became, the greater the proportion he would have received. These payments amounted to more than the termly amounts paid for his services and financially enabled him to continue at the college.

Given George's experience, his popularity and the esteem in which he was held, Jane might have dipped her pen nib and written in admiration of her father and his life choices to this point. In stark contrast to her view of Mr Collins (*Pride and Prejudice*), she would very much have approved of the honourable use of his time and his wisdom and prudence in making the most of his 'gentleman's education'.[25] In giving himself over to the service of the college and the development of his abilities, and in building upon the opportunities presented by his membership of the university in order to better provide for himself, she would surely have applauded him as one far above those who merely served out the requisite number of terms, took their BA and left. From this vantage point, George himself may well have been looking ahead to a time when he could perhaps envisage himself standing for election to the position of vice president or president.

Another 'encouragement' to stay as long as he had may well have been a very profitable source of additional earnings as college tutor. Only some fellows were given this role and as well as being perhaps a marker of his experience and status in the college, it also gives us an insight into George's perceived abilities and professional experience. Given that the role was intended to educate college students in religion, ensuring that they had the required doctrinal understanding, George's appointment to this role would reflect a good reputation for his own understanding and also his mentoring skills. Permitted and awarded solely at the discretion of the college president, 'tutors' were not on the payroll of the university or college as such, but were paid at source by those of independent means. The role could earn hundreds of pounds over the course of a year as it would have been possible to have more than one tutee at a time. Tutors would guide and nurture each student academically and pastorally, and help them to navigate every area of university life, even aiding them in the management of their finances.[26] In order to act as such a guide, a tutor would have needed to possess not only critical knowledge but also a high degree of personal integrity, both in the eyes of the college and also the parents beyond the college gates.

It is thought that George was marked out for this role, and that he may well have tutored James Langford Nibbs who enrolled nine years later than George in 1758 at 19, an older age for a student, before he left to get married two years later. He was most likely to have been a gentleman-commoner on account of the fact that his 'cautions', the deposit laid down when a student matriculated as an indemnity against a student going into debt with their 'battels' or bills, were larger than some at £20 for the year.[27] This was an indicator that his family was wealthier and could underwrite James' potential debts to a higher amount, rather than the fact that the president who had admitted him thought that James ran a higher risk than another student of incurring any debts. At 21, James was to come into all the inheritance of his deceased father and whilst a resident of St John's, he was granted a coat of arms in 1759, a status symbol confirming his family's pedigree. It has also recently come to light, in a discovery made by Professor Devoney Looser, that it was George who conducted the marriage ceremony for James and his cousin Barbara Langford at St Clement Danes Church in London on 12 February 1760.[28]

What is also true is that George helped James a few days before that date, on 8 and 9 February, in regard to managing his inheritance and how it should be divested in the event of his death. George was named in an indenture as a co-trustee, acting in law to ensure that James' family's ownership of their estate would continue and that, in particular, payments to his new wife Barbara would be protected. The overall proposal and premise in the legal document was that George, in line with James Langford Nibbs' wishes, was to be a part of the group of people nominated to oversee the transfer of ownership of the Haddon or Weeks and Popeshead estates in Antigua to James' future descendants. If James were to die George would have had to administer his plantation estates on the young family's behalf.[29] George is listed as residing at St John's at the time of this agreement and this would therefore make it all the more plausible that he had indeed been James's tutor. This level of involvement with a tutee's financial administration would have been very much in keeping with the sort of task that a tutor may well have helped with. Moreover, George always sought to be useful and was a proven guardian of principles and duty. At this time in his career, he makes quite the impression. A highly respectable, capable and reliable supporting adult, a tutor was deemed to possess the necessary skills and gravitas for a situation like this. A pillar of the college, able to shoulder responsibility with integrity, it is clear that the college president believed that George was someone a student could turn to for advice, in confidence, and be sure of certain help, in times of need. The other co-trustee was Morris

Robinson, a solicitor, who would have had the experience and qualifications to oversee the legal side of the role and act as advisor in this capacity for any legal matters arising. His appointment placed George firmly in the role of educated guide, a respected and trusted pastoral advisor, rather than being responsible for any legal advice.

The fact that James's father had been a 'gentleman of Antigua' raises the reality of the conditions on which 'gentlemen' made their fortunes on the island at this time. Enslaved people were a very real part of the building of that wealth and it is here that George has been examined for his involvement in the Nibbs family affairs. James' descendants seem to have sold both the estates on to others just over ten years after his death, around 1806.[30] When the Haddon or Weeks Estate was laid out in the will of its second subsequent owner, made twelve years after the death of James, seven enslaved people were named in regard to the estate.[31] In October 1835, following a change in the law, a claim for £3,701 14s 4d was made in respect of Popeshead, or Langford's, as the second Langford Nibbs owned estate was called. There were 305 enslaved people named in relation to the estate at this time.[32] This number changed slightly over time, but it categorically places enslaved people and the ethics of how the profits and gains were made at the centre of the inheritance which George was theoretically involved in overseeing and safeguarding under the law. George's role, as laid out in 1760, was concerned with being ready to give support, advice and administrative help directly to James' future offspring in regard to upholding the terms and conditions legally governing their interests, as laid out in James' marriage settlement. We have seen that his involvement as a trusted and educated adult was typical of the role of tutor, although their friendship and links were to grow beyond this. It is a truth that needs to be acknowledged, however, that George was involved in supporting Nibbs' family in receiving an income which, although they were legally entitled to it, came directly from the profits of a sugar plantation whose workforce was comprised of enslaved people. As George was at school in Tunbridge with the sons of businessmen away in the West Indies, he must have been aware of the reality of the situation he was dealing with, to some degree. However, any views he had must have been shaped and influenced by the context of the times in which he lived.

Jane's views towards slavery were clear and stand in stark commentary against George's administrative involvements. Through her genius way with words and turns of phrase, her seemingly oblique and 'coincidental' uses of names or places, Jane Austen demonstrated a greater understanding and education about the business of a 'merchant', as she said society called them. Even though she wrote in a time when the nation's attitudes towards slavery were changing, for example, with the establishment of the Society for the Abolition of the Slave Trade, ideas and petitions had not yet evolved into passing Acts of Parliament. This did not happen in full until well after both George and Jane's lifetimes. Gabrielle White, in her book *Jane Austen In The Context of Abolition*, agrees that an awareness and care for the abolitionist campaign would have been 'natural' for Jane.[33] However, it was a subject to be approached with great care so as not to inadvertently spark a setback to any legal advancements or to dent the education of public opinion. It has been pointed out that the very title of *Mansfield Park*, Jane's novel which makes so many references to the slave trade, evoked the name of Lord Mansfield, who significantly ruled against an argument for slavery in 1772: a milestone in the process towards full abolition of slavery. Mrs Norris, from the same novel, shared her name with Robert Norris, a late eighteenth-century slave trader, as did Mrs Elton (*Emma*), whose maiden name was Hawkins. In *Emma*, Jane makes references to Jane Fairfax and her situation as being involved in 'governess-trade', all mentioned within a strange conversation with hints made in relation to the slave trade.[34] Fanny Price (*Mansfield Park*) similarly always appears trapped in her situation, albeit an improving one and in a totally different context. She too is controlled by a ruling family at the beck and call of all their wishes for her behaviour and movements, until at last she is able to break free and show them her value and worth which does, in fact, outclass theirs.

In *Mansfield Park* a direct link is made between the economy in Antigua and Uncle Bertram's finances. The implication is that these factors on the West India Estate are now so pressing that they seem to be causing her Uncle Bertram a lot of trouble. In the face of financial losses, he is called away in order to attend to his interests there, taking his troublesome heir, his eldest son, with him. In the case of the real-life Nibbs family, James' eldest son, also called James, got himself into difficulties brought about by his own lifestyle choices and behaviours, and eventually he was disinherited in favour of James senior's younger son and siblings.[35]

Mansfield Park later focuses upon Fanny's uncle's surprise return when she tries to talk to him about the 'slave trade' and highlights that she alone, amongst all the others, showed any interest in talking to him about it. Our hero Edmund expresses his shared wish that she had raised the matter further, but Fanny points to the fact that her enquiries were met with complete silence. Her uncle is an intimidating, domineering personality and yet Fanny bravely dares to address this economic situation, which his own daughters, or sons, despite their own superior educations, fail to do.[36]

That silence is an uncomfortable one and deliberately so. We are left wondering why no one with greater authority in the group questions Sir Thomas. Yet the novel later hinges on the terrible task of saying 'no' to this patriarch, when he practically coerces and chivvies Fanny into agreeing to marry Mr Crawford.[37] Fanny is left trembling and exhausted after her excruciating conversation with him, yet her integrity unfolds as the shining example to all of the family. The implication is that his values and priorities really do bear scrutiny and that much pain could have been saved and much greater service done to his children, and others back on his estates, had they been called into question much earlier. Something that Sir Bertram himself later laments.

It is a matter of great intrigue and interest also to think what Jane Austen might have portrayed through the poignantly unfinished plot line of Miss Lambe, a mixed race West Indian heiress, in her unfinished manuscript segments of *Sanditon*. A novel concerned with the country's contemporary obsession with health and its quest for curing itself by the sea, we may well have experienced more of Jane's views and thoughts on other aspects of the 'health' of the nation.

Closer ties to slavery would go on to surround George's children in the future. Legacies of British slave ownership have been found in relation to those living close by and in their social circle, including James Holder, the tenant of Ashe Park.[38] He was someone whose company Jane really did not enjoy and, in her letters, she once lamented her bad luck whilst awaiting the arrival of her friends for a ball there. Being holed up with him alone in the drawing room for a full 10 minutes, her letter gave the impression of one of those situations which in reality is only minutes long but seems in the imagination to be hours. In the excruciating moments before the other guests entered, she kept her hand firmly on the door handle willing someone, anyone, even the housekeeper, to arrive and relieve her from being alone in his dreadful company.[39]

Within the family circle other revelations of links to slavery have also come to light. George's eldest son, James, named perhaps after Nibbs, went on to marry Anne, the daughter of General Edward Mathew. Born in Antigua, he had been the governor of Grenada and commander in chief of the West Indies, and owned estates, including enslaved people, on the island of Dominica.[40] Even when James' wife died, the family, of course, remained close to him as grandfather of baby Anna Austen and continued to receive payments and contributions from him towards her upkeep.

After Jane's death, when Jane's best friend Martha married her brother Frank, he famously lost out on an inheritance that had been tacitly understood in the family to be coming his way in the future. His aunt Mrs Jane Leigh-Perrot, née Cholmeley, who had married his mother's brother James, owner of an estate called Scarlets in Berkshire, had intended to leave her home to him on her death. Yet she took a great dislike to Martha and lamented Frank's involvement with her. She could not countenance Martha as mistress of Scarlets and deplored that Frank was taking advice from such quarters that she could not abide. She gave Frank £10,000 and severed him from inheriting her estate, bestowing it upon James Austen's eldest son James Edward, Martha's nephew, his mother being Martha's sister. This strange yet clear dislike taken against Martha could be linked to Martha and Frank's stance against the slave trade. The couple's Christian faith was the bedrock of their identity, both separately and together, and as such their principles against the abhorrence of slavery would have been cemented as an immovable and integral foundation of their life's values. Part of the inheritance held by Mrs Leigh-Perrot came directly from her father's plantation estates which was amalgamated with those that her mother inherited from her second husband Mr Workman in Barbados, including the enslaved people therein.[41] It may well have been the issue of slavery and Martha and Frank's view of it that drove the final wedge between them and saw the inheritance going to a different branch of the family.

With his future children taking a very clear stance against slavery, perhaps there is an understanding of the true nature of their father's nominal involvement in Nibbs' affairs. Perhaps we see his intentions echoed in the perceived kindness of one of Jane's most beloved heroes, Captain Wentworth (*Persuasion*). He too steps in to aid the cause of a widow, albeit an impoverished one, which Barbara Nibbs senior was not. In his actions we get an insight into how helpful administrative assistance could be to a bereaved woman who might otherwise fall down on her luck. With all the red tape that could ensue when dealing with international affairs, Captain Wentworth is applauded by the narrator for his efforts, for his bravery and perseverance. It could very well be that Jane saw the same in her father's case; he had been acting as 'a determined friend' even though, when all was said and done, this was a decidedly concerning state of affairs.[42]

In any event, back at St John's, life, as it had tended to do previously for George, took a different and unexpected turn. His happy, settled and comfortable routines at Oxford were interrupted – this time by love. George had met Cassandra Leigh, the daughter of a clergyman, the Reverend Thomas Leigh, incumbent of the living of Harpsden. A fellow at All Soul's, Oxford, he was a member of the wealthy Leigh family of Adlestrop, Gloucestershire, the very same that were, as is most likely, caring for young George Hastings. It is often thought that the happy couple's paths crossed at the university, perhaps when Cassandra was visiting her witty Uncle Theophilus Leigh, master of Balliol College, who had already had some dealings with George over the statutes business. However, what seems far more conducive to the course of events that followed is that Cassandra's brother James Leigh, who had added the name Perrot to his own in order to be in line for an inheritance within the wider family line, was a student at St John's at the same time as George. He had matriculated a few summers later than George at the age of 15, when George himself was around 20 years old and by then long confirmed in his fellowship status. James graduated with a BCL (Bachelor of Civil Law) in 1758 and George may well have been present at James' graduation in support of his colleagues in the law department. George was studying for his degree in divinity at the time so they may well have bumped into each other in the library or other common study places. George was also serving as assistant chaplain for the college and dean of the arts undergraduates; as a striking figure with a high profile amongst the student body, he and James must have seen each other around college on a regular basis, for example, when family and friends were visiting and socialising during the weekends and out of college hours. They may even have been well acquainted. It seems very likely therefore that this was how George might have been introduced to Cassandra, and that the added bonus of having two relatives close by might have legitimately increased the frequency of her visits and thus George's opportunities to spend time getting to know her. Those dark eyes, handsome complexion and neat but evocative hair had time to work their magic on Cassandra, and her conversation had time to weave around the heart and mind of our gifted academic. In 1763 George had a portrait taken of himself; exchanged as a gift on their engagement, it bore a permanent reminder of those bright eyes and his handsome features highlighted by the elegant addition of a powdered wig.[43] The following spring, George and Cassandra were married by special licence at St Swithin's Church in Walcot, Bath. It was April 1764; George was 33 years old and his wife was a lively 24-year-old. Cassandra's sister Jane Leigh and her brother James both attended the wedding. Simultaneously, George wrote a letter to his Oxford college, resigning his position as a fellow there, a note of which was duly made, as per tradition, by the president in the college register. James himself married just over six months later so maybe, just maybe, he had very much been in a match-making frame of mind at this time and had taken a contented interest in facilitating such a happy attachment for his sister.

Chapter Five

Our Steventon Home

In the spring of 1764, just prior to his wedding day, George made his way to the parish of Steventon to take stock of the rectory and to make plans for him, his wife and their future. Part of a larger consortium of land owned by his patron and distant relative Thomas Knight of Godmersham, Kent, Steventon was a small parish. Near the source of the River Test, part of the Basingstoke Hundred, it had historically stretched approximately three by three and a quarter miles.[1] Set amongst the North Downs, in rural Hampshire, it nestled amidst gently sloping hills of chalkland meadows where sheep grazed and crops like oat and barley grew. In the decades preceding George's arrival, there had been a population of about 80 people which, in the course of his career as their rector, would rise steadily to a healthy 153.[2] As recently as the 1740s, the Steventon parishioners were still paying tithes, traditionally a tenth of their yield, in kind and the pervading community desire of old was that their rector would 'not be extortionate' in his expectations.[3]

George immediately took an interest in every detail and aspect of his new role and in the community that he was to serve. He started by taking stock of the state of St Nicholas' Church and its records. At this time church record-keeping was at the mercy, whim and capability of the rector. As a highly educated and organised man, George immediately took to writing up a fair copy of the current parish register out of a book said to have been compiled originally by his predecessor, the Reverend Henry Haddon. However, Haddon died in 1743 and was succeeded by William Payne and later Stephen Abthorpe before his cousin Henry relinquished the position, so it is possible that they too had a hand in recording some of the original information. The book, since lost, must have fallen short of George's required standards either in organisation, legibility or condition. He made a better copy in his clear, neat penmanship.[4] The records went back as far as 1738 and recorded baptisms and burials. George kept these all mixed in together, in chronological order in the same document, and from 1764 onwards he kept each page signed at the bottom in his own neat hand.

On arrival at the parish, the church records were not the only thing in a fragile state; the building itself was also in disrepair. The steeple tower had come down in a recent storm and the roof, badly damaged with exposed decaying timbers, was found to be too weak to support it.[5] George took the pragmatic decision not to rebuild either a steeple or a new spire, avoiding the expense and disruption. Instead, he arranged for the bells to be reattached and the roof to be redesigned and remodelled above them with vents to allow their sound to escape.[6] Hence, the church would have looked very different to Jane than it does to us today.

It also quickly became apparent, and perhaps rather more graphically in real life than in any previous correspondence with his benefactor Thomas Knight and his curate Thomas Bathurst, that moving directly into the rectory was nowhere near a possibility. To begin with, the couple and their young charge, George Hastings, now aged about 7, were to lodge at nearby Deane Parsonage. The incumbent, William Hillman, lived in the better-appointed Ashe rectory. Deane was approximately 1½ miles from Steventon and very walkable, in good weather at least, as the country lane – a muddy cart track between the two – could get very disrupted when the weather turned for the worse. George's Uncle Francis had also purchased for him the livings of Ashe and Deane. George would be able to add whichever became vacant first to his portfolio and thus his income. He was lucky to have had a living on offer, for many who left university in Oxford might have expected to languish in the office of curate for some time. As Mrs Jennings points out in *Sense and Sensibility*, many could only put off marriage in the hope of a living for so long before succumbing to accepting any type of income at all, however low.[7]

As Jane was quick to focus in on, some livings or salaries attached to the post of rector were more lucrative than others. Hence, for example, such subservience from Mr Collins (*Pride and Prejudice*) to Lady De Bourgh as observed so wryly by Lizzy Bennet.[8] Certainly, George and Cassandra would not have been able to get married without such a living. Luckily for them, George's Uncle Francis had continued to show kindness and generosity, so helpful as the lands and property belonging to George's father that he expected to take his share of in due course were still tied up with his stepmother Susanna, and he would not become eligible for them until her death.

However, securing a living was not a simple process. It was dependent upon waiting for the incumbent to depart, which usually meant upon their death or if one was lucky, their retirement. The urge to settle for a low-paying curacy in one's desire to get married would not only have been the stuff of Jane's characters' lives, but also a reality for couples eager to set up home together. George and Cassandra had no choice but to exercise patience. Everyone hoped that they might be recommended to someone in possession of an advowson, the right to nominate a rector to a parish. In reality George was very lucky in having been chosen by his distant cousin's spouse and lucky again to have his uncle's support waiting in the wings. As it was, when the livings became available, it was no guarantee of the high life, and as gentlemen who had the power to bestow one, such as Colonel Brandon (*Sense and Sensibility*) might observe, it was no standard of living that might tempt *them* to hanker after it.[9] On the other hand, it was a profession which came with an income and accommodation and with that a place of some social standing and respect within a community. It is no wonder that Mr Wickham (*Pride and Prejudice*) had *his* eyes on the sort of prize that he imagined Mr Darcy senior might be able to present him with one day.[10]

Uncle Francis' purchase, moreover, was a generous act, seeing as an advowson was on the whole a more valuable asset to the seller than to the recipient. The owner could demand a price that suited their own pocket and sell to the highest bidder. The purchase price could end up being far higher than the tithes and payments that it might actually be comprised of, as John Dashwood (*Sense and Sensibility*) and his business-focused mind certainly worked out in the case of Delaford.[11] Indeed, poor Edmund Bertram (*Mansfield Park*) was considered to have missed out on the intended family living set aside in everyone's minds for him when it was cashed in and sold. Its monetary value was deemed necessary in order to pay by way of Edmund's pain for the pleasures that his older brother Tom had pursued.[12] Sometimes all one could purchase or aspire to was holding a living in lieu of the chosen recipient, working it until the new incumbent came of age and claimed it and all its benefits as their own.

So, George had the security of knowing that not just one but two livings were coming his way, yet he did not have the confidence of a Mr Collins who could, and did, boast of his own good house and good income on his search for a good wife.[13] In *Northanger Abbey*, when the verbose and grandiose General Tilney rocks on his heels contemplating with pride his ability to provide such a living that would in itself see his son Henry comfortably off, Jane reflects her wary understanding that this was not a given or a certainty for everyone entering the clergy. All that could be hoped in the Austens' case, as in most others, was that the living at Steventon could be improved upon, as Uncle Francis hoped his addition would prove. If anyone had the mental resources and drive to achieve this, it surely would be the little orphaned boy who had risen to the top at St John's College.

However, the value of a living was more to George than pounds, shillings and pence. He had demonstrated a commitment to his vocation in taking holy orders before he had any secure knowledge of or desire for a particular living. As Edmund Bertram states, even if he had had an inkling of a preferment coming his way, this need not have been a cause to question his motivations; it may even have encouraged him to continue and press on with his calling.[14]

The fact that some might view this choice as shunning the opportunities of the shiny side of life would not have put George off either. In his role as usher at Tunbridge he had already been schooled in the art of avoiding any ostentatious forms of dress or lifestyle. He had stood firm on his honour as a seeker and supporter of truth and right, both when working for the school and in his role as junior proctor at the university. What is more, George must still have been experiencing some suffering from the sting of separation from his siblings and the loneliness of the loss of his parents. This was another motivation for him as he moved to create a stable, safe and secure base for his own new family. Never having settled into a home of his own before and having spent most of his life living in an educational institution, it is poignant yet not surprising to see how George threw himself into creating a viable and comfortable home for himself and his wife.

In the autumn of that first year, however, tragedy struck. Little George Hastings had become very ill and died of 'putrid sore throat'. Mrs Austen was devastated as she had really taken the little one under her wing and become very fond of him. Family legend asserted that she felt as great a grief as if he had been her own son.[15] His poor father did not hear of his death until his return in 1765 when it is reported that the first thing he was told on disembarking from his ship was that his child had died at George Austen's rectory. Surprisingly, there is no burial record at Deane or Steventon. George's grandson James Edward Austen-Leigh (also known as JEAL) concurred that with George keeping fastidious and faithful accounts of such things, it must therefore mean that Hastings junior was not buried at either place. Perhaps the young boy was repatriated to the Hastings family burial plot at St Peter's Church in Daylesford or, as JEAL believed, to some other location at the request of the family. Or perhaps, family conjecture, that the little boy was taken somewhere else for his health and subsequently buried there is true.[16] It is possible that the concerned Austens sought the medical help of a specialist in a larger town or city and that he died there.

Unlike Mr and Mrs Edward Ferrars (*Sense and Sensibility*) who sat out one month in the relative luxury of Colonel Brandon's mansion house whilst their parsonage was prepared, things were very different for George and Cassandra. For a start, George's mother-in-law, Jane Leigh, widowed that same year, had joined them at Deane Parsonage (a little house that would become notorious in the family for the difficulties that living there presented) and was with them for four whole years. In that time George and Cassandra's first three children, all sons, were born. James was born just a short time after their marriage, in February 1765. George's firstborn son and heir, he was perhaps named after James Cawthorn, George's Tunbridge School mentor. Or perhaps his namesake was the younger James Langford Nibbs, who became his godfather. With son George arriving 18 months later in August 1766 and Edward 14 months after that in October 1767, the parsonage now contained three boys under three years of age. George certainly had a growing brood and the bustling atmosphere of home must have reminded him of life back in the boarding school. It cannot have been lost on him that he had also just passed the age his father was when he died. Provision of such familial security must have gone a long way to healing his heart a little more from the sadness of being orphaned so young.

George's mind held a clear vision for their future Steventon home. However, bringing it up to a standard that would suit his way of living took a long while. In the meantime, the parsonage at Deane must have been full to the brim. The rectory at Steventon was not to be fully ready until the summer of 1768. No doubt finances had a lot to do with the slow progress of the renovation; indeed, George's bank account shows that he was still to make two substantial payments to the Reverend Hillman even though they had vacated. It just so happened that a sudden much larger injection of funds materialised that year in two unexpected instalments. Firstly, George's stepmother Susanna died in January. Under the terms of his father William's will written in the pre-Susanna days, this meant the release, at last, of the property which George and his siblings had been set to inherit. As per his father's wishes, the land and the three buildings were sold, and the proceeds were shared three ways between Philadelphia, George and Leonora. A timely help in more ways than one, with the knowledge of this extra future income George would have been able to afford to spend in the present and finish the outstanding work on a much-needed home for him and his growing family. Now finally settled with a family of his own to nurture and be nurtured by, the death of his 80-year-old stepmother marked some sort of closure on the pains of the past.

George did indeed transform the place and would continue to do so. There was even a carriage sweep invented just as Elinor and Edward Ferrars and the Tilneys (*Northanger Abbey*) had the imagination to include.[17] Packing up all their worldly goods onto carts and horses, Cassandra's elderly mother perched in amongst their belongings and the children, George moved into the first permanent family home that he had had since those hazy days of his early childhood in Tunbridge.

Certainly, there were challenges in fitting up the rectory at Steventon. It was set at the foot of gently sloping hills in a little valley of sorts and, as such, was very liable to flooding. At times George must have had deep concerns over the place, but he continued to carve out a creditable home for his growing family. The fact that in later life his daughter Jane would wish a 'comfortable parsonage house' as the fate of her niece and family speaks of a nostalgia for a truly settled home, a tribute to the life that her two parents created together.[18] Yet the mocking laughter of a scoffing Robert Ferrars (*Sense and Sensibility*) also reminds us of the impracticalities and inconveniences that a typical parsonage could present.[19] Seeing as it was not in the perfect location, unlike the parsonage so fortunately located in a village such as Highbury, and neither was it comparable to life in an abbey such as Northanger or the ancestral seat of the Leigh family at Stoneleigh, it is a credit to Cassandra that she too fully engrossed herself in creating a life for her and her family in such a humble abode.

With her ancestry, Cassandra could have aimed higher in the marriage stakes; certainly, Jane's Kitty and Lydia Bennet (*Pride and Prejudice*) would not have countenanced a courtship with a clergyman, although Fanny Price (*Mansfield Park*) and Catherine Morland (*Northanger Abbey*) may well have begged to differ and might even have envied Cassandra such an elegant, eminent catch. All the blessings which Uncle Francis' patronage had brought him, his place at Tunbridge, his gentleman's education, his fellowship at Oxford, and all George's scholarly endeavours and commitment perhaps had added to his persona and handsome countenance in order to align the stars for him and Cassandra. George would always have needed some sort of profession to elevate his station in life and to provide for himself and any family. Maybe, with his intellect, a career in the law might have suited him, although perhaps the army might have felt 'too smart' for him, just as Edward Ferrars had once shuddered at the thought of a military career.[20] George's attendance at St John's, where most were fitted for a life of service under holy orders and a minority for a career in the law, may have meant that Uncle Francis and the family were keeping their options open for either future career. Perhaps, though, the fact that others in his family circle were being prepared for the Church coupled up with George's own preferences even from an earlier age. This professional pathway, whenever and however it had finally been chosen, even if George had not been 'brought up' for the Church, was a direction which matched both his intellect and his vocational values and one he had definitely decided upon by the time he had put down his own roots at college. Through his achievements George now stood apart from his humbler beginnings, and like Mr Charles Hayter in *Persuasion*, he set himself in motion on a pathway to happiness, not only towards a career but also to a family circle of his own of some standing.[21]

Jane certainly had fun with her characters and the whole idea of married life in a parsonage, imagining the pride and prejudices attached to running such an important house in the parish. Mrs Norris's (*Mansfield Park*) comments in regard to creating the right reputation for the rectory and her obsession with organising the most perfect pantry puts us in mind of the day-to-day organisation of such an abode.[22] We can easily imagine how it might become a role ripe for an author's eye. Jane, of course, would go on to become familiar with many clergy and their homes, yet in her novels we see glimpses that might well be looking back at Steventon life, a portrait of her parents' view on how a home 'should be', one that we can see her delight in. After all it is not difficult to imagine that as in the words of Miss Maria Bertram (*Mansfield Park*), the Austens were aiming for 'a tidy looking house' despite all the children that were to fill it, and we can just see George and Cassandra standing at the door as we pass by, two 'very decent people' indeed.[23]

In late August of their first year in the house, Cassandra's mother Jane died. On 1 September George held the funeral service and buried her in the chancel. She was memorialised with a tribute stone placed close to the altar in the village church near their new home. The inheritance from Cassandra's father, including £1,000, would be released to her by February 1769. George and Cassandra pooled all their funds and invested it all – some £3,350 worth – in annuities with the South Sea Company, which was primarily set up to handle the debt of the government in 1711. Its attraction lay in that it paid back a guaranteed dividend or annuity each year to shareholders. Historically the Company had whaling and fishing contracts as well as lucrative trade relations with South America, but in the 30 years previously it had also been involved in supplying slaves to Spanish colonies. Set up in competition with the Bank of England, it was mainly a vehicle for managing national debt and as a government-backed scheme, it would have seemed a safe and sensible investment, rather more solid that placing one's money in a lottery scheme.

Meanwhile, back in London, Elizabeth Hinton, the widow of George's Uncle Stephen, died, and her widower, Mr Hinton, and latterly also his new wife, charitably continued to take care of Leonora there. George made payments for her upkeep and their sister and Mr Hancock did too, for Hancock made mention of his 'great Chearfulness' in doing his duty for Leonora in a letter to his wife. Mr Hinton's actions drew his praise too, and Mr Hancock thought that under the circumstances he had 'behaved very nobly.'[24] However, an unsurprised disdain with Stephen's widow's attitude, not unlike that which had prevailed in George's heart from his dealings with her in the past, was evident when he passed further comment on the fact that she had not left anything in her will to her niece-in-law.[25] George's bank accounts show that he continued to support his younger sister when the second Mrs Hinton was widowed. Leonora stayed with her and her new husband, also a bookseller, Mr Stephen Austen Cumberledge, in Paternoster Row until her death in early 1783.[26]

At home in Steventon, George took a great pride and joy in improving all aspects of the house, and by the time he had finished his efforts drew more than a little admiration from the hearts of his offspring. Sitting alongside the lane to North Waltham with around nine cottages for neighbours dotted about similarly on either side of road, the house occupied the spot nearest the turning into Church Lane of St Nicholas. A location such that Catherine Morland might hope would prove 'tolerably disengaged' from the rest of the village.[27] The original vicarage, which Jane might have had in mind when describing Mr Elton's 'old and not very good house' (*Emma*) had been built as long ago as the late fifteenth century.[28] For the last seventy years of its life, the house had maintained the same frontage, with windows either side of a front door. It had been extended at the west end and at the back, over a cellar. Previously, in 1697, there had also been two barns on the site. George gradually refurbished the house so that there were five useable rooms on the ground floor with seven rooms above and three attics.[29] Inside, George had learnt from the best at Tunbridge in how to set up rooms ready for occupation, fit for purpose and of a certain elegance whilst avoiding gratuitous expenditure or luxury. As a result, others later looked upon the inside as rather sparsely finished with a noticeable lack of cornices, and beams that were barely concealed behind their whitewashed finish.[30]

George was a dab hand at making his money stretch further, ensuring that with every purchase for the house from John Ring's shop in Church Street, Basingstoke, he swapped back a few pieces of furniture in exchange.[31] John Ring was not only an auctioneer with a furniture shop – he was also a cabinet maker, carpenter and joiner, quite capable of reupholstering a chair or repairing a table. He offered the perfect range of services for every pocket.[32] Certainly, when compared with the records of his eldest son James's expenditure when he took up residency in Deane Parsonage in later years, there was a distinctly frugal air to George's accounts and a noticeably indulgent one to his son's.[33] George, unlike James, did not go in for buying many mod-cons or ornaments and he did not make 'unnecessary' purchases. Anything George bought had a function and a purpose. Money was parted with on a need-by-need basis, even down to buying single forks and knives at a time. His home was elegant in a functional way and he had a firm grip on what would go in it, recycling anything of worth that no longer fitted with the family's needs and repairing anything that could be used for a little longer.

George had an eye for a bargain or a money-saving idea, but he also had taste. He bought select yet elegant pieces that had a practical use, and he was adept at choosing wood, even a cheaper one that could be tinted to look like something of better quality without attracting the higher price tag which went with it. Bedrooms were fitted with bedsteads, tent beds were made up by John Ring's men, and there were useful yet tasteful touches such as the oval or square mahogany-framed looking glasses.[34] George was fastidious about selling back things to the store for resale or repurposing as a way of raising funds to finance his present needs. As soon as a bed and bolster or a tent bed was no longer needed, it was sold back to John Ring. Each item received was carefully annotated in their ledger under George Austen's account, and the precise amount of money deducted from the cost of any newer purchase. Over time George sold back all manner of household items, including fenders, store grates, dining and card tables, mahogany chairs, armchairs, glass plate and window curtains (striped, checked and green.)[35] These reveal his enjoyment of good furniture and his and Cassandra's shared taste for softer furnishings and interior design, even down to their choice of window shades, curtains and carpets.

George's and Cassandra's choice of furniture must have occupied their thoughts and conversations to such an extent that it wound its way into the consciousness of their children as Jane often remarked upon their purchases in her later letters to her sister. George also shopped around, buying some of his furniture from a Mr Bayle at Newbury. As was the way of things when waiting for something to be made or finished, it could take time and there could be many unforeseen delays. Jane wrote of her brother James having to step in and chivvy along Mr Bayle, who seemed to have been of quite an unpredictable temperament, which may or may not have been influenced by alcohol. The whole relationship was one that Jane's humour and wit makes merry with in her letters.[36]

Perhaps Jane was used to not always sharing the taste and fancies of her parents when it came to furniture, but she acknowledged that neither were they always either independently or jointly happy with their purchases. She commented on her own surprise at everyone liking the delayed set of new tables very much.[37] Formed of two ends with a centrepiece overlayed in glass, Jane was taken with its aesthetic as well as its practical use. In the same letter Jane reveals the family also had a Pembroke table – a smaller mahogany table with sides that folded down when not in use and that contained a useful little drawer underneath – and a sideboard which would have had useful drawers too. The simple pleasures of being able to keep valuables safe seemed to delight her mother which in turn tickled Jane. Typical of George and Cassandra's 'use not, want not' attitude, when the new furniture arrived a current piece was immediately repurposed in another room. According to Jane, the senior Austens were also waiting on another piece of storage-type furniture, a chiffonier, which had a drawer and cupboards as well as a useful countertop or shelf. Every item had to earn its space and place in the Austens' home. Buying a lot of furniture at once was a large expenditure and atypical of George's financial personality, so they must have come into some money, just as they did in 1791 on the death of kind Uncle Francis; at that time, after more than three decades in their home they had a total upgrade to their downstairs living space. Jane's reflections and frustrations in having to wait upon their decisions of what to buy and where to put it can be heard in the echo of Emma Woodhouse's triumph (*Emma*) in purchasing and placing a modern round dining table in the family home. Once achieved, Jane took equal joy in persuading her father out of his habits and into eating there instead of at the Pembroke.[38] Perhaps George had a penchant for this prandial routine. The senior Austens' fondness for such a table gained it another special mention, reprised once again in *The Watsons* who lived like the Austens in a similarly ranked parsonage. They too featured a Pembroke in pride of place.[39]

This was not the first time that the house would have experienced a metamorphosis. It was often reimagined as the needs of the growing family changed and as the finances of the Austens ebbed and flowed. Family members who visited Steventon as children remembered that the front door opened straight onto the 'common' parlour where Mrs Austen would often be encountered completing some sewing task or other. In addition, facing out to the front of the house, there was a best parlour, or dining room, and the front kitchen, and towards the back of the house sat another kitchen, the stairs and George's study, with a little bay window that looked out onto the garden.

Initially, the bedrooms and the attics were fitted up for practical use as sleeping accommodation, but as time passed and needs changed, the rooms and their uses would be frequently reassessed. In later years, when grandchildren arrived, rooms and furniture would be altered to welcome and accommodate them too. In July 1795 when both Anna, James' daughter and Fanny, Edward's daughter, were just two years old, George purchased a child's chair made from cherry wood with a comfortable rush-woven seat.[40] By the time George's daughters, 'the girls' as he continued to refer to them, both reached their late teens and beyond, George gave over a part of the house just for them. One of the bedchambers above the dining room was redecorated and restyled to be used by the girls. It was directly next to their bedroom and the whole look and atmosphere of it made a huge impact on Jane's niece Anna whose senses must have been piqued at the time to be able to recall the room in so much detail into adulthood.[41]

They named it the 'dressing room' and Anna recalled a painted press, a wardrobe-type structure with shelves for linen that backed onto the bedroom, opposite a fireplace, which one presumes, unlike the old schoolroom that Fanny

Price adored as her own little nest, was actually lit for warmth when needed.[42] Jane and Cassandra loved the room and even in their twenties they spent the bulk of their time there. Jane gloried in having this space for themselves and trilled with the happiness of having their own room, feeling so much freer and 'elegant' there than downstairs with her parents in the parlour.[43] One imagines that she too felt all the benefit of having a bigger space in which to walk about and think in as Fanny did. Perhaps, just like her, Jane too had a few little plants to water and care for as she ruminated an idea of two. We know that Jane's creativity revelled in the space and atmosphere that this little environment permitted. We hear of items that reflected both the girls' personalities and interests but also George's elevated economic status for not every parsonage had a pianoforte or a daughter's day room with shelves for actual books.

Anna remembered one of the oval looking glasses above a table where rested two oval Tunbridge ware sewing boxes. Tunbridge ware was a highly skilled and unique decorative craft in which wood was cut and laid so that the exposed ends visible on the surface created a mosaic effect. Designs could be simple or highly intricate. The craft originated in Tunbridge, George's home town, and quickly spread via the tourist route to Tunbridge Wells. The provenance and inclusion of such an object in the girls' room is a touching link to their father's roots. Anna must have been very taken with the boxes and surely loved playing with them as a child. She could recall every last detail about what was inside. Jane too must have fondly remembered the boxes for it is in a similarly designed box that Harriet Smith (*Emma*) stores the treasured relics of her communications and associations with Mr Elton.[44]

There was a scant carpet too, rare as not many rooms in the house possessed any carpet at all. Anna talks of the décor as cheaply and plainly done, but the paper bought from John Ring was always thoughtfully and tastefully chosen for its colour and value for money. It was the freedom to express themselves however they wanted without fear of reproach, condemnation or eavesdropping that made this room so famously important to Jane that family members later recalled Steventon as 'the cradle of her genius' as a writer. According to Jane's niece, up here, out of the reach of her parents' regimes, there was an unchecked 'flow of native homebred wit' which provided the room with its real charm and attraction for the young women and their invited friends. What a boon this room was to Jane. What a gift from her father to give over such a space to his daughters. What an investment in both her personality and her personhood. A generous and unusual step to take, this support and nurture of Jane was critical to her. It was a catalyst and encouragement to work on what would become her novels as, in 1795, she began *Elinor and Marianne* and in 1796, *First Impressions*.

George's improvements at Steventon continued outside and developed steadily over time as the family's needs and desires changed. He and Cassandra created a thatched mud-effect wall for the garden and grew hedges, firs, elms and fruit trees, all intended to act as a cocoon, effectively shutting out the wind.[45] The back of the parsonage was truly 'enclosed in its own neat garden,' just like the one at Uppercross which Anne Elliot (*Persuasion*) was so familiar with.[46] Family members remembered this pretty spot with joy and gladness, especially the view looking directly out from George's study at the back of the house. There was a little cucumber patch near to a well to the left and then a wide grass walk up the middle with rows of strawberries planted either side, usually bathing in the sunshine there.[47] The sun's rays were captured and tracked by the sundial at the end of the path, no doubt reminiscent to George of the one back at Tunbridge School. It really did have all 'the best embellishments' just like Mr Parker's original home at Sanditon.[48] Mrs Elton's long and detailed commentary on the life of the strawberry at Mr Knightley's estate in *Emma* comes to mind too, and one wonders if George might have often talked proudly of his own knowledge of this fruit or even his cucumbers, or if he and Jane had walked there together.[49] Arising at the back of the garden was 'a green slope' just like the one Jane later described Catherine Morland rolling down in her childhood.[50] This little turfed terrace, as it was known, was a matter of interest to the whole family with much discussion and deliberation about how it should be planted up with beech or ash, larch, thorns or lilac.[51] It was flanked by a grove of trees that contained a walk. The layout was set in just such a way as we see referenced in one of Jane Austen's earliest writings, her short story of *Frederic and Elfrida*, in which the two lovers meander from the parsonage through a grove of poplars, rather than the Austens' elms, and en route to a 'verdant lawn' rather than surrounding fields, but still in a 'sweet village' where Elfrida's father is rector.[52] Yes, as Mr Elton in his own parsonage at Hartfield might relate to, Steventon may not have had any blessing in the form of its location, being like his very close to a road, but over the years one could definitely concur that it had been 'very much smartened up by the present proprietor.'[53] George was still investing in the gardens as late as 1800, some thirty-six years after they first set foot in the parish. For all the natural simplicity of the place which may have delighted a visitor such as Jane's Fanny Price, he continued to develop a new plan and ideas for a new enclosed garden to the right of the elm walk area. He showed the sort of pleasure and creativity in his aspirations for his grounds which Caroline Crawford (*Mansfield Park*) might have found surprising for a country parson.[54] The talk of the household was whether there should be apple, pear and cherry trees, a boon for their own ciders and fruit wines, or whether to plant it out with larch, mountain ash and acacia.[55] For George's grandchildren, this part of the garden was the most fun because near to a bench next to the gate for the wood walk was a weathercock mounted on a high pole that scratched and 'scrooped' in such a way that delighted them, if not the other occupants, and lived long in their memories of this happy place of their childhoods.[56]

Chapter Six
Community Cleric at Large

T he best part of all was that George now had a home into which he could invite his family. George and Cassandra both wrote regular letters to his siblings, and those that survive are warm and personalised, quite remarkable in the light of all their years of separation. George and Cassandra were particularly close to his stepbrother William-Hampson and his wife Susannah in Kent. In May 1770, George wrote such a kind and caring letter to his 'sister' Susannah, inviting her and her daughter Philly to stay whilst her husband was away for an extended period.[1] He thoughtfully made all the arrangements for transport, sparing her the cost and providing the means for her to get away. On her return home, in July, the pair exchanged friendly letters once again, this time whilst Cassandra was away. She was looking after her sister Jane who had just given birth to a son, a little earlier than expected, notes George – in fact, whilst Cassandra was still on her way to her sister. George wrote in a relaxed yet eloquent manner, sharing facts and details, warmly and thoughtfully including Susannah in all the family's news. He wrote about missing his wife and lamenting such a quiet and lonely life without the usual hustle and bustle of their normal way, a rhythm of life he had been used to, having lived in busy institutions all his younger days. He added that his boys were coping, perhaps surprisingly, really rather well and were simply glad of any kind attention from anyone; he was sure that they would not miss him one bit either should he have been absent himself – as is a child's happy way.[2]

The content of George's letters meld with an intimate tone and show a closeness to his sister-in-law. Open, honest and kind, laced with humour, wisdom, Christian faith and a calm, practical sense of the world. It is clear he was intent on sharing nuggets of information that he felt she would particularly enjoy, including a gossipy notification of a feud between two locals. In this letter we also gain a valuable and rare insight into the health of George junior. Approaching his fourth birthday, he had experienced fits in the past and George's words lament that they could not be too hopeful of ever expecting a full recovery of his health. His sad but empathic reasoning that at least they knew that he 'cannot be a bad or a wicked child' seems to comfort George as he writes, and reveals a tender compassion towards his son's fate. He finishes with a more hopeful topic, a promise to visit in a future summer with his wife, whom he won't let leave without him, and therefore with the whole family, as *she* won't leave without them. George's letter invites us to look upon a tender home life centred on the strong bonds of his family relationships in a pervading atmosphere of nurturing care.

The following summer, in June 1771, Henry Thomas was born, the first of George and Cassandra's children to be born and baptised from Steventon Parsonage. He was followed just under eighteen months later, in January 1773, by their first daughter, Cassandra. George was prompt in visiting and privately baptising newborn babies of the parish, publicly receiving them into the Church within the next month. That summer of 1773, Cassandra senior was so excited to invite Susannah and her family to meet the youngest two additions, her pride and joy wreathed around her happy words. By the end of the summer, Mrs Austen was newly pregnant again and this time Philadelphia was planning to visit, no doubt to lend a much-needed pair of hands to her sister-in-law. Although the Austen children were cared for at home for the first three months of their lives, they were, as was common practice at the time, subsequently nursed by another family, the Littleworths, in their home. A local family, the children customarily lived there until they could toddle about and were visited daily by either George and/or Cassandra. These visits were combined with parish work and the care for the three elder boys now aged 6, 7 and 8 living at home. The Austen household's life was getting busy. Hancock, Philadelphia's husband, who had returned to India to work on his business interests, could not stop himself from scoffing at George, passing on what he perhaps thought of as a witty message in his letters about the mounting costs incurred by this growing family: 'I fear George will find it easier to get a family than to provide for them; pray give my love to them.'[3] Frank was born the following April and Jane some twenty months later in December 1775. It was happy news to end the year, following the sad news of the death of the aforementioned Tysoe Hancock whilst still out in India. Thankfully, George and Cassandra had been with his beloved sister, who had returned to Europe, as she heard the news of her husband's death. This was truly a comfort to her, a widow, facing a period of grief and uncertainty, starved of any updates or further details on account of the distance.

The very next day after Jane's birth, George wrote to Susannah and William-Hampson. In his joy and relief at her safe delivery, his self-deprecation and gentle humour were once again to the fore. He began with a joke poking fun at himself and Cassandra as aged parents and the possibility of his siblings questioning their ability to predict their due date, anticipating their confusion and mirth at his expense. He talked lovingly and wistfully, full of hope at the 'present plaything' and 'future companion' for their daughter Cassy.[4] Ever the family man, at the same time, George had the presence of mind to enquire after his nephew who was in Jamaica, where the Hampson family owned a plantation. He also responded to his stepbrother's enquiry regarding a St John's College fellowship. George's nephew James was about 16 years old at the time. Always looking to interject with a note of whimsy, he also mentioned friends known to the Walters who were visiting locally and his hopes for a ploughing contest as a bit of fun for them as well as his parishioners. However, the frost he mentioned in passing, in the time-honoured British tradition of discussing the weather, did not let up as he had hoped; in fact, it deepened into something quite severe.

January became one of the coldest winters on record; the temperatures in Hampshire were as low as minus 18°C and snow came, went and returned in a cycle of freezing temperatures and fog.[5] February was windy with gales, the weather not letting up. As a result, parish records show that George could not welcome Jane officially into the Church until April, a noticeably longer time lapse than was usual.

When Jane was 3 and a half years old, her 'own particular little brother', as she called Charles John, was born. His godfather was John Cope Freeman, George's cousin on his maternal side. This branch also owned a plantation in Jamaica and John may have been the relative who paid for Philadelphia to go to India.[6]

George, aged 48, now had a family of six sons and two daughters, a far cry from the 6-year-old orphan. He had possession of the inheritance from his father, a close family circle of his own and regular contact with his brother William and sister Philadelphia. His youngest sibling Leonora was safely cared for in the home she had always known. The recipient of a gentleman's education, he had now progressed into his career. As the incumbent of the living of Steventon parish, he was now firmly and securely settled; his boyish days were far behind him and he was free to fashion his own future, master at last of his own destiny.

Having been on the receiving end of his uncle's generosity, he now in turn became a great source of comfort to his family. Following the death of Tysoe Hancock, George was called upon to use his experience and intellect on behalf of his niece Eliza, just as he had done all those years ago for his tutee Nibbs. He was appointed co-trustee of the trust fund given to her by Warren Hastings, alongside John Woodman, brother-in-law to the same. Mrs Ann Woodman was Cassandra Austen's childhood friend. Eliza expressed herself as dearly fond of her uncle and in May 1780, now aged 19 and living in France, she sent him a miniature portrait of herself.[7] However, as she entered her third decade of life, he began to grow concerned for her. She was about to marry Jean Capot de Feuillide. Both her great-uncle Francis and George concurred that this was not something they considered in her best interests. By August, George was growing rather agitated at the prospect of such a connection. His fears were not just for his niece but for his sister, and he lamented that they would be isolated as a result of the pairing, not only sacrificing their friends in leaving their country behind permanently but worse by perhaps even forgoing their religion.[8] By Christmas of that year, George had not had reason to change his mind and was genuinely worried.

George himself was no stranger to money worries. His income from his parish duties was valued at £100 and the rectory at £11, not much more than the rate for a curacy and not considered very much by the family and those in the know at the time. Tysoe Hancock had been right about one thing: paying for the needs of a growing family was not easy. The Austen couple's reality reflected that of Fanny and Edmund in *Mansfield Park* who, as in Jane's words, had by now been married long enough that an increase in their income was something they were looking for.[9] In the most timely and necessitous of moments, in 1773, the living of Deane, formerly purchased in trust for him by his Uncle Francis, had become vacant on the death of the wealthy Reverend William Hillman who had generously made Deane Parsonage available to George and his family on their arrival in the area. Before his Uncle Francis, as patron, presented George to the position at the end of March, three local rectors stepped in to plead his case. Clergy were not permitted to hold more than one post; indeed, pluralism, as this was known, was frowned upon. It was thought that clerical duties could not be carried out to the requisite standard if a rector was spread too thin. In George's case the rectors of Dummer, North Waltham and Worting wrote to the Lord Bishop of Winchester, the Lord High Chancellor of England, and the Archbishop of Canterbury to confirm the value of the livings. Deane rectory was valued at £10 and the parish was reputed to be worth £110 per annum and Steventon rectory was in the king's books rated at approximately £11 with a £100 yearly income. They also sought to clarify that the two parish churches were so close together, within 2 miles of each other, in fact, and that as such they could quite legitimately be covered by one minister.[10] On 1 April the mandate to induct George was sent to the Archdeacon of Winchester.[11] Another milestone had been reached. George might not have quite been the 'country curate, without bread to eat', so famous in the judgemental mind of Sir Walter Elliot (*Persuasion*), but things had got very difficult there for a while.[12]

George was a very diligent clergyman who noted all marriages, births and burials carefully into the appropriate parish registers. His time at Steventon spanned a period of the registers being left to the care and conclusions of the rector, but as time progressed the Church began to introduce proformas and to lay down guidelines for record-keeping. Church registers were most likely kept at home in the rectory for safe keeping rather than at the church, and some parts look to have been completed in what has come to be regarded as a female hand, which could possibly have been his wife Cassandra's or either of her daughters. George always ensured every detail was present and correct, and he signed his name at the bottom of each page with a neat signature 'Geo: Austen Rector'. Later, in one of the forementioned marriage registers, Jane's love of imagining and writing got the better of her and she 'borrowed' the opening pages that gave advice and guidelines on how to complete the registers. Jane wrote herself in as the bride in three different sections, comically playing about with the names of the groom, inserting three different characters in the role. Henry Frederick Howard Fitzwilliam of London, Arthur William Mortimer of Liverpool and good old Jack Smith all appeared on the forms. The name Fitzwilliam, of course, later became known to us as the Christian name of one Mr Darcy. Some have thought that this might date Jane's romantic daydreaming on the pages of the specimen marriage register sheets to about 1796 when she would have been 21 years old. However, Fitzwilliam may well have been lurking in her mind as a possible name for a character for a few years prior to that, for the officially printed marriage register forms were introduced in about 1754, so the form filling may have been more of a childish pursuit, one that captured the imagination of a creative pre-teen who was already tucking into her writing experiments with enthusiasm around the age of 12.[13]

In an early short story, *The Three Sisters*, Jane proved her expert knowledge of the pre-marriage administration process when she had her two lovers discuss the merits of the special licence and the marriage banns.[14] She drew upon her knowledge of the logistics of her father's clerical job, both as a vocation and as one of the 'preferred' professions of the upper classes, and weaved them between farcical comedic moments. In her story *Love and Freindship*, Laura marries her sweetheart Edward with her father popping up to perform the ceremony within the flash of a few seconds of the proposal. It turns out that he is not even ordained, has not passed through the many echelons of training from sub-deacon to deacon before becoming a priest, not served a curacy or gained any living. In the space of a cleverly crafted sentence, which mirrors the momentum of the plot, his lack of degree or training is brushed off as just an administrative discrepancy not worth worrying about, for as the joke makes clear he had been brought up for the Church.

In the Steventon marriage register covering the period of August 1738–July 1753, there were seventeen weddings. The rate remained more or less steady during George's tenure from 1764 to 1801. In the year George retired from his day-to-day duties and handed them over to his eldest son James, there were thirty-seven. Names appear there which may have fired the imagination of a young author on the hunt for titles for her heroes and heroines, villains and villagers. They included neighbours from the pages of local history such as Harwood, Bennet, Parker, Elton and Collins! In Jane's short story, *Catharine or the Bower*, the heroine is friends with two Miss Wynnes, 'daughters of the clergyman of the parish,' roles that Jane and her sister Cassandra knew intimately and understood the duties of, from supporting special events in the church to helping their father with the record-keeping.[15] One entry in the Steventon marriage register was for Cassandra and George's niece, Jane and Cassandra's dear cousin, Jane Cooper, who married Thomas Williams RN, in December 1792. Jane and Cassandra were to be present in a formal capacity as her witnesses and signed their names on the documentation, this time with genuine reason. The bride had been living with the Austens following the death of her widower father that summer. It must have been a very poignant affair, made all the more personal as Tom Fowle, an ordained minister, one of George's former pupils and Cassandra's new fiancé, presided over the proceedings.

During George's incumbency he carried out the services and offices of his role with humility, gravitas and great respect. There was no organ or choir stall, so he would most likely not have had to sing with, or for, the congregation as he might have had to as assistant chaplain at the chapel of St John's College, Oxford. Services would have included prayers, Bible readings and sermons. The latter were often influenced by the 1662 Book of Common Prayer which suggested seasonal prompts, topics and themes, and provided related readings and Bible verses as inspiration. George may have preached sermons shared locally by others or written by celebrated preachers of the day, but he also wrote his own. We know that a book was passed to his grandson James Edward Austen-Leigh which listed the texts of some of his sermons and some of those given by his maternal great-grandfather, the Reverend John Lloyd. The topics of George's sermons would have covered a wide range of Bible verses and themes, but in this little book they are all related to the four Gospels.[16] Today, from the reminiscences of his great-granddaughter Emma Austen Leigh, we know that at least one of George's sermons survived for some time and that he had carefully annotated on it the dates and locations when he had delivered it, totalling seven times at Deane and eight at Steventon.[17] It is intriguing to speculate what this sermon may have addressed. Author George Tucker believes it to be taken from Psalm 5:9, a text which exhorts the Christian believer, in no uncertain terms, to greater command of themselves in word and deed.[18]

As a trained and experienced teacher, with a vocational pull at the core of his heart, George may have given extended sermons. He preached once, possibly twice, at Steventon each Sunday but most likely once in the morning there and once at Deane in the evening. He may well have taken the opportunity to explain and expound either on a theme denoted in the church calendar, or as he dwelt amongst his congregation on a topic that he felt matched the needs of his parishioners. If the chatty conversational style of his letters is anything to go by, he would have been able to interject some light humour with local references and anecdotes to help get his message across. When Caroline Crawford in *Mansfield Park* scoffs at the thought of sermons 'worth hearing', she implies that many were not. Her pointed judgement against anyone daring to write their own, rather than having the 'sense' to preach celebrated versions such as Blair's, might well have been an in-joke once shared between Jane and her father.[19] In the context of his everyday life, poking fun at this element of his job would have made much sense to George and his daughter and been a great source of humour for them both.

Jane herself was clear in making judgements of both the sermon and the sermon giver. She respected a clergyman who could preach with 'ease & collectedness' as, after many years fulfilling the role, George must have done.[20] In her mind, speaking with sincerity and conviction could assuage other peculiarities or idiosyncrasies. In her later years, despite being brought up within her father's very clear-cut traditions, she was not totally against even the Evangelical branch of the Church, although she could be taken by surprise by an overly enthusiastic style or a little over-the-top eager and earnest preacher. She preferred a mix of 'reason and feeling' to the other end of the scale, a turgid and heavy delivery with a 'want of animation'.[21]

It has been asserted by the Reverend Michael Kenning, rector of Steventon between 1992 and 2010, that with the plain walls and distinct lack of decoration in the church at the time, there was not a lot for the congregation to be distracted by visually, which may also have helped them to focus on George's sermons.[22] Perhaps Jane was reflecting on this and playing on family jokes that compared the younger generation of sibling clergymen with her father's generation when Edmund Bertram comments on how little the 'art of reading, a clear manner, and a good delivery' had been studied among those who took holy orders 'twenty, thirty forty years ago'.[23] George's training in the art of delivering a persuasive speech, of reading with feeling and reciting back with careful emphasis at Tunbridge School, coupled with his knowledge of biblical content developed further through his delivery of the Waple lectures at St John's, must have truly added great credence to his abilities as rector. He must have made a positive comparison with others in his profession, especially those scattered across country livings endowed by prejudiced preferences for near connections or sold to those who could pay the highest price but perhaps were not the best candidate. His powers of critical thinking and depth of knowledge, as evidenced not only in the written style of his sermons but also in his spoken delivery of them, must have rendered each divine service at Steventon and Deane worthy of even Mr Crawford's (*Mansfield Park*) praise. Certainly, when we read of Mr Howard in *The Watsons* so highly praised for his reading skills, we understand that he had the intelligence, sensitivity and good sense to deliver a simple reading that, in its sincerity of form, touched the hearts and minds of all who heard him. When Jane wrote of Mr Howard as reading like a 'scholar and a gentleman', she must have had her father, who might then have influenced her brother, in her mind's eye.[24] Although Jane adored the theatre and drama, and became very knowledgeable and assured in her own definition of what made a good or a bad actor, she was clear in her depictions of clergymen such as Mr Elton (*Emma*) and Mr Collins (*Pride and Prejudice*) that the overaffected delivery of a sermon at the lectern or in the pulpit was not something that could ever be equated with a sense of good taste: a view which would have corresponded with her father's.

As per his commitment made at his ordination, George adhered to the language and traditions of the Church in which he had been trained and relied upon the experience he had gained at St John's College. George used the King James version of the Bible, that was, according to its own first page, 'appointed to be read in churches'. It contained the formal language prized not only by the Church establishment but later viewed as the only true version insisted upon in their homes by his own family. This was especially true of his son Frank, who, perhaps with a touch of nostalgia at the memory of his own father reading from it, would not countenance the use of any other version. George donated a large, brown leather-bound copy with gilt detailing to the spine and the cover, printed in 1793, to St Nicholas' Church. This beautifully printed copy is amazingly still in existence today and has continued to be used right into the twenty-first century.

The expectations of a parishioner's commitment to fulfilling their obligations to church services was something that Jane enjoyed exploiting in her imagination, no doubt drawing on either her own experiences, or conversations overheard from others as she grew up with the Church as her centre of gravity, exerting a force over her time and her sense of duty. She may have been fortunate to have attended church with some of those whom Edmund Bertram describes as the more discerning and educated of worshippers and she may well have been able to discuss the merits of her father's preaching. However, when characters such as Caroline Crawford lament the length of a boring sermon or service, or the ugliness of rectors both past and present in Jane's novels, she highlights this difference in the calibre of the clergy and the luck of the draw on which worshippers were on the receiving end. Luckily for George, he was well known, almost famous, for his handsome features and good looks into his older age as well as in his youth, which no doubt added to the compelling nature of his presentations. Although, as Sir Walter Elliot quite rightly pointed out, albeit in his preoccupied exaggerations, George's looks were also at risk for as a clergyman he was 'obliged to go into infected rooms.'[25] Perhaps in his lifetime, Jane and her family enjoyed teasing their father about villager comments about his handsome features, and references such as these would have brought all those memories to mind.

Although we know that from time to time the church building was repaired, it would probably only have had a rustic floor and, for the most part, would have lacked heating. As a result, in winter the sermons were probably a little shorter. However, the tenants of Manor Farm, the residents of the manor house that sat behind the church, may have been a little cosier. Their box-pew may well have moved around the church; some think it might have been at the chancel end opposite the piscina and some that it may have been placed next to the only fireplace in the church, giving the Digweed family a comfortable perk of the place during their worship.

The question of where the box-pew might have been located is not helped by the fact it is also unclear which altar George – dressed in his cassock, black scarf and perhaps his university hood – would have used or where he might have stood to deliver his sermons. There are two 'piscinas', one under a surviving, simple, narrow, arched, non-stained-glass window where an altar is placed today, and one behind that, along the same wall, in the chancel. A 'piscina' is the name Anglicans gave to a small, shallow basin that was traditionally placed near the altar for washing the priest's hands or any items used when giving Holy Communion. As there are two at St Nicholas' it poses the question of whether there were once two altars, or was one for more private, or smaller, services in the chancel? The silver chalice and paten that George used during Holy Communion, stamped with the date 1663, still exist today.

Jane herself was a committed and dedicated Christian. At home at the rectory, George would have read out the day's apportioned Bible verse for his family. He would probably have taken his cue from the direction laid out in the 1662 Book of Common Prayer that gave a suggested Bible reading for each day and a collect, a simple and succinct prayer focused on a theme or intention, with perhaps some additions for the Austen children from their father. The Austen family would have spent time in meditation, prayer and reflection on a daily basis, a family ritual that embedded itself into Jane's way of life and into her novels too. This was a practice which a domestic chaplain in a large country house would have led for the family, a custom that Fanny Price held so dear it was one which evoked precious memories for Jane.[26] When her own family were in mourning or in need, she turned to the comfort of the words and the ritual as an appropriate way to channel strong feelings and to find solace.[27]

Jane herself attended church regularly, even when away visiting relatives; indeed, if she or one of her friends ever missed church, it was a point to be mentioned in her letters. Inspired by the teachings and family traditions of faith modelled and laid down by her father, she also wrote her own prayers, three of which survive to this day. The Reverend Kenning notes how Jane shows her own knowledge and understanding of the Bible and, indeed, the Book of Common Prayer when she narrates Miss Bates in *Emma* misquoting Psalm 16 when reflecting upon her 'goodly heritage' in sharing in the generosity of the Woodhouses.[28] Her well-educated and more upwardly mobile characters such as Henry Crawford certainly possessed a knowledge of, if not a respect for, the qualities of the liturgy.[29] The deep understanding of the sacred texts which Jane used in her novels came directly from the family culture of Christian teachings and faith instigated, embedded and instilled in Jane by her father and the example he set. His sense of vocation, of religious duty and purpose influenced Jane's own Christian walk and way of life.

As rector, George was motivated to bring moral benefit and direction to his parishioners through his teaching and explanation of the holy texts. Moreover, through the expression of his faith, both privately and publicly, he wished to show with sincerity his dedication to Christianity, that he might be an example to, and of use to, others in living out the values that he preached. Jane saw examples of the clergy all around her, later in her brothers James and Henry, but also in local representatives and those of other members of her family. Yet her father's dedication was something she came to view as honourable and worthy but not typical of his profession. The fact that George resided in his parish and preached there regularly, not just every once in a while, was something with which she imbued her more worthy clergy characters in her novels. The integrity of the truly dedicated rector as asserted by her own dear Edmund Bertram is prized by Fanny Price. His elevation of residency as the highest ideal is something that both she and Edmund's father, Sir Thomas, viewed as the only dignified and honourable way of things. Jane took care to have her hero point out that it was certainly the only way to gain such exemplary personal knowledge of a clergyman's allocated flock of parishioners, and that a resident rector was in fact the only one who could completely meet their needs, their specific 'wants and claims'.[30] In later life Jane herself lamented that a talented and valued preacher in her brother Edward's local church had to pack up his life and return to one of his other churches on account of not being able to rely on his curate to carry out the offices in his absence. Indeed, this curate was so poor at the job, the parson was returning to take up full-time residency as it was the only way to eject him.[31]

Once resident in Steventon, George himself worked largely unassisted for most of his tenure, giving over his place to his son James as curate on his retirement nearly forty years later. James would go on to a career in the Church and George's son Henry who, having followed his father to St John's College, just like his brother James, eventually took holy orders after professional careers in both the militia and banking. He was curate at Chawton, Jane's later village home, in 1816 and, for a period of time following James' death in 1820–1822, Henry also resided as rector of Steventon until his nephew Edward Austen Knight was of an age to take up the post, as it was by then in his own father's gift to give. In reminiscences of his father, Henry put great store by the fact that George had resided in his parish for four decades in the 'conscientious and unassisted' fulfilment of his duties.[32]

When Jane gave a voice to Edmund Bertram on this matter, it had an air of memoir about it too. The virtues of the vocationally driven and spiritually committed country parson who might buck the trend of the city cleric with a purer interpretation of the role make a poignant portrait of George as rector. In Edmund's speeches we see the value that George placed upon the role, that of discharging one's foremost duty to God and to one's fellow man. His vocation was aimed at delivering upon his beliefs, using the influence of the position to affect those in his care both 'temporally and eternally' (even if that did sometimes mean spending a lot of time listening to the needs of others to the detriment of having time for oneself or one's family, as Caroline Crawford once lamented).[33]

With all the opportunities to witness the clergy first-hand, to observe them in their public roles and to hear their conversations behind closed doors, it was quite something when a clergyman of a more distant acquaintance attempted to influence Jane on her portrayal of a minister. In a strange happenstance, a fellow alumnus of her father's Tunbridge School, James Stanier Clarke, one-time naval chaplain and librarian to the Prince of Wales, approached Jane Austen to invite her to visit the prince's library at Carlton House in London. He informed Jane that the Prince Regent had copies of her novels and that she would be very welcome to include a dedication to him in her upcoming novel, *Emma*. In the correspondence that followed, James also attempted to coerce Jane to write about a clergyman who had a very similar biography to his own. His lapse into a small personal rant about his own perceived mistreatment in the role must have made Jane and her family chuckle. They knew the foibles of the Church for sure, and they had also seen how hard their father had worked and how diligently he had sacrificed himself in discharging his role over nearly forty years. George would have used his relational connections to build his reputation and perhaps lobby behind the scenes in line with his quiet yet diligently ambitious bent. Creating a character that wanted revolution rather than evolutional change, a parish parson that would openly challenge the senior priest or campaign for the doing away with tithes was not really the spirit or the approach that would influence Jane's message. It was not a suggestion that Jane was receptive to portraying. Nevertheless, James petitioned her forthrightly and repeatedly on behalf of his ideas. In fact, the example was one so opposite to the style of influence Jane received from her father that she pounced upon his ideas as a parody, including them in her 'plan of a novel.'[34]

George's vocation elevated him in the eyes of his daughter, his family, his parishioners and his community. As they made his acquaintance and interacted with such an educated and scholarly gentleman, they automatically associated him with wisdom and assigned greater weight and gravitas to his decisions and opinions. Anecdotally, we learn that locals called upon him as arbiter in private discussions and arguments.[35] His authority in the pulpit combined with his character and reputation, and spilled out into a wider public role in regard to local law and order. The countryside at that time held its own petty sessions and quarter sessions overseen by magistrates and justices of the peace. In addition, at a more local level, the lord of the manor or his representative would hold its own annual court leet, which dealt with any crimes committed within the local community, and the court baron, which recorded any issues between tenants. This included the transfer of lands from one tenant to another as had happened when the Hellier family handed over the parcel of land to George on his arrival in the parish.

The courts were usually held on the same day in a public place such as an inn, although sometimes in smaller parishes they were held at the manor house itself and would often both take place on the same day. The local community were very much involved and George could have been fined if he had not attended.[36] Moreover, as a well-regarded and respected leading member of the parish community, he would have had an important role to play in supporting the proceedings, overseeing decisions and even acting as a witness or juror if required. His very presence, which encapsulated his known character, his integrity and his intellect would have added a layer of respectability and calm to these events. In addition, in his clerical role, he would have been able to assert his authority by confirming all deaths, births and marriages affecting any of the transactions of the day. Unfortunately, the manor court rolls for Steventon at this time are in too fragile a state to be read. They were written on long parchments bound together at the top and then rolled like a scroll and bound. For each session, there would have been a list of tenants included at the top of the page and then the business of the meeting was laid out underneath. They were often written in Latin and required a degree of legibility and penmanship, making it highly probable that George was called upon to write up or check over these important minutes.

From his earlier involvements in organising matters regarding the library at Tunbridge School with the Skinners' Company, statutory matters as a junior proctor at Oxford University and legal matters in his work as an executor of trust funds, we know that George held fast to his principles on these occasions. He relied on his values and acted upon his gut instinct. In these types of highly organised, highly structured procedural settings, he was a stickler for process and was diligent in ensuring that judgement was dispensed carefully and correctly. He was resolute when it came to upholding ethical and legal standards, and was able to make decisions and stick to his guns with stubborn conviction. In Jane's imaginary world, Mr Knightley (*Emma*) shared George's involvement in parish matters, even serving at perhaps a slightly higher level as a magistrate in the county coordinated quarter sessions. Mr Knightley's discussion of such matters with his own brother gives a small insight into the reverberations of such conversations both around the village and the Steventon rectory.[37] According to the proud boastings of Mrs Elton (*Emma*), the rector might expect to be badgered by the local magistrates and overseers as well as any churchwardens, although in Mr Elton's case we are encouraged to laugh at the idea of anyone seeking his opinions and advice.[38] Young Henry Tilney too (*Northanger Abbey*) had to ensure he was available for parish meetings and for parish business, above and beyond that of his Sunday services.

From time to time, George had to make lists, take inventories or compile rolls recording certain details concerning parishioners and their community. He was required to send in local information in answer to government surveys, carry out paperwork relating to visitations from the bishop and update his parish registers, which he considered as all part of the job.[39] George's replies to the visitation questionnaires have an air of eloquence. His careful sentences uniquely combine detail with succinct clarification in a manner which reveal both his education and his personality, especially when read alongside returns made by neighbouring ministers.[40] In regard to these public interest commitments, however, he also involved himself more privately behind the scenes. His warm-hearted pastoral nature combined with his connections, and just like Mr Woodhouse (*Emma*), he was renowned for helping locals find situations and positions to suit them. He wrote letters to local employers such as the May family of brewers, enquiring into and applying for positions on behalf of his parishioners. He kindly intervened as much as he could, hoping and helping to improve the lot of the younger generations in his community just as he would do for his own children. Thus, he combined his concerns for the diligent communication of sacred teachings of his faith and office with practical and down-to-earth support for his parishioners.

Chapter Seven
Farmer Austen

I n addition to the monetary wealth, or the lack of it, that George gained from his parish role, he held a high status amongst his parishioners, perhaps uniquely elevated to a higher position than most other rectors would have commanded. Alongside his scholarly achievements and intellect which had already added to his striking character and integrity, he also possessed a kindred link with the absent lord of the manor, Thomas Knight, who owned the whole estate but did not reside there. As such, George was a cut above the ordinary country clergyman and even his 'chief parishioners', as his grandson referred to them. Truly a pillar amongst men locally, he would *almost* have been ranked amongst the squirearchy, that is definitely thought of in the same bracket in terms of calibre and gravitas as the tenants of the manor house, the Digweed family. Within the small Steventon community, he would have been defined and respected as a gentleman, and although he was employed as a rector, as was recognised by later family members, he would have become a 'centre of refinement'.[1]

However, George's humble beginnings and precarious financial status, coupled with his educated mind and manners, would not have given rise to the type of overconfidence and haughty arrogance caricatured by Jane in her Mr Collins (*Pride and Prejudice*). Jane must have revelled in the cringeworthy attitude with which he interacted with the local gentry and upper echelons. How she and the family must all have giggled and teased her father with the thought of *him* wandering straight up to a Mr Darcy-type figure in their lives.[2] The thought of their father George doing anything so out of step with social niceties, or daring to carry himself in any way above his station with any overemphasis of the 'authority' or 'rights' of his role, must have caused hilarity and no small degree of banter.[3] Having the leisure to make his life all about himself and a means to shoring up comfort or keeping up appearances of any status, as Mr Collins and even Mr Elton (*Emma*) were wont to do, could not have been further from the truth of George's life and situation.

In reality, George's £231 a year living plus tithes was still a small income. As Caroline Crawford points out to Edmund Bertram in *Mansfield Park*, there was no way to really 'distinguish' oneself as a clergyman as one might have hoped to do as a soldier, sailor or lawyer.[4] There were only a certain number of burials, births and marriages for which George could have counted on the extra guineas. The glebe lands at Steventon – lands set aside in an English parish for the sole use and income of the church and its incumbent – were considered very small at an estimated three acres, and traditionally had been spread out in small parcels of land amongst other farmed plots. Generously, Thomas Knight granted George the use of the 200 acres of Cheesedown Farm in the north of the parish, just south of Deane Gate.[5] A local farmer, Mr Hellier, also signed over four acres, containing a building, a barn and a garden for the rector's use in return for 2s a year.[6]

It was in this way then that George became even more visible amongst his parishioners. As he merged the duty of rector and the role of farmer, he believed he could more easily impart his ideals and values as a Christian because locals had more opportunity to witness him on a day-to-day basis, rather than just once or twice a week in church. He discharged his parish duties visiting those in need but in spending more time amongst the villagers in a farming capacity, he and they had the opportunity that Edmund Bertram described as only possible in the more intimately configured country community. That is, the villagers of Steventon and Deane truly got to know his 'private character' and through the challenges and frustrations, the problems and practical necessities that the seasons posed for the agricultural way of life, they got to observe his general 'conduct' in a way that perhaps rendered his role as Christian influencer even more successful.[7] George already had the moral high ground as set out by Jane's own Sir Thomas Bertram (*Mansfield Park*) in that he did not only 'do the duty' of Steventon, riding over there from some other place to temporarily bed down for a Saturday night; treating his parsonage like some sort of second home in order to take the Sunday service and read some prayers; and having stayed around for a few hours then returning to some other, presumably more comfortable, life.[8] In living *and* working amongst the parish, George was able to take his Christian duty to another level of service. In this way he would have had his ear on the ground and developed a sensitivity to the needs of his flock by directly participating in their shared way of life. He would have had ample chance to confirm himself as their sincere 'well-wisher and friend', and to express and convey in real life those messages and spiritual encouragements for love and good works which he sought to explain in church each Sunday.[9]

George's decision to improve his income by taking on the role of farmer had a huge impact on his life, taking up a large proportion of what would otherwise have been his leisure time. His thoughts now had to consider and reflect upon the major influence of the fate of local crops and livestock on his family finances, far above and beyond any impact solely on the rate of his tithes. It has been estimated that in fact George received between 33 per cent and 50 per cent of his entire annual earnings from the farm.[10] The developments in agriculture at the time, such as increased mechanisation and the application of modern theories and approaches to farming the land, alongside political ramifications caused by new laws governing the enclosure of land and the price of crops, were the context in which George spent his day-to-day operations on the farm. As a closed parish under the ownership of Thomas Knight, George would have been protected to a certain extent from the prevailing political whims that other rectors might fall foul of. Nevertheless, farming matters, especially his fluctuating income year on year, would have occupied his thoughts, his mind and his conversations. All in addition to, and alongside, his time spent on composing his sermons or other parish duties, which he diligently fulfilled.

Jane absorbed much of this talk and grew up knowledgeable about investments and profits, failures and crises that might impact upon those whose income and livelihood derived from the land. In *Sense and Sensibility*, Elinor's brother John laments at length the cost to him in enclosing land, complaining about the drain on his resources that such an expenditure might have, and mentions in passing his buying up of farmland adjoining his own.[11] She leaves the implication and reality hanging in the air – for this was land that would in one effective sweep have been taken away from the local villagers. Previously, common land was legally being hedged off for private cultivation and thus private profit. Land once considered too poor in quality to cultivate in earnest, where parishioners would have previously been permitted to graze their animals, was now hedged off. Now if they dared to enter, any villager would be charged with trespassing and fined. With the sale of a farm right out from under the reach of any local inhabitant in situ, local sources of financial support could be lost to those already most in need of it. For example, where poorer families would have habitually been used to exerting their gleaning rights after a harvest, the women and children would now be forbidden to collect any scraps of crops left behind. Food that had for a long time provided staples in the diet of a population already at the mercy of food shortages and scarcity would now be out of reach.

Juggling resources and prioritising the needs of the farm were a feature of many a conversation, not just those in George's study with his steward and bailiff, John Bond, but also amongst the pages of Jane's novels. Sparing the horses was a particular reality, as noticed by Elizabeth Bennet (*Pride and Prejudice*) and exploited by her mother when the latter sought to delay her daughter Jane on a journey to Netherfield. Forming part of Mrs Bennet's schemes, she hoped that her exaggerated concessions in favour of prioritising the farm's needs might mean that a carriage journey to the hall would be out of the question. She was not being authentically altruistic but was contriving a potentially profitable prolonged stay for a sickly Jane caught up in the bad weather on the way.[12] Likewise, when Mary Crawford enquires after the use of a horse and cart from local farmers for the delivery of her harp, of all things, right in the middle of the harvest, she meets with a passionately felt negative.[13] Jane pokes fun at her and in one stroke reveals an urban dweller's ignorance of country ways and a lack of any understanding of how the calendar of the seasons governs life on a farm. At the same time, this signals the influence of her upbringing on her own detailed consciousness of this way of life. Fanny Price (*Mansfield Park*), however, is a heroine very much in touch with her knowledge of the countryside and is portrayed as all the more heroic and naturally pure for being in possession of such intelligence. She may have lacked the education of her cousins, but she could assess from one quick glance when riding by in a carriage the quality of the soil, the cattle and how the harvest was progressing.[14] She noticed the details, the things that would have mattered to those whose living was determined by the land, things that Jane had had brought to her attention through her father's farming interests.

George had arable land, as well as some cattle, pigs and sheep. His steward and right-hand man John Bond would help him when choosing the sheep to add to his flock. Mr Digweed, the lord of the manor renting from the proprietor, Mr Knight, had a gentleman's agreement with George that when the sheep arrived, they would choose one after each other, letting them skip out into their care. When George once commented on the particular quality of the random allocation they had gained that year, John admitted with a wink to giving one or two a quick and timely nudge as they made their way out of the gate.[15] Mr Martin, the handsome and kind farmer in *Emma*, also had a prized flock on the farmland that he rented from Mr Knightley. His wool commanded a high price and enjoyed the best reputation, an astute observation by Jane Austen on not only the purpose of a working farm but also how such things were held in a fine balance, and how the scales of the worth of the farm in any one year could tip, either in the family's favour or in someone else's.[16]

Jane gained insight into the qualities of the farmers and landowners she saw about her and their characteristics and values filtered down into various elements of her characters. When imagining an older Mr Martin, she pokes fun at his potential ignorance of the airs and graces necessary in a more genteel, social world, and blames this on his overwhelming obsession with the fortune of his farming business and his blinkered focus on the bottom line and staying in the black.[17] For George and the farmers around Steventon, investment and return would have been their daily concern, and their hopes for a profitable year were the reason getting them up in the morning. Just like Mr Knightley and his estate bailiff, William Larkin, George and John Bond's minds would have been full of these matters too. They had to be if they were to ensure a smooth transition from season to season and navigate the market forces at play, and the weather, not only on their own farm, but also in the collection of tithes from the parishioners – their farming neighbours.[18]

This had not gone unnoticed by Jane over the years that she had spent seeing her father toing and froing, and witnessing the many comings and goings of his steward and others in his study. In fact, Jane took delight in laughing at the profession of farmer. Despite how hard they worked and everything they did for their communities, she found there was still great scope for teasing them about the position they held in the social hierarchy. Poor Mr Martin is summarily dismissed by Emma as a possible suitor for her friend Harriet as she feels she sits well above the status of any yeoman farmer.[19] George himself was not a yeoman, but they were a social group whom some considered akin to a gentleman, many overseeing large areas of farmland. They and their families were of an elevated social status, much higher than that of a labourer. George being viewed as a gentleman by the community gave him some overlap in terms of their shared agricultural experiences. In this regard, as well as giving Jane ideas for her imagination to develop and expand upon, mentions of farming and farmers, 'whether on horseback or on foot' were an opportunity for a healthy joke aimed in the direction of her father and the neighbours she grew up around.[20] For poor Mr Martin, despite any admirable disposition, honourable character or amiable qualities, had no chance of succeeding in winning Harriet's hand, in Emma's mind, simply because he would never amount to anything more than 'just' a farmer. If the farmer already occupied a lower rung on Emma's marriage-market ladder, then the farmhands, the ploughboys, would not even have made it to the first step. Part of the chorus in life, the background to the farmer as the main protagonist running the show, Jane even included them in a little song she wrote as part of one of her scraps, entitled *The First Act of a Comedy* included in her *Volume the Second* of her *Juvenilia*.[21] The ploughboys sing along, acting as a little comic refrain to the other characters. The group of lads Jane would have witnessed walking behind the cattle as they prepared the soil for sowing, or sat atop hay bales on the waggon after the harvest had all been safely brought in, gathered perfectly in her imagination, unified as one, a character poised on the edge of the scene with intrinsic comedy value.

Certainly, George could have held his own in discussions with Mr Knightley and his brother John, and matched their knowledge and enthusiasm topic for topic, be that the planting up plans for each acre for the following season, or the mundane but important tasks that became the bane of a farmer's life: those relating to drains, fences and trees.[22] Jane must have heard many conversations like these buzzing in the background of life at Steventon and she used them to good effect when outlining her characters' personalities and realities. Even when news of Mr Martin's betrothal to Harriet does finally reach Emma's ears, her response is a hilarious gentle swipe at the one-tracked mindedness of farmers and their teams. She chides Mr Knightley that perhaps he is only confused and has made a mistake, and that actually in reality, rather as in the normal way of things in their conversations, the two were distracted together by their usual subject matter, talk of drills and farm machinery or the 'dimensions of some famous Ox'.[23]

When Admiral and Mrs Croft take up residence at Kellynch Hall in *Persuasion*, they take a real interest in admiring all the pastoral aspects of their new estate. Enjoying what for them is the novelty and idyll of the rural way of life, they spend a lot of time outside taking in their new surroundings, wandering the fields at their leisure and pausing to admire the aesthetic of their crops and livestock. Although they are depicted as taking an interest in the wonders of their new world, they also reveal how little they understand of the reality of this way of life. It was an environment to be enjoyed at *their* convenience, but perhaps now they would also become fully aware of all the inconvenience, of the work and effort – at all hours, in all weathers and all year round – necessary to maintain this picturesque scene.

It is in the midst of the work of the country farm, at hay harvest that we first meet Mr Heywood in *Sanditon*. Standing amongst his labourers, overseeing and directing the proceedings, we hear of how healthy and good-looking this middle-aged 'gentleman-like man' is. One cannot help but wonder at this, another glimpse of George, leading and supporting his farm workers at one of the busiest times of the year. If only we could get a closer look at this man's handsome face and striking eyes just to be sure it is him.

The nitty-gritty of farming life was a continual topic of conversation amongst the family too, even into the adult life of George's children. Great pride was taken in the killing of a pig or the bounty of a crop, and Jane was asked by her father on many occasions to pass on messages about the fate of the farm in her letters, particularly to Edward, who, by then, was running his own estate and farmland. Successes such as the praise of George's mutton by a worthy neighbour ('the finest … ever ate'), the buying of sheep for a good price, or the selling of one of record-breaking size were passed on to brothers and sisters, even when they had grown and left home, a representation of how much this news filled George's mind and life.[24]

Nothing was sugar-coated – the farm was not a fairy tale so the reality of farm life was communicated too, such as the death of a lamb or a lament that a pig could be no bigger due to the end of the rearing season.[25] Such was the measure of how much of an understanding of their farm life was interwoven within the fabric of Austen family life. That this was the news that mattered to George and that he wanted to share underlines just how integral to his life and self-identity the farm's success became to him. Indeed, sharing his bounty and sending a ready-salted pig to his daughter Cassandra was a source of glee and gladness of George and Cassandra as parents.[26] For George it was also a way to bond with his son over a topic of mutual interest. George would even poke at Edward for more news of his pigs and would encourage him with a little bit of competition, sharing news of the interest and passion that a local landowner, Lord Bolton, was developing, even down to his commitment to constructing impressive pigsties.[27]

The senior Austens' pride in their agricultural achievements and their farming prowess was telling and a tribute to their joint devotion to one another and to their way of life. The level of determination and diligence that they invested in Cheesedown Farm, all whilst George was performing his clerical and parish duties, took hard work, perseverance and loyalty to the cause. George had found an ally in his wife, a co-worker to share his absolute commitment in his goal of taking care of his family. Cassandra became very knowledgeable about farming matters, another source of information through which Jane could absorb observations of daily life. Not only in her father's presence, but also in her mother's would she have heard of the varying lifecycles of different crops and good and bad harvest prospects. Harvest time would have taken over the whole of the Austen household and community, with extra workers drafted in, sometimes even from outside the village, which would mean hosting and feeding them too.

In one of her frequent letters to Susannah Walter, Cassandra discussed her hopes and expectations for their wheat, oat, peas and barley.[28] The crops would have provided food for the family, but were the staples of George's farm meant for sale and income, for market profits, and, as such, were not the sole claim of home consumption. Some of the rejected oats and peas may also have served in some cases as fodder for the animals.[29] Like George, Cassandra now talked openly of the work involved in reaping and rejoiced that they had managed to get it all done in just one month. Her expert knowledge of the importance of getting in the harvest as quickly as possible is matched by her interest in the weather forecast and its implications, which she interpreted for the impact they could have on the ripening times and the final quality of their produce. Where Cassandra really excelled and took charge was in the dairy. In her letters she wrote with real pride of her success with her cows. She revealed her detailed understanding and management of her cattle, including an awareness of the variance in their different breeds and how this individuality might bring different assets or the converse. She was also aware of how calving and breeding would affect a cow's use at different times of year. She showed such joy and delight in celebrating their productivity and that the family had more butter than they could use.[30] This is perhaps one of the most telling examples of how great a wife for George Cassandra truly was. She truly partnered with him in building up their assets and their business. Encouraging the family to visit, she passed on the anticipation of her husband's joy in being able to show his stepbrother all that they had achieved, all his lands and his livestock. Finally, in Cassandra, George had a rock, a supporter at close quarters on whom he could rely and with whom he could begin to jettison those feelings of abandonment and loneliness and instead celebrate their successes and hopes for their future.

Jane grew up knowing that her mother ran an excellent dairy. Her comments to her sister in one of her letters about a new maid's total ignorance being a bit of a challenge in their family speaks volumes as to how slick an organisation their family dairy was and how much of a family trait and skill running it became. Her final thought, that the maid was to be taught everything, leaves us in no doubt that she would need to be, that it was a real feature of the household's working life and a fundamental need for anyone who was part of the parsonage team and that also there might be a period of intense schooling ahead for the said maid from Mrs Austen herself.[31] One might almost imagine this knowledge being something like that passed on to Mrs Norris by the housekeeper on her visit to Sotherton Manor House in *Mansfield Park*.[32] Mrs Austen knew all about poultry, if not pheasants, and could also have passed on a huge amount of information in any conversation involving cows, a dairy and recipes for cream cheese.

It might even have been a joke at her mother's expense when Jane snuck in the mild lecture and instructions from Lady Catherine de Bourgh (*Pride and Prejudice*) to young wife Charlotte Collins on how to husband her cows and her chickens. If Lucy Steele (*Sense and Sensibility*) had lived nearby, no doubt she too would have been tempted to avail herself of Mrs Austen's hard-fought-for bounty. Interestingly, though, with George's ancestors of old being linked to the ancient clothier families of Kent, there is no mention relating to information surrounding any trade in the wool produced by George's sheep. However, spinning crafts were still part of the wider Austen family's way of life, as they were for some of the women and families in Steventon village too.

With the farm being such an important part of where, and how, George derived his income, he might well be forgiven for investing his capital in the running of it, rather than adding more and more to the parsonage itself. If young Henry Crawford (*Mansfield Park*) had ever visited, he may well have suggested some of his 'improvements' to the Steventon rectory as he had done to Edmund Bertram's at Thornton Lacey.[33] Luckily, the farmyard itself was a little removed from the rectory or else it would have no doubt drawn Henry's scorn. Jane's knowledge of Deane Parsonage is evoked in her character's reminiscences of what an unrespectable abode may contain. The building was often lamented amongst the family as a low-rooved conglomeration of uneven floors and inconvenient rooms and seems to attract its share of Jane's wit here under Crawford's eye.[34]

The idea of 'improving' their home was something that George had attempted for very practical reasons but that he had done on a tight budget and with all his experience of making do and mending that the Skinners' Company had taught him back at Tunbridge School. Having any home at all was such a luxurious concept, even if the bare bones of it might echo the 'vulgar compactness' as Henry saw it, of what for them was a farmhouse as much as a parsonage.[35] In this case, Jane's use of the wealthy man's penchant for their pipedreams, for their extravagant gestures towards introducing the picturesque into their estates was such a far cry from the needs and opportunities afforded to a farmer, even if it were the 'residence of a man of education' that Henry's visions aspired to convey.[36] No doubt this passage echoed the banter of the Steventon household of Jane's youth. These unfulfilled fantasies were so out of their own league as to be laughable, such a witty joke to be shared amongst the family, and with the added feature in the novel of defining Henry's character for readers with pinpoint precision.

Jane enjoyed poking fun at herself and her sister too, feeling their shared deep-rooted affinity with the farming community. She delighted in playing upon and revealing the stereotype of the ubiquitous 'mere farmer's daughter, without education' who might, she notes with a wink to the reader, as Miss Emma Woodhouse (*Emma*) implies, just be the most terrible catch in the marriage-market and well below the notice of the good of society.[37]

Chapter Eight
Schoolmaster Austen

In the early spring of 1773, George was struggling for income. The rate at which money was coming in from the farm was unpredictable and changeable, and consequently the amount earned from Steventon parish tithes could also be quite small. His bank account with C. Hoare & Co. for February shows he had gratefully received substantial financial help from his brother-in-law James, just before the happy and timely arrival of his presentation to Deane the following month.[1] However, not one to rely on others when he could help himself, talented, experienced and ever resourceful George also put his scholarly acumen to work. James, his eldest and intelligent son, was now 8 years old, approaching the age when George himself had first been sent off to Tunbridge School. His younger brother Edward was 6. Having decided that it would be a shame, as much in George's case as in Mrs Weston's (*Emma*), that 'one who so well knew how to teach, should not have their powers in exercise again,' especially if a little income could be come by from it, George and Cassandra opened up their home as a mini, family-run boarding school.[2] There was no organised school for the poor in the parish at that time and there would not be until the turn of the century. Even then, it would prove the parish as a small one in Jane Fairfax's (*Emma*) calculations as there were even fewer than twenty-five pupils, averaging only about ten per year in its opening decades.[3] Just like Mr Howard (*The Watsons*), who had turned his hand both to tutoring and the Church, George returned to the combination of careers he had been used to when usher at Tunbridge School and curate of St Giles', Shipbourne Church in Kent. He offered this opportunity, for approximately £35 a year per pupil, not to parish children but to the sons of local gentry and clergy as well as those of contacts they themselves had built up. George and Cassandra took pupils right into the heart of their home; George's Hoare's Bank customer ledgers show that they usually hosted about four at a time, with a view to educating them and, if appropriate, preparing them for their university applications.

In summer 1773, Cassandra wrote of one such pupil, a very young boy about 6 years old, with learning difficulties, called Lord Lymington, son of the Earl of Portsmouth who had just started with them. Sadly, he was not to complete his education as his mother later became concerned about his speech development and withdrew him from the Austens' care.[4] Other boarders were also the sons of wealthy gentlemen known personally to George and Cassandra. These included his tutee and friend from his St John's days, James Langford Nibbs, who sent his son George to study under perhaps *his* namesake. Some were sent by friends such as the Reverend and Mrs Fowle in nearby Kintbury who sent their sons Fulwar-Craven and Tom. Other boys were sent under the sponsorship of clergy, such as Croft, paid for by the Bishop of Exeter. Friendship and personal recommendation accounted for other boys becoming pupils. Sir William East, who sent his son Gilbert, was a near neighbour of Cassandra Austen's brother James. A young Vandergesten was the son of another of James and Cassandra's friends who hailed from Cane End in Oxfordshire. A close working associate of Warren Hastings, this link confirmed not only the childhood friendship of the Hastings and the Leighs from their days growing up so close to one another in Oxfordshire, but also the confidence that George's reputation and educational qualifications inspired in them all. The boys, just like young Hastings all those years ago, wound their way into Cassandra Austen's heart. Vandergesten junior, even as a 14-year-old, impressed her with his manners and disposition.[5] Boarded in the house amongst the Austens' growing family, Mrs Austen fully supported her husband in his entrepreneurial venture in a very practical way, acting as a pastoral housemistress and joint carer for the boys, just as George's grandmother Elizabeth had done all those years ago at Sevenoaks School.

Education was a lynchpin for George, one of the fundamental values upon which he had built his own life and a respect for which ran in his blood, passed on perhaps even in his DNA from his grandmother. Perhaps this turn of events brought a source of comfort to George, a sense of connection and a nostalgia for a father whom he had known for such a short time. He was also, of course, returning his living conditions to the routines that ran inside him like clockwork and must have reminded him of his former life as an usher at Tunbridge School. Jane would later joke that her father had his own very clear views about routines, particularly those surrounding mealtimes. Pointed references to dining times, such as Lady Denham's (*Sanditon*) preference for early eating and the lengths to which Mrs Weston went to keep her son-in-law Frank's poor mealtime punctuality a secret from Mr Woodhouse, suggest it may well have been a shared family joke referring back to their father's stickler-type nature and his set views concerning the etiquette of daily prandial habits.[6] Eating with a few more mouths around the table would not have been an uncomfortable inconvenience to George who had experienced so many such gatherings both at Tunbridge and Oxford.

Jane was born into observing the world that George had created. Caught up in the atmosphere of his daily workload, she witnessed him instilling the virtues of learning and scholarship into his pupils. She overheard the pride and praise from her parents in recognition of each pupil's progress and achievements, as Catherine Morland (*Northanger Abbey*) did and she absorbed a great deal of the philosophy and educational culture as valued by her father.[7] Edward Ferrars (*Sense and Sensibility*) was scolded and scoffed at by his younger brother for what *he* saw as the misfortune of being sent, upon the advice of his uncle, a *Sir* Robert no less, to the home school of Mr Pratt, for a 'private' education instead of going to one of the prestigious public schools as he did. Believing this to be at the expense of Edmund's future and social development, the younger Robert never ceased to blame and criticise his mother for making such a choice.[8] Jane is no doubt lampooning the 'public' education system here which actually failed many. Through the tale of these two brothers, she demonstrated the blind prejudice against a school like her father's, run by a kind and experienced teacher who, along with his vocation as rector, had much of meaning and true worth, in short, principles to communicate to his pupils. We are told that, separate to what his brother believed, Edward was already blessed in disposition and abilities by nature, just like George, and that his understanding was improved by the education he received.[9]

In fact, one of the pieces of the puzzle which leads us so to mistrust and pity Miss Lucy Steele (*Sense and Sensibility*) is when we discover that she has lacked any type of education, formal or informal, at home or at school, and that the failure to provide it has left her stunted and ignorant, socially maimed and quite simply out of Elinor or sensible society's league. The sad irony is that it was at her Uncle Mr Pratt's home that she met Edward, whilst he was still a pupil there. If only she too had been invited to the school table, laments Jane.[10] Colonel Brandon (*Sense and Sensibility*), an educated and sensible man of great means, a hero in Jane's world, deeply regretted that he was not able to offer such an experience to his ward, seeing the value of such personalised oversight by a caring and upright rational parent-type figure as opposed to the pot luck of leaving for and learning in some educational establishments.[11]

When Marianne Dashwood (*Sense and Sensibility*) is recovering from her dangerous fever after the breakup betrayal of Mr Willoughby, she vows to throw herself into music and reading as the antidote to her devoted obsession with him.[12] She (over)ambitiously vows to read every day for six hours for a whole year. A typically enthusiastic and perhaps a very Marianne type of emotionally determined response, but reaching out for education and knowledge as a supportive foundation for future survival was something that

George had grasped hold of at an early age and, although here lightly mocked, it was a positive mindset that Jane received from his influence.

We see the very same value reflected in the heart and mind of one of Jane's most iconic and beloved heroes, Mr Darcy himself (*Pride and Prejudice*). In order for a woman to be authentically accomplished in his view, he believed that she had to have improved her mind by 'extensive' reading, alongside her possession of other attributes relating to art, music, dancing and foreign languages.[13] In a rare and candid insight, Mr Darcy underlines his belief in the need to improve oneself but concedes that there are some defects which education cannot vanquish. Later we discover that some can only be truly overcome by love.[14]

For Jane, too, education and particularly the use to which one did, or did not, put it was important. Using education to modify and improve oneself, to tame and ultimately master one's own nature in order to be commander of oneself was a 'spiritual' matter for Jane and her father. The pursuit of knowledge alone as a tool for improving the mind was not enough. Using that knowledge, especially of oneself, offered through the insight that education provided, was an outworking of their Christian duty. It was their faith in action. Education in this respect was a tool to be applied in order to improve oneself through the renewal of one's nature, mind, manners and comportment by word and deed, all the better to serve one's God through serving one's community.

In Jane's works we are introduced to a number of protagonists who received a misguided education with disastrous consequences for their character. Sometimes this was because any teaching was provided by incapable and bad educators. Edmund and Fanny in *Mansfield Park* reasoned that a mind could start out wonderfully with a bright future, and be 'tainted' and 'injured' at the hands of a rogue or dubious influence.[15] We learn, for example, that the positive development of Mr Collins' (*Pride and Prejudice*) natural state failed due to the poor quality of his early education by his father. Sometimes, in addition, an individual's own failure to engage with educational opportunities when they were available, as was likewise the case with Mr Collins, could derail any improvement and halt the amelioration of an individual or group. If this state of affairs was coupled with the future promise of easy gains, of assured prosperity, then the ensuing lack of purpose, of a goal which needed effort in order to be attained, could mean that the person involved risked ruination of character.[16] Or worse still that they might be lost beyond the reach of the powers of education. Perhaps then, as a result, they might be ever forced into social faux pas humiliating themselves and others, such as was the case on a regular basis with Mr Collins and Mr Elton (*Emma*).

Once the gap between two people's levels of education was opened up, as observed by Fanny Price of herself and Mr Henry Crawford (*Mansfield Park*), that divide could not be breached, and no further connection between the two could ever be forged without want of training and re-education on the side of one or the other. Yet, if they had each received an education similar to each other's level, then just like Mr Martin's sisters with young Harriet Smith (*Emma*), there might be no social disapproval or awkwardness and their relationship might be sanctioned, deemed acceptable and free to flourish.[17]

For Jane, able to observe her father's approach to teaching and learning so closely, the question of the style and form in which schooling was arranged and delivered was a legitimate one to be posed. Jane and Cassandra were taught the basics of their letters and numbers at home by their mother as was the custom of the time. Cassandra was a gifted and talented artist and Jane could play the piano; however, Jane loathed the whole concept and reality of visiting masters, criticising them in her letters and encouraging us to laugh at Lady Catherine de Bourgh's (*Pride and Prejudice*) insistence on them and to rejoice in the happy day when Catherine Morland saw them banished from her home forever.[18] Jane also enjoyed lampooning and loathing the governess. This was perhaps a comment on their scope and status, rather than their common personal attributes or intelligence, as later in life she had a very good friend, Anne Sharpe, who performed the role for her brother Edward's family at Godmersham Park. The idea that a young girl of the upper classes might have been badly neglected in not having a governess was one that Jane liked to exploit and rail against. Her father taught his sons at home, none of them being sent away to Winchester or Westminster College as his grandsons would be. He, of course, was extremely qualified for the role himself, but it undoubtedly saved them money too and such a financial cost may well have been out of their reach. Jane's complete rejection of the requirement for governesses for girls goes beyond just the expense of them. In her disdain for them and Elizabeth Bennet's (*Pride and Prejudice*) total ambivalence to not having one, there speaks an opinion that they were not indispensable.[19] Her referral to the fear and revulsion in Jane Fairfax's mind at the prospect of becoming one revealed Jane's all-round view of the unsatisfactory nature of the post for all parties.[20]

Jane talks of Catherine Morland enjoying the same pursuits as boys, rolling down the banks at the back of her home and probably as Jane did, playing cricket with her brothers and sisters.[21] The implication is that she learnt through play and the exploration of her environment. In putting this type of early education in a positive light, setting it in nature and the open air, Jane made the whole method seem a much more natural process in itself.

A developmental one, personalised to the learner and more apt for the age and stage of a child's young life; Jane describes it with such feeling in her words that it could well be she either joined in with her father's pupils and her brothers, or sat wishing she could. Jane found this much more enlightening than some of the other activities on offer to a girl of her age, designed to nurture her in gentle femininity and submission to the needs of others, such as caring for small animals or taking care of the plants.[22] Jane wrote later too of the pains and strains of teaching a young child to read and form their letters. She even has one of her heroines, Catherine Morland, compare the experience to torment, regretting the hours of struggle that she both witnessed and experienced under her mother's guidance.[23] With Jane's disdain for this role, we know that certainly she never held any aspirations to be a teacher or a governess herself. In fact, she felt quite the opposite.[24]

A decade into the life of George's school, the landscape of their home life looked somewhat different. James had matriculated at St John's College in June 1779, the same month that his baby brother Charles was born. Attending under a founder's kin fellowship attained through his mother Cassandra's family line, James was enrolled in his father's college. He had gained a prized scholarship which must have been George's delight as both his teacher and his parent. In joining St John's, he too would receive the same preparation for a career in the Church as his father had before him. Frank and Henry now became the focus of George's teaching skills as they joined the ranks, both becoming his pupils. This was a period of time which Frank recalled in later life with great admiration and gratitude for both the scholarly prowess and patient, nurturing capabilities of his father.[25]

Jane herself had recently been sent away to school aged just 7 years old, along with her sister aged 10 and her cousin Jane Cooper aged 12, to their cousin's aunt, Mrs Cawley, who had a school in Oxford – a privilege that cost George £20 in payments to Dr Cooper and the headmistress.[26] One of Jane's school books has survived from that time, a 'primer of fables' with an inscription of her name and the date, believed to have been written by George, on the outside of the front cover.[27] The book must have been used at home too because written in her young hand inside the back cover is the message 'mother's angry, father's gone out'. A poignant little missive which inevitably invokes the question: what were her parents arguing about, and where did George go and why? Did he go out because his wife was 'angry' or was she angry because he had gone out?

George and Cassandra had not initially considered school for Jane, believing her too young to go, but family legend reports that Mrs Austen resolved the situation because of Jane herself. They drew the conclusion that the same little girl who had wandered over the fields with her little brother Charles in tow, even as a very young child herself, would not in reality bear to be parted from her beloved sister.[28] Wherever Cassandra went, Jane insisted that she had to go too, much to her mother's exasperation, a frustration that would follow their relationship for a very long time and occupy Mrs Austen's thoughts in regard to Jane's future path.[29] Where indeed would she end up once her sister were to marry one day?

However, Jane did not enjoy being at school. In considering Mrs Weston's prospective parenthood, Miss Woodhouse *longs* that Mr Weston's child might not suffer the fate Jane herself did, being wrenched away and banished from home to school. Emma's hope is that in being a girl, the new child need not suffer but might yet be saved from the same fate as a son in this case. Emma talks up the advantages and delights of an older Mr Weston having the 'freaks and the fancies' of a 10-year-old daughter to brighten his home life.[30] Which, alas, was not Jane's luck. Jane was writing here of hopes for a fictional father who had suffered having his own son adopted away into another branch of the family. Perhaps Jane never could look happily on the decision to send the Austen girls away from home to such a place.

It is not surprising that Jane held this particular view, however, as in their own case, disaster soon struck. In summer 1783, Mrs Cawley moved her school from Oxford to Southampton, and all unbelievably without telling the parents of any of the children that she was doing so. Typhus spread throughout the port city and all three of the girls fell ill. Mrs Cawley did not inform their parents of this either, and it was only when Jane Cooper wrote to her mother, Cassandra Austen's sister, that the adults became aware of the situation and immediately brought the girls back home. Horrifically and tragically, the illness was much more violent in adults. When Mrs Cooper contracted the disease from the girls, she sadly died.

In 1785 the Austen girls were sent away to school once more. Again, they joined their cousin Ann, this time at Madame La Tournelle's Abbey House Boarding school in Reading, now The Abbey School. Biographers do not concur whether or not George afforded his daughters the position of parlour boarders, as Harriet Smith would become. This would have meant further expense and was very much the experience of the minority in a school. However, it is possible that perhaps they were able to benefit from this position, receiving a little better food as they ate breakfast and supper with their headmistress in her parlour in their first year as George's accounts show that he paid over double the amount to Mrs La Tournelle in this period compared to his later cheques.[31] Mrs La Tournelle was the stuff of legend, a prime candidate for one of Jane's later stories. She had a cork leg and was not even French – in reality, she was just plain old Sarah Hackett. Originally employed as the French teacher, in truth she could not even speak the language very well and her name had functioned to add a little authenticity to her in the role. At her school, the girls were taught a little French, music, reading, writing and needlework – at which Jane excelled but their time was not as tightly timetabled as in some schools in London, for example, or indeed as it would have been at Tunbridge School. Her schooldays lingered in Jane's memory nonetheless and were tinged with the tang of the fears and frights of being put on the spot and made to learn. Young Fanny Price has her own set of flashbacks to being quizzed and questioned on her understanding of English and French that filled her with the trepidation of a young pupil put agonisingly under the spotlight.[32] Theirs was not a broad and balanced curriculum but neither were there painful lessons of comportment or Latin conjugations. The school is often quite fondly compared to Mrs Goddard's School (*Emma*), which was value for money for families, and a place where girls might be reasonably occupied and 'scramble themselves into a little education', as Jane liked to say.[33]

Memories of schooldays at the Abbey House School in general, and of Mrs La Tournelle in particular, were that she encouraged a love of drama and theatre, of acting and actors, and this suited Jane right down to the ground. The rest of their time was spent left to their own devices and the girls wiled away the term laughing amongst themselves, reading and strolling around the abbey ruins and gardens. They left at the end of the school year in 1786. The girls had been, as Jane's Mrs Norris might put it, 'given an education' but whether this was intended to help them 'settle well' in the future 'without farther expense' – in other words, to be married to another suitable provider – or whether it was because Steventon Parsonage had been full at the time and their beds had been rented out to fee-paying pupils is a valid question.[34] Whether the investment in their education would pay off in regard to the former aim was one thing, but in scrutinising George's accounts books at Hoare's Bank, we can see that the boarders' fees made a positive, welcome and timely difference to the family's financial situation.

Aged 11 and 13 respectively upon their return, neither Jane nor Cassandra were assigned any form of apprenticeship or preparation for a future career as a governess – much to the relief of Jane perhaps and also to her parents' pockets. Neither though were they ignored by their intelligent mother and father who sought, amongst other matters, to teach their own values to their young charges. There was a pervading 'university of life' culture present among the Austen family themselves, and they were famous for their intelligent banter around the table or wherever they were gathered throughout the house. In quite the opposite of young Catherine Morland's family experience, George would never have been so laconic, or so happy, with only a pun when a little conversation might be entered into. Neither would Jane's mother with her way with words and sense of humour have stopped after the utterance of just one sole proverb.[35] Their limericks and puzzles beautified their conversations, and intellectual stimulation of every kind abounded in every interaction between the members of the family. James, a talented poet and writer, had started *The Loiterer*, a student-produced periodical at university. He was now 21 and it is said that he recommended reading and encouraged Jane in her home studies when back visiting in between terms. Now that he was completing his degree and embarking on studying for his MA, he must have been both admirable and stimulating company for his inquisitive wordsmith of a younger sister. Edward was now 19 and about to set out on his own form of extended education on his grand tour of Europe. Henry, aged 15, was in the final years of his own preparation for a place at St John's College, working hard in anticipation of the scholarship which he too was to gain. Frank was just about to leave home as he had enrolled at the Royal Naval Academy in Portsmouth. Only 12 years old, he was about to take a bold new step for the family and set out upon his own adventures. Being so close to both Jane and Cassandra in age, his departure must have been a wrench, albeit that they were filled with pride and hope for his future. Charles still only aged 7 remained, now under the watchful care of his father, and began his own particular forays into education. The intelligent wit that led to the creation of family limericks, word puzzles, enigmas, charades, jokes and comments was free-flowing and fuelled by an increase in the proportion of adults in the family, as well as the addition of three or four schoolboys from outside. This was a time when, as well as challenging the young pupils to practise their powers of persuasion in readiness for their school disputations, the Austens also injected their particular brand of wit. Perhaps over lunch the group even challenged and demanded of one another 'one thing very clever, be it prose or verse, original or repeated – or two things moderately clever – or three things very dull indeed', as the bored rogue Frank Churchill suggests at the Box Hill picnic in *Emma*.[36]

George collected various pieces of equipment both for his own interest and for use in teaching. These included a microscope and a globe, revealing a forward-thinking and intellectually curious approach to both curriculum and learning methods.[37] The microscopes would have been used to view insects, plants and vegetables in detail with the level of magnification adding awe and wonder for George's pupils to the study of the world about them. The globes had a mathematical use too as they were a way to explain both latitude and longitude, and showed an emerging understanding of the measurement of the world's topography. This was particularly useful for any of his pupils who may have been preparing for the navy. In his own study book at the RNA, Frank had to complete many mathematical equations and solve many problems relating to latitude and longitude.[38] Globes had traditionally been collected by gentlemen for some time and were often used as status symbols or ornamental furniture, a talking point. However, in George's day, they were also becoming more accurate in mapping the known and as-yet-unexplored world. Used for facilitating interesting conversations about the world, especially perhaps about various contemporary navigators and explorers and their expeditions of discovery, they would have been a useful 'philosophical' teaching tool. The 18-inch terrestrial (rather than celestial) globe was made by the renowned and respected mathematical instrument makers, the Adams family, who would go on to count King George III and his family amongst their customers. They even produced sundials, so George may have purchased the one for his garden here too as, in addition, he possessed a smaller version and other astronomical instruments including a compass which he kept in a black shagreen case.[39] The Adams' family business was in Fleet Street, the same street as George's London bank, Hoare's Bank; it was an area that he would have known well and when he had business in town, he would have perused their shop and offices and acquainted himself with their products and technology. George's accounts show that he did indeed make a purchase in June 1779.[40]

Chapter Nine

The Library

With 'only' a small group of pupils boarding at a time, it was most likely that George took over the larger parlour with the pupils sat either at the main dining table or arranged in chairs or stools around the room. However, tucked away at the back of the house, George had his own study, to where even the youngest of family members noticed he would escape to avoid all the hustle and bustle of the parsonage comings and goings. He, like Mr Bennet (*Pride and Prejudice*), could quite happily shut himself away in there with his books and be unaware of the passage of time.[1] He may have taught some of the boys individually or in smaller subgroups here, perhaps with a chair drawn up to his mahogany library table. They may even on occasion have glimpsed his Tunbridge School gilt pen up on the mantelpiece or tucked inside one of his library table drawers as they sat at their own work. Any visitor would most likely be surrounded not only by books but also by the tasteful works of art that adorned the walls, some donated by grateful parents of past pupils. In her later letters, Jane mentioned such offerings from the Nibbs and East families. Most recently it has come to light that George owned two paintings by the renowned Welsh landscape artist Richard Wilson RA, also the son of a clergyman. Wilson painted views of Britain and Italy and his work was highly rated. Those in George's possession depicted the Italian countryside and a river scene with crumbling ruins in the background.

Gentlemen of taste at this time often fashioned themselves a library and furnished it with interesting artefacts and collections. In George's scholarly past he was, of course, used to having a private space which he could dedicate to his passion and respect for knowledge and academia. Both as an usher at Tunbridge and in his rooms at Oxford, George had grown used to the atmosphere and benefit of having such a room of his own. The memory of the discussions with James Cawthorn surrounding their vision for a library, such an important addition to the school, makes the whole investment in this room far more personal and poignant.

As in similar libraries of the time, George may also have displayed some coins or medals or anything that might attract interest in the study of England, of classical civilisation or the wonderful world of nature. Status symbols such as these would have been an indicator to others of George's academic gravitas and his particular social standing as well as his personal interests. When Mr Woodhouse (*Emma*) made a visit to Mr Knightley's home at Donwell Abbey, he was treated to a similar experience but on such a grand scale we are left in no doubt as to the wealth of the owner. He was presented with plentiful collections of medals and cameos as well as exotic shells and corals from far flung places, indicating through this hint of foreign travel the grandeur and social standing of their neighbour.[2] This extrapolation of Jane's father's experience is entertaining and aspirational, not remotely in the reach of George, but as it would turn out, very possibly something that her brother Edward would one day be able to indulge in on a grand tour of Europe. Having grown up with great reverence and appreciation attached to libraries as a child at Steventon, he was to be unimpressed by the library at Zug in Switzerland in August 1786 but would take note of the manuscripts held in the Ambrosian Library in Milan in June 1790. On his very first ventures through the Swiss Alps, his childhood home would remain foremost in his mind. Of all things it is the strawberries found at the bottom of a glacier, reminiscent no doubt of the ones viewed from George's study, that he marvels at.[3]

George himself had a profound fondness for reading and over the years he developed this space into a quiet haven filled with books. By the end of nearly forty years in their Hampshire home, these amounted to more than 500 volumes by Jane's own estimate. Not quite the large library room that Northanger Abbey could boast but still something not experienced by the average Steventon citizen, this collection of costly covers would have indicated George's level of education and taste as well as his gentlemanly status amongst the locals. George purchased many of his books from John Burdon Bookseller in College Street, Winchester. John was a respectable man involved honourably in his trade and his community. He worked hard and had nine children of his own to raise. He and George would have found much to respect in one another. George was able to keep abreast of Burdon's new publications on offer and sales of certain titles as the shop conveniently advertised its wares in local newspapers, including the catalogues of books for sale acquired from deceased reverends and other gentlemen collectors. This, of course, was something that Jane's Anne Elliot (*Persuasion*) might have read and understood as she had the task of making the same such inventory when her family had to vacate Kellynch Hall to make way for Admiral Croft and his wife. It would be something wonderful indeed should a similar catalogue for George's library ever come to light.

The shop held a particular interest for George. Its location was, as the address suggests, very close to Winchester College; indeed, its main source of income was in supplying the college, its masters and pupils with maps, books and stationery. Selling educational books specifically aimed at the teaching of Latin, Greek and Philosophy, and other texts necessary for either religious instruction or preparation for a university career, meant it was the perfect provider for George in his roles as both schoolmaster and clergyman.[4] Being able to purchase books at all was a nod to George's wealthier status, but he also needed these volumes to help him in his teaching post. In this instance the shop's particular specialisms and expertise was combined with a large trade in second-hand books which rendered these expensive textbooks a little more affordable for George. The Burdons prided themselves on selling books cheaply and widely promoted generous discounts for schoolmasters.[5] They even accepted books for exchange, a happenstance which strikes a chord when considering George's habits in regard to furniture. This clinched Burdon's position as a preferred supplier for George and later his sons too, and it may account for part of the reason why George was able to continue to indulge his passion and buy books even after he had stopped teaching and times were financially a lot tougher.

In addition, the proprietors also operated a bookbinding service. Binding a book was an expensive option, but the fact that the shop offered this service as it printed books written by and for the college itself meant that texts could be purchased at a range of prices according to their final physical state. Papers could be sold loose, stitched together, bound in boards or vellum and, at the luxurious end of the scale, even in calf leather. The service was flexible and bespoke, older books could be repaired and books could be covered after purchase, even from another source. For an additional price bespoke details could be included – perhaps the purchaser might like lettering on the spine, ruling and tooling to the covers, marbled endpapers or even red sprinkled edges. Handily the shop also sold all that one might need as a scholar including quills and pens, ink and paper, and for anyone with, say, a daughter aiming to improve her musical accomplishments – sheet music.[6]

As time went on, George would invest in further library furniture too. A man who did not have a lot of money to spare and who never really splashed out on frivolous purchases, in spring 1795 he undertook to prioritise the funding of a personal project. His study acquired a large bookcase which came complete with a set of two locks and two sets of keys each. Two of John Ring's men were employed for a total of three weeks to build and install it in situ. This is most probably the bookcase later referred to in a sale of furniture from the Austens' property as possessing six doors and measuring 8 feet by 8 feet.[7] It was made of deal, a cheaper wood that once stained could look like mahogany or a better quality of material than it was. This was a clever way of getting an excellent finished look for a much more affordable price. There was also a smaller bookcase. Whenever books arrived in the house, bound by the bookbinder at the back of Burdon's shop, there was great excitement. As well as the unpacking, there was great rejoicing by Jane and her father when the books were carefully placed on the bookcase. At this time, books were typically purchased without covers and having them bound was a costly luxury. Having books rather than a bundle of loose papers not only preserved and personalised their copy, but also compressed the papers into satisfactorily neat little versions; Jane wrote joyfully to her sister that it made it so much easier to house them upon their shelf.[8]

All of this expenditure at once and on items that were for a more personal than needfully practical use was a very rare occurrence and did not at all reflect George's usual spending patterns. The timing of his purchases is also interesting, coming as they did towards the end of twenty-three years of teaching in his home domain. Perhaps the new makeover for his own room was a reward for all his services to teaching because within a year George was no longer receiving any payments for pupils and his study had once again become his very own. It may have been decorated to that taste which Jane refers to in *Mansfield Park* as being in vogue fifty years ago, with its dark mahogany and shining wooden floor under a rug, but it certainly denoted a man of taste and epitomised her father's personal style; a place to which she was drawn.[9]

At the same time as all of the bookcase work, George ordered chocolate-brown paint, blue paper and brown paper and a pair of two blue-striped window curtains with lace trimmings.[10] A month later, when the construction in his own study was completed, he also purchased some Scotch carpeting in a tree pattern and some more in buff and blue and had a large carpet made up. Le Faye agrees that these items chime with Anna Lefroy's description of Jane and Cassandra's upstairs dressing room makeover. Just as their father was re-investing in his own library, he was also recreating a similar room of their own, a space to nurture his daughters. George's establishment and investment in a separate space for Jane and Cassandra recognised their needs as apart from others in the household and it was a watershed moment in their own young adult lives.

A notable expense on George's account was to a company called Penlington, a tallow and chandler maker who supplied George and his family with candles.[11] The family, of course, would have needed these for reading at home around the fire in the evenings or in their rooms and to assist them on their way to bed. Wax candles in the schoolroom of one of her connections were boasted of by Mrs Elton (*Emma*). It is not a given that George had these. Beeswax, and later wax made from a substance in whales' heads, were a boon and a real development in candle technology, not only because they burned more slowly and the light therefore lasted longer but the fat did not spit or smoke or smell like cheaper animal fat or tallow would do. Using candles of this calibre anywhere in a house was a marker of wealth and extravagance, and prized as a luxury, another indicator of the importance that George placed upon an evening spent in the company of a good book.

Jane was always a very welcome visitor to her father's study. George allowed her to read anything she wished to; all of his books were at her disposal. No doubt she was guided to those pointed out to her by her brothers but also by what she saw and heard George reading himself. In addition, the books themselves beckoned her. She was free to peruse and discover her own favourites for herself. The atmosphere was calm and safe, quiet and nurturing, the perfect setting to get lost amongst the words and worlds of a writer. Jane could sit and read here with her father close by, perhaps whilst George sat writing one of his friendly family letters, pondering a sermon or a lesson plan, or marking some of his pupils' Latin. The image of him and his escritoire seared into her mind's eye and was captured forever in her imagination. We see one just like it belonging to Augustus' 'unworthy' father in her early story *Love and Freindship*. In this case Jane had her young man steal a good deal of money from it.[12] At other times Jane could sit at George's feet whiling away the time in Richardson or Cowper whilst he remained in his armchair by the fire musing over his latest set of farming accounts pulled from the bureau's chest of drawers. Jane had someone to mentor her just like Fanny Price (*Mansfield Park*) did. George, like Fanny's Edmund, was someone to 'encourage her taste' and with whom to discuss what she had read. The time spent in reading in this manner not only enriched her imagination and entertained her, but it also expanded her word power and broadened her understanding of the world. As Edmund would say, her time spent reading there, perhaps curled up in a chair or lying on the carpet, was 'an education in itself'.[13]

Contrary to Lady Catherine de Bourgh's (*Pride and Prejudice*) 'concern' over the neglect of the Bennet girls' education, Jane found plenty amongst her father's bookshelves, in what Catherine Morland (*Northanger Abbey*) might call his storehouse of knowledge, to sharpen the intellect of someone like Elizabeth Bennet (*Pride and Prejudice*) or herself who 'wished to learn.'[14] George's library was a place to which Jane was drawn. The peace that filled this intentional space, the lack of 'disturbance' was the same as that found by Fanny in her adopted, quiet, abandoned schoolroom and again with her sister Susan upstairs in the Price's noisy Portsmouth home.[15] Fanny's penchant for her books and belongings might have put Jane in mind of her father's secluded study and the one he created for his girls.

Jane's passion for storytelling from a young age may have come into its own even in her early years, squirrelled away with groups of girls at the Abbey House School, helping her to find her niche, to feel a little more settled in. Stories were Jane's happy place, nurtured in them as she had been even earlier in *her* childhood than most young people of her time experienced. Indoors at home with the Austens was generally centred on family routines. There might be one long visit in the morning but apart from that Jane found time to herself in which to read. Once she had finished with her own duties in support of the household, perhaps running errands for her mother and father or overseeing aspects of life behind the scenes of the dairy, she could head back in and bury herself in a novel, a travel guide or even a newspaper.

Recent research has shown Jane had an encyclopaedic knowledge not only for Richardson's *Sir Charles Grandison* but for the celebrity aristocrats, nobles and gentry of her day. The headlines of the newspapers brought her into closer contact with those she had read about in her father's travel guidebooks. Putting faces to the names she had heard of, even as far north as Yorkshire, Jane was able to soak up suggestions from which to title her leading gentlemen and ladies. As young as she was, Jane had a heart for a dramatic storyline and shut up away with her best friend Martha at the tender age of 12, she had learnt that real life could be just as outrageous as fiction when she was scandalised by the revelation of the history of Martha's cruel grandmother, Lady Craven. We see from Jane's entry of 'Fitzwilliam' in the Steventon marriage register that the glamour of names spotted in newspaper headlines and columns had already merged with her imaginings. Janine Barchas' recent research in her book *Matters of Fact in Jane Austen* argues that Jane, far from dampening down the sharp-eyed wit of her *Juvenilia*, went on to develop it in conscious and clever ways in her future novels. For a contemporary reader, the names Jane was using would have rung all sorts of bells of understanding. This intuitive genius for expanding upon and extrapolating celebrity in cunning literary ways was sparked by a love of reading and inflamed by reading materials left lying about on her father's library table.

The family at Steventon dined early, about 3.30 pm and then drank tea together at 6.30 pm. Jane later lamented this difference, comparing it unfavourably to the more sophisticated tastes of a later supper at Edward's home Godmersham Park.[16] She enjoyed making the most of both the humour and slight humiliation in this arrangement when imbuing old Mr Watson (*The Watsons*) with the same foible, a fancy for an early dinner out of sync with the hours kept by most others in polite society. Once, when Jane returned to Steventon from her brother's home, expecting to arrive well after George's supper time, she knew that her father would not be able to wait for her. She knew that in spite of the commonly held eating hours, he would no doubt still be eating at his preferred habitual time. With her tongue firmly in her cheek, Jane acknowledged in family letters the hopeless cause of expecting him to wait for her and dutifully gave him her permission not to do so.[17]

In the evenings after supper though, the family would gather around the fireplace where George would read to them all. This was where the conversational qualities, charms and characteristics of the Austen family would really come to the fore. The animation and sense that these conversations provoked is reminiscent in Mr Bennet's grief at the loss of Elizabeth and Jane from the family circle.[18] The profound poignancy he feels at their absence at such a valued family time evokes the precious Steventon evening atmosphere that meant so much to her father and to Jane. These times, gathered together with a good book and good conversation, became such nostalgic memories for Jane, a tradition in which she felt a closeness and a bond with her father. It was a practice which the family continued at every fireside they frequented in their future homes, and a topic, therefore, also too ripe not to be picked when it came to choosing a setting for her stories. As early as her late teens, Jane penned a tale (*Love and Freindship*) that had the same such quiet conflab around the fire in the grate, but this time it was interrupted by a knock on the door so loud that it broke into the conversation and demanded attention.[19] The amusing considerations that occupy the family's thoughts at this occurrence, as to who might be knocking and why, infused with both wit and intelligence, were of a tone and type that would have served as an in-joke. A spark of recognition of themselves in the weighing up of such a situation, the familiar repartee of presenting one's arguments, with their individual points of information, their own pros and cons and different perspectives and points of view. All their own commonly used words were there, ricocheting off the page for the knowing Austens to see and understand and to laugh at, to be entertained by.

George and Jane's love of reading and moreover their shared interest in their reading matter sheds a unique light onto their relationship. As one of the major reasons for their closeness, it gives us an insight into the bond they shared. They would simultaneously read titles, passing them back and forth to one another and to friends and family, even as often as when they had finished a section or chapter as well as when they had read the whole thing. They then fell into discussing the merits and failures of the work as they saw them. One such example was *Fitz-Albini* written by the brother of Jane's dear friend, their neighbour Madam Lefroy, wife of the rector of Ashe.[20] Jane had originally objected to her father buying it as she knew that her friend did not particularly rate his latest work. However, she overcame her reticence, perhaps drawn in by her own curiosity as to what it might reveal about people that they knew.

Neither of them enjoyed the book very much and George was disappointed. Jane, though, confidently commented that she was not at all surprised at how it had turned out. This whole experience was formative for Jane. Following the family traditions of questioning and debating, at 23 years old Jane showed competence in her critique of the work and could eloquently state her position on it in conversation. Encouraged by this type of reading and discussion with her father, along with her experience of writing her own creations and her extensive personal reading, Jane was very clear as to the weaknesses introduced by the author. In reading this book with her father and discussing it with him, she articulated her view to her sister that it was too autobiographical in its opinions, mirroring the author's beliefs and personality too closely in each character. In taking this opportunity to review the writing style and construction of the work, she also revealed her emerging understanding of what made for a good read in terms of characterisation, plot and structure.

George and Jane also collaborated on which title to choose next and shared their hopes and expectations for a book. Once again, they either commiserated or confirmed their opinions with one another once finished. They read Boswell's *Tour of the Hebrides* and *Life of Johnson* (Dr Johnson's own prose being Jane's favourite, according to her brother Henry's biographical notice of her), as well as the poems of Cowper: a particular pleasure for Jane and something George liked to read to the family after dinner.[21] Jane treasured up these readings in her heart and when Fanny Price is homesick for Mansfield Park, it is to Cowper's *Tirocinium* that she turns.[22] For Jane the memory of her father's reading would be forever associated with a real sense of home even when escaping into literature that took her further away in her imagination or even, perhaps, thanks to her French-speaking cousin Eliza de Feuillide, into the realms of other languages too. She read *Les Veillees du Chateau* by Comtesse de Genlis, moral tales for children, although whether both she and George read the same book together on this occasion is not known, and her letter on the matter does not make it truly clear if she read the French version or the translation.[23] Her exotic cousin certainly helped to broaden her tastes and understanding, as did Jane's visits in later life to Edward's beautiful home at Godmersham Park. Here she made the most of his vast library. The thought of this library bringing both Jane and her father so much pleasure is a poignant insight into their relationship. Jane made sure in *Northanger Abbey* to list the ingredients for a heroine's training in relation to literature and included a compulsory reading of authors such as Pope, Gray, Thompson and Shakespeare. Young Catherine Morland read these in her late teens. This could just as easily have been Jane herself in her father's study.

For all his scholarly reading, though, George also enjoyed those 'horrid novels' which Jane revelled in enjoying too, despite the literati of her time looking down on anyone who read them, especially the head of a household, as either at risk of melting their minds or being brought into degradation by them. Jane defended her family's love of this emerging genre when considering joining a circulating library near her village. In a letter to her sister, she discussed her plans, noting that the proprietor, one Mrs Martin, was at pains to point out that there were all types of literature available to readers in her library, not just novels. Jane enjoyed laughing at this sales pitch, intimating in her letter that as she and her sister both knew, there was no need to make this point on their account as the family were all perfectly happy with their reputation as readers of novels.[24]

One such novel which George borrowed from the library was published around the same time that Jane was writing about Mrs Martin. Called *The Midnight Bell*, it was a Gothic tale of a hapless and at times tortured soul, Alphonsus, sent away suddenly from the family seat, Count Cohenburg Castle, by his mother.[25] We accompany him as he embarks on a quest which brings him into contact with all manner of people including the love of his life and bandits. Thrillingly, throughout the story we see him experience all sorts of 'Gothic' encounters. With the moral of the story being to suspect suspicion itself, the tale is a chaotic romp that leaves the reader on edge, wondering what might loom out of the gloom at any moment. In the final part of the story, in order to overcome all the 'horrid', Alphonsus has to wake up to reality and face his fears. He has to transition back into his former world, in order to understand what has actually happened in real life and to lay claim to his rightful inheritance.

Novels that highlighted the supernatural or focused on the mild horror of a dead corpse were thought inferior in content and style and less worthy than more classically acclaimed works. Having lauded the works of Pope, Gray, Thompson and Shakespeare, Jane also highlighted the iniquities cast as aspersions over the Gothic genre in particular, but also novels in general. She has her reader squirm at the scorn with which novels were customarily treated and how both the authors and their readers were almost shamed into denying they had anything to do with them. However, in *Northanger Abbey*, Catherine Morland and her new friend Isabella Thorpe thrill each other in discussing their reading and include *The Midnight Bell* in a list of seven books that, at Isabella's urging, Catherine puts straight onto her 'To Be Read' pile. In their exaggerated enthusiasm, Jane both laughed at and with these stories and their readers in a kindly way, although perhaps Isabella Thorpe's near-expert knowledge of an entire back catalogue of this and only this genre should sound a warning bell somewhere. Much better perhaps a friend like Miss Eleanor Tilney with whom one could talk about all sorts of reading matter. In sending up the tropes of the Gothic novel, Jane revealed the knowledge of the books both she and George read and showed that they too could laugh at themselves, not taking the books too seriously either. Enjoying them for the escapist fun that they were, Jane and George could read them in the round with all their other sources of reading, and they could balance the serious and the sacred with the farcical and romantic.

However, that being said, in having a heroine who loses her grip on any education she might have had that may have saved her from her indulgences, one who got too giddy and carried away with the plot lines and events of her beloved fiction, Catherine Morland puts us in mind of the equally afflicted Don Quixote. Cervantes' knight-errant was a gentleman who read so much of *his* favoured genre that his own brain shrivelled. He, like Catherine, also became powerless in the wake of his own imagination. When his mind was infiltrated in a similar way, this time by books on chivalry, Quixote was unable to hold onto a consciousness of the differences between fiction and real life any longer. The two became dangerously and absurdly blurred into one. Catherine Morland began to imagine that terrible and fearsome acts had been carried out at the Abbey by General Tilney against his wife. Quixote too began venturing into a virtual reality, living his imagination out in real time, accompanied by his sidekick, Sancho Panza, and his horse, Rocinante. He deluded himself into embarking on a quest to protect all, especially his sweetheart Dorothea. He conjured up imaginary enemies and, on one occasion, launched himself at his foe, confusing windmills for attackers. Catherine too allowed her imagination to lead and she followed with all the emotional suspense that only a truly immersed reader might experience until thankfully she was pulled out of her macabre reverie by the appearance of the young Mr Tilney. A hero who was able to read novels, defend the reading of them, 'The person, be it gentleman or lady, who has not pleasure in a good novel, must be intolerably stupid', and yet not let the education of his character be overcome by any pull they might exercise over him as a reader.[26]

Two years before the letter in support of her shared love of the novel, Jane's name was published in a list of subscribers towards the publication of a novel by Fanny Burney, *Camilla*, published in 1796. Burney is singled out, heralded and defended in *Northanger Abbey*, albeit in an ironic tone of voice, as one of the best observers of human nature, an author who possessed great skill as a writer. When we are confronted with the brother of Catherine's new friend, Mr Thorpe, as her possible suitor, we are horrified. Apart from any other reasons to distrust and discount him, we are immediately alerted to his disdain and his ignorance as he trumpets his opinions about novels. From his lack of understanding and readiness to patronise and decry these favourites, we know at once that he is a fellow not to be trusted or relied upon. That, in short, he is unsuitable.[27] Indeed, we come to a similar, clear revelation upon the character of Sir Edward Denham in *Sanditon*. His misunderstandings and unhealthy penchant for the villain of the literary piece are enough of a hint for us to cast him aside as hero material.[28]

Camilla would go on to be one of Jane's all-time favourites and she took delight in quoting it and making literary comparisons between herself and Burney's heroine in a letter to her sister the very year when the book would have been foremost in their minds and conversations.[29] Jane enjoyed this experience, even perhaps seeing her name in the printed list of supporters as well as receiving her copy. In later life she subscribed at least once again in support of a forthcoming book, this time *Two Sermons by Reverend Jefferson*, a citizen of her father's home town of Tunbridge.[30]

When Harriet Smith (*Emma*) seeks to endear her beloved Mr Martin as a worthy suitor to her match-making friend Emma, we are privy to her praises and promotions of his reading abilities and taste. There is a comic moment hanging on her earnest assurances to Emma that Mr Martin has never read any of the 'horrid novels' and had, in fact, never even heard of them until she mentioned them to him. So anxious is Harriet that Emma thinks well of her Mr Martin, she does not realise that Emma might have thought more highly of *him* if he had never read them and decidedly never would, and perhaps Harriet too for that matter. Harriet revealing that he is now determined to read them as soon as possible blindly risks playing into Emma's hands and provoking her judgemental ways.

In regard to the revelation of him reading the *Agricultural Reports*, we learn that, just as Emma would have expected, he was a professional and diligent farmer wanting to improve himself and, by implication, his farming and financial profits. However, the mention that he has read Goldsmith, a friend of the eminent Doctor Johnson, and that he read Vicesimus Knox's *Elegant Extracts*, not only to himself but also aloud to his mother and sisters after dinner, quickly raises his profile and level of education up a notch in the mind of the well-informed reader of the time and especially the Austens.[31] Emma and Harriet themselves, in collecting and copying out selected verses, puzzles, riddles and charades into their own notebook, attempt to include an addition from these *Elegant Extracts*. Emma announces the fact to her father with some pride.[32] She is eager to impress her father with this addition to their project. The author of the *Elegant Extracts*, Vicesimus Knox, was approximately twenty years younger than George and yet they shared so many experiences in common. He too was a Fellow of St John's College, Oxford, before he married and in 1778–1812, he was the headmaster of none other than Tunbridge School. He was an eminent scholar of English Classics and was highly regarded both nationally and internationally for his own publications. In his role as headmaster, he had focused his own intellectual powers on preparing his scholars and his book *Elegant Extracts*, a compilation of prose and later poetry, was intended as a compass to direct their minds, hearts and spiritual steps through reading edifying examples of excellent literature. Written and compiled around 1787, George himself put so much store by their usefulness and worth that he commended them specifically to his son Frank when he left home to take up his first commission on a ship at sea. Jane too was familiar with this family favourite. It would have been her father's approbation of this compilation which sang off the pages to the family at the mere mention of the text here in Jane's story.

Jane enjoyed the tradition laid down with her father and her wider family of reading and discussing, dissecting and critiquing a book so much that she became part of a book club, something that we now understand the attraction of. She was very proud of her own little group and saw the emulation of it by others as both flattering and a waste of time because they could never be as good. Taking part in these discussions with neighbours and girlfriends must have always taken her back to those days amongst the bookcases in her father's study and those long (thanks to their early dining) evenings of her father reading and her family conversations by the fire.

Settled into a good book in his reading nook in his study, George could take sanctuary from the clamour of his outside world of farming and parish duties and also gain a little peace away from the hustle and bustle of his teaching and his own household. He too, like Jane's Mr Bennet, might be happy to tolerate his family with its noise, liveliness and business in the kitchen, the parlour and the drawing room, safe in the knowledge that he had this quiet place to which he could withdraw.[33] Perhaps he too, like Mr Bennet, could lose track of time when reading there and his reason for having a penchant for an early supper was so that he could spend his evening in this tranquil state of mind. When Elizabeth Bennet seeks an audience with her father, they often convene in the quiet stillness, the foundation of his world, his anchor of a place, his book-lined study. The atmosphere that comes off the pages of these scenes is the memory imprinted upon Jane's sense of the security offered by the relaxed gravitas of such a place. Hence, the horror with which Tom Bertram's (*Mansfield Park*) actions might be met when he decides on an outrageous whim that his father's room will serve perfectly as a 'green room' to their adjoining billiard room-cum-theatre, and shows no thought at upending it and changing its use. He sees no harm and no disrespect, but Jane and her family would have. His suggestion that 'all' that needs to be done is to simply *move the bookcase* would have been unconscionable to Jane and her family.[34] It would have been tantamount to sacrilege, an act that would have felt like a violation to her father, showing an egregious lack of respect and privacy. It would certainly have angered and hurt George deeply should any of his family mess about with his beloved bookcases in his special room. In just two swift sentences mentioned in a by-the-by sort of way, Jane reveals so much to us about the character, or want of it, in Tom Bertram.

It would be no trifling matter as Tom suggests it to be, not at all; in fact, we know from the swiftness of the prose alone that it would be quite the opposite, that the warning signs are there, and that it would actually be much cause for alarm. When the Austen family members seated around the fire read this scene, there would have been a sharp intake of breath and more than one shared knowing look.

When Sir Thomas Bertram does return unexpectedly, he is much surprised to see candles burning in his personal room, thus intimating that it has been used by someone else without his knowledge. It is not simply the use of expensive candles that scandalises him. He *immediately* spots that the bookcase has been moved and his surprise could only ever be expected by an Austen to give way to deeper feelings. From the moment of the realisation that so much has occurred in his private space, in his absence and without his permission, it is never going to bode well for the perpetrators involved.[35]

That Mr Darcy (*Pride and Prejudice*) has a reputation for frequently buying books is not just a factor in defining his financial status for the reader; it also places him at the heart of Jane's esteem, fostered by her respect and love for her own father. A hero who fosters a love of books, of learning, of reading, is a rational creature, and his reverence for literature and for surrounding himself in it as a heartfelt duty, a legacy to be carried on in honour of previous generations and in readiness for the next, is an attractive quality indeed.[36] Conversely, the opposite, highlighted in the continuation of the scene, is also true, with Miss Bingley's father having left her so few books to read, it is no wonder that she can only make scathing comments about reading. Mr Darcy himself refers to such short-sighted provision as neglect. Miss Bingley's cold heart, consigned to her by a lack of parental education in regard to the habit and joys of reading, is confirmed when she sarcastically and falsely declares a great preferment of reading. We realise, ironically as readers, that as she yawns and discards her volume, what has passed was only a cheap ruse, her half-hearted attempts of using and abusing reading as a tool for wooing. Miss Caroline Bingley's desire for an 'excellent library' of her own one day is revealed as purely being for show, as a status symbol and not because of any real passion or devotion to reading on her part.[37] Her inner thoughts and motivations reveal a gap between the caring educative approach of Jane's father in regard to nurturing her education through reading, and the soulless and empty gesture of the wealthy attempting to buy education simply by owning books just because they can.

When we meet Sir Edward in the few fragments of *Sanditon* that we have been given, we learn of a person who truly had access to a range of reading materials, a plethora of them, a true assortment and abundance from the ancient to the modern. This should have inspired him to taste and decency. In his shunning of novels as evil influences, we might expect then a refined wisdom to have taken hold in his heart and mind. However, through the prism of his cold interpretations, with the lack of guidance and discussion about what he has read from a sensible and intelligent source, such as Jane had, he is left with a skewed, distorted view of their messages and misconstrues the lessons that are there to be learnt.[38]

We feel the disappointment in our heroine Emma Woodhouse and lament her father's weakness in not pressing her to attend to the attempts Miss Taylor no doubt tried to pursue with her in regard to reading.[39] In learning that Emma got her own way in most things, especially with her doting father and since her mother died, we understand that a passion for reading was not something that sat naturally in Emma's heart or mind. Studying and reading took intellect, which no doubt she had, as her match-making imagination proved, but also commitment to the cause. Unfortunately, such a weak enthusiasm for reading more than a few chapters with Harriet must have been due to some earlier lack of self-discipline when she herself was a pupil. In not being able to study for any particularly beneficial length of time and in choosing to opt out for an easier way to educate, guide and persuade Harriet, we can intimate that she did not pursue or attend to reading with much passion or perseverance herself.[40] In this small detail we feel a sadness as George and Jane would have done and hold onto hope that this might be something in her future.

Jane uses reading as a litmus test for the suitability not only of a romantic partnership but also for friendship. If Emma and Harriet are not able to read together, what will the quality of their shared conversation be like? Reading for Jane was such an intrinsic part of relating. Sat around of an evening listening to a book being read or reading aloud themselves was a way of building strong social bonds for the Austens. Spending time on such an edifying activity, they were taught ideas and thought processes that would serve these readers long into their futures. Even as a very young writer, Jane tries to establish a friendship connection in her story *Catharine, or the Bower* between Kitty and a Miss Camilla Stanley. However, their clash of understanding and taste, even in regard to commonly read popular books, reveals a chasm that will be hard to bridge and is only widened when other topics come into view.

Books were fundamental to the quality of Austen relationships, fortified by the family traditions surrounding them and by the time spent at leisure in her father's study. In Jane's youthful writings they can be used for comic and dramatic effect when defining adult/child relationships. In *Catharine, or the Bower*, for example, we see the provision of books used against a younger relative. When a young man randomly kisses young Catherine's hand and runs off, she is left bemused. When her aunt, Mrs Percival, who has seen what happened, then launches into a tirade against Catherine, she rants at her over what she claims has been the total waste of all her efforts to have her educated. The anger that Mrs Percival throws at Catherine is wrapped in accusations of ingratitude and the poor innocent girl is held in contempt. Mrs Percival throws in her face all her supposedly kind gracious gifts of books, the unregulated use of her library and the loans from her neighbours on her behalf. She bemoans all the copies of educational tomes she has supplied, including Blair's *Sermons* and Hannah More's *Coelebs in Search of a Wife*.[41] No matter that she had misunderstood the situation, education has become a rod to beat the younger relative with. The very fact that she would do this reveals a major flaw in Aunt Percival's character.

When Isabella Thorpe suggests, with maybe a hint of arrogance of her own, that perhaps Catherine Morland has not read a certain book because of her mother's forbiddance, we feel a chill wind for this friendship begin to blow with the harsh allegation that her parent was lacking in this way. Catherine is quick to negate any negligence and just laments her lack of opportunity with no supply of books coming into the house. She also mentions that one was a title beloved by her mother. This particular one was read in its seven-volume entirety again and again by Jane in her father's library; *Sir Charles Grandison* by Samuel Richardson. Jane became a fount of all knowledge on his characters whose depiction struck a chord with her taste.[42]

For George Austen, books had a purpose; they could educate directly through their transparent messages that might reveal more about the world around about, or through deeper critical thinking they could enable the reader to move to a higher plane of understanding and moral behaviour. Equally they could be for pure entertainment where the development of one's creative imagination could only be a good thing. Through the volumes George made available on his bookshelves, he broadened and equipped Jane's understanding. Through the combination of his conversation and reading materials, he avoided her overstudying and losing herself as Mr and Mrs Musgrove feared for Charles Hayter in *Persuasion*.[43] In fact, through the wide variety of sources

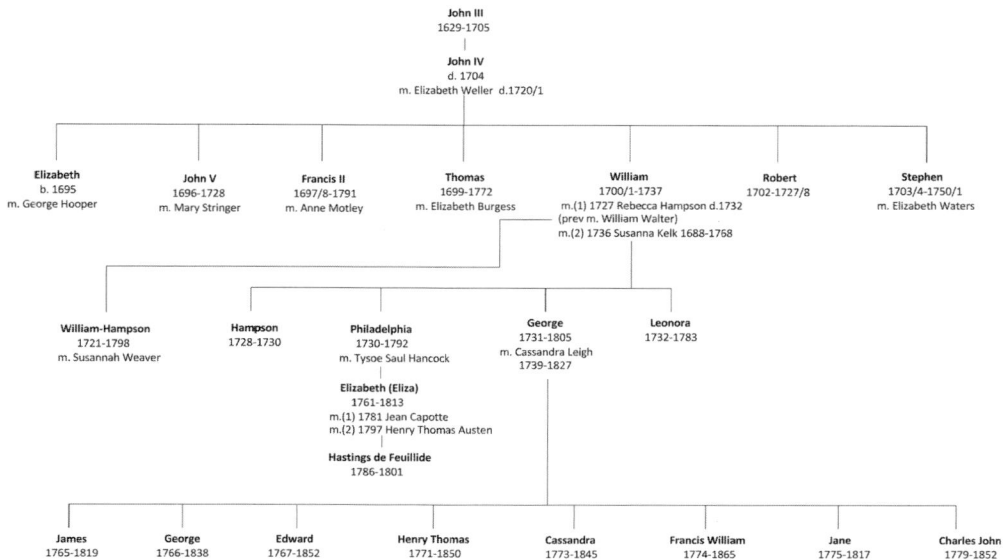

George Austen family tree. (*Joshua Wheddon*)

Horsmonden village sign.
(*Author's own photo*)

Austen family memorial, St Margaret's Church, Horsmonden. (*Author's own photo*)

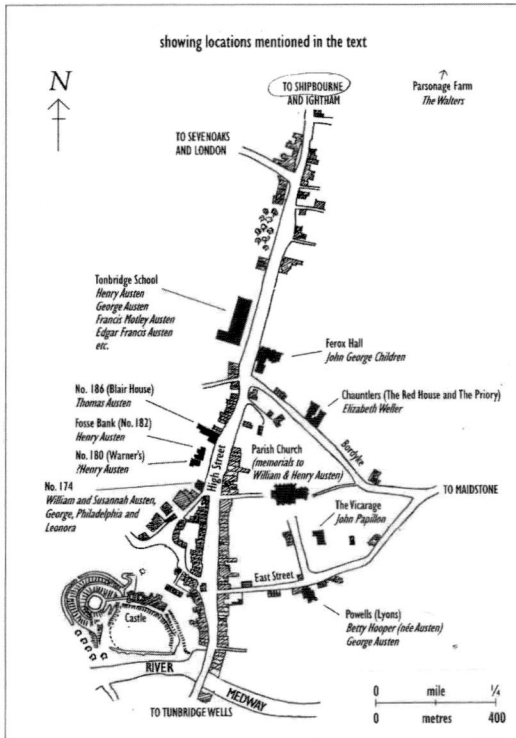

A map of Tonbridge c1750. (*Used with permission of Margaret Wilson, author of* Jane Austen's Family and Tonbridge (*2001*). *Photo by Nicky Liddell Photography*)

Example of a publication by Stephen Austen.
(*Courtesy of Hathi Trust*)

THE

PRACTICE

AND

THEORY

OF

INOCULATION.

WITH AN

ACCOUNT of its SUCCESS.

IN A

LETTER to a FRIEND.

By THOMAS FREWEN, Surgeon,
at Rye, *in* Suſſex.

Magna eſt Veritas, & prævalebit.

LONDON:
Printed for S. AUSTEN, in *Newgate-Street.*
MDCCXLIX.

Tunbridge School c.1824. (*Photo by Nicky Liddell Photography*)

Picture of Tunbridge School room until 1864. (*Used with permission of The Tonbridge Historical Society*)

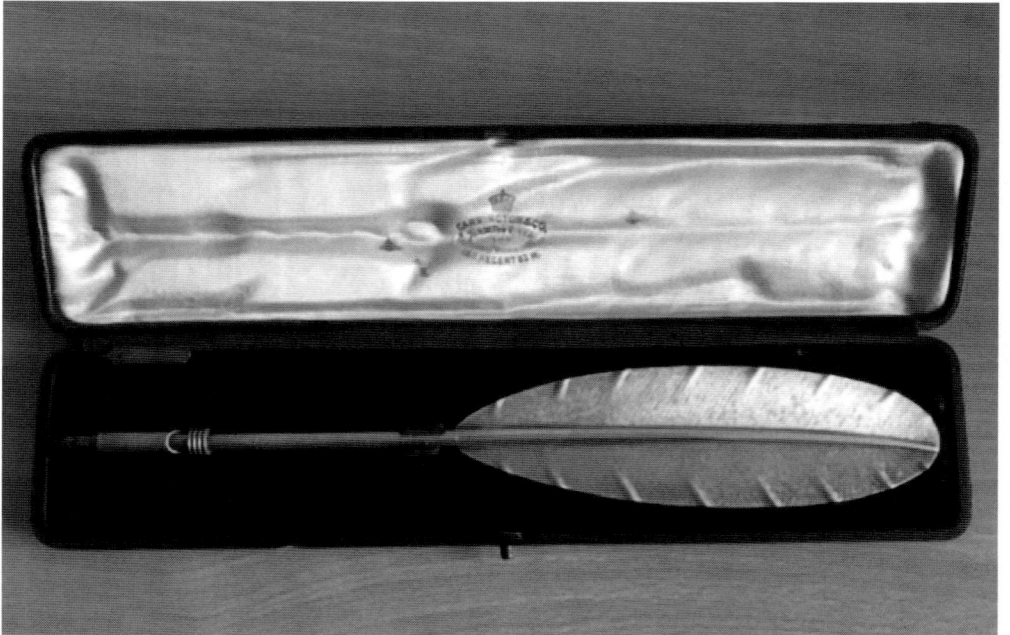

Tunbridge School Pen Prize. (*Courtesy of Tonbridge School*)

Tunbridge School Commons Box.
(*Courtesy of Tonbridge School*)

Miniature of young Reverend
George Austen. (*Jane Austen's
House, JAH319*)

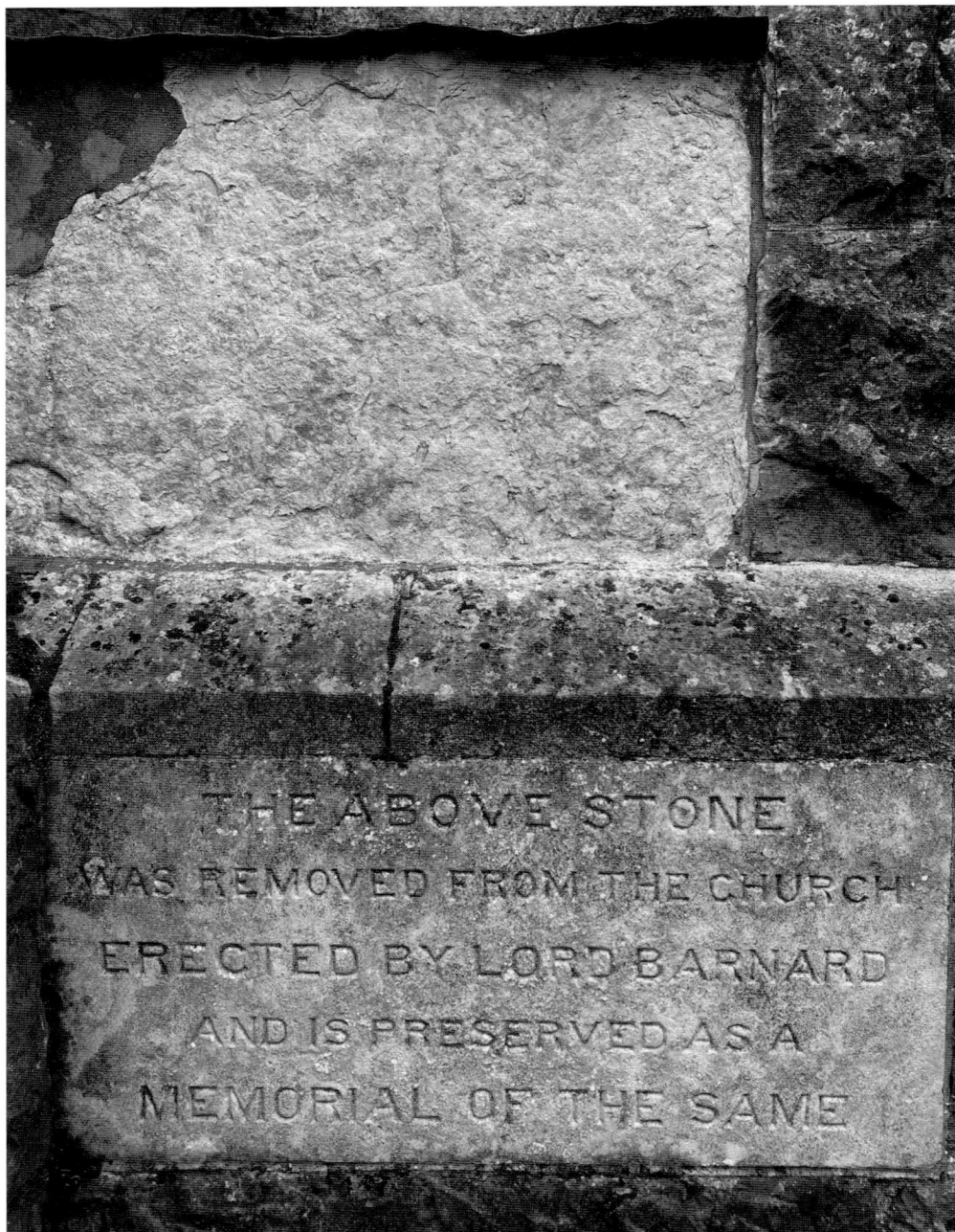

THE ABOVE STONE
WAS REMOVED FROM THE CHURCH
ERECTED BY LORD BARNARD
AND IS PRESERVED AS A
MEMORIAL OF THE SAME

Memorial cornerstone from 1722, St Giles' Church, Shipborne. (*Used with permission*)

St Giles' Church c.1722.
(*Used with permission*)

Tunbridge School with library c.1830, drawn by T.M. Baynes, engraving by H. Adlard. (*Photo by Nicky Liddell Photography*)

St Nicholas' Church, Steventon. (*Author's own photo, with kind permission granted by St Nicholas' Church*)

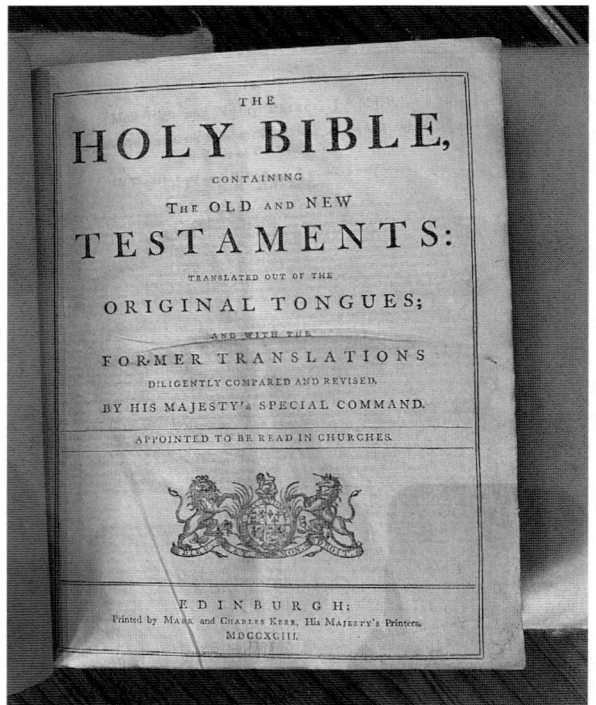

THE

HOLY BIBLE,

CONTAINING

The OLD and NEW

TESTAMENTS:

TRANSLATED OUT OF THE

ORIGINAL TONGUES;

AND WITH THE

FORMER TRANSLATIONS

DILIGENTLY COMPARED AND REVISED,

BY HIS MAJESTY's SPECIAL COMMAND.

APPOINTED TO BE READ IN CHURCHES.

EDINBURGH:
Printed by MARK and CHARLES KERR, His MAJESTY's Printers.
MDCCXCIII.

King James Bible donated by the Reverend George Austen. (*Author's own photo used with permission of Jane Austen's House*)

Chalice used by the Reverend George Austen. (*Used with permission*)

Baptismal entry for Jane Austen signed by George. (*Used with permission of Hampshire Record Office, 71M82-PR2*)

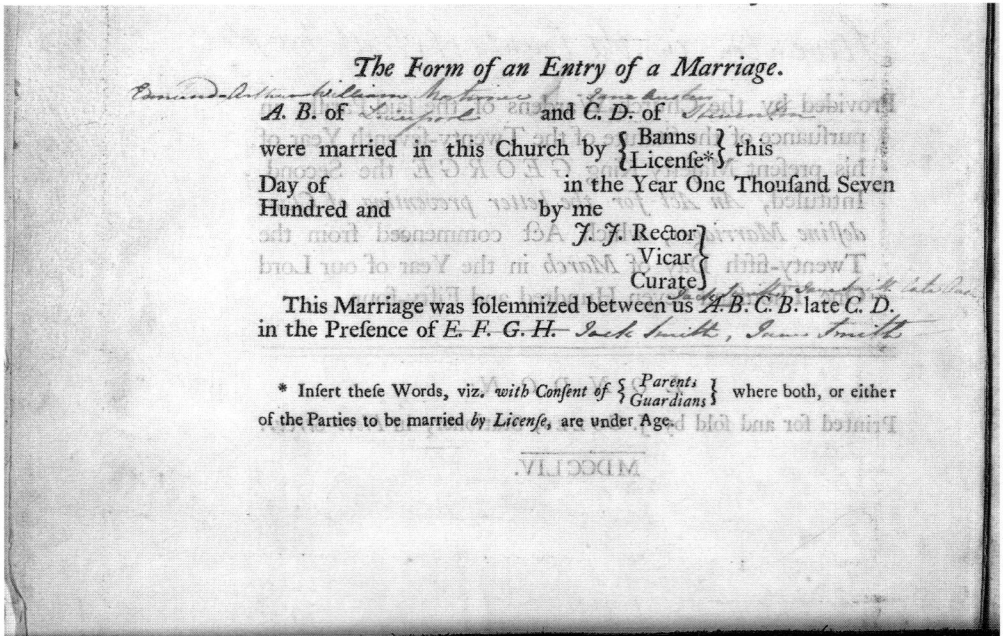

A marriage featuring Jane's fictitious entry. (*Used with permission of Hampshire Record Office, 71M82-PR3*)

Cross-stitch of
Steventon rectory.
(*Author's own work,
picture by Nicky Liddell
Photography, pattern by
Riverdrift House.* (TM))

The Reverend George Austen's bureau and bookcase. (*Author's own photo used with permission of Jane Austen's House*)

A painting once owned by Reverend George Austen by Richard Wilson (1713–1782). (*Used by permission of present owner, Natalie Jenner*)

P&G bookshop, Winchester. (*Photo by Madelaine Smith, used with permission*)

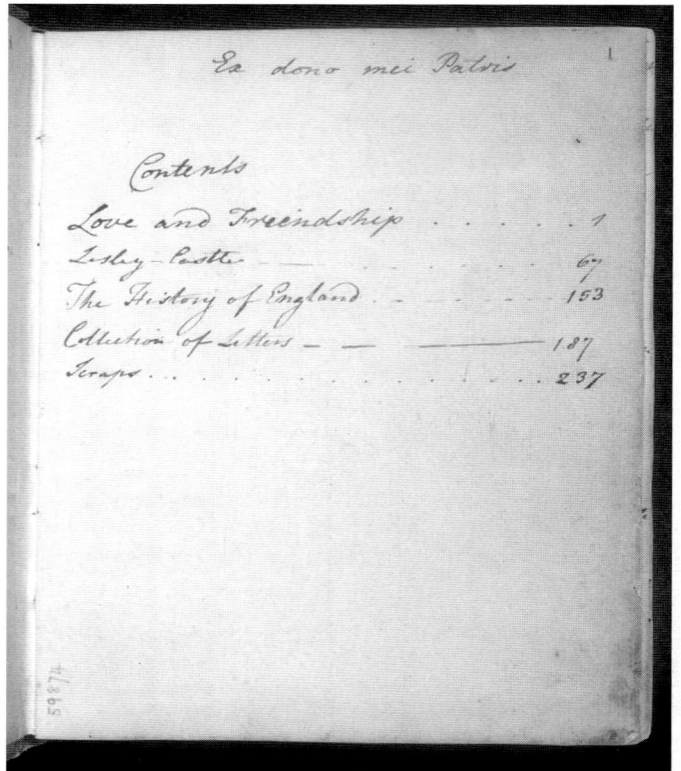

Volume The Second, Latin
inscription by Jane Austen.
(© *The British Library Board,
Add MS 59874, folio 001/recto*)

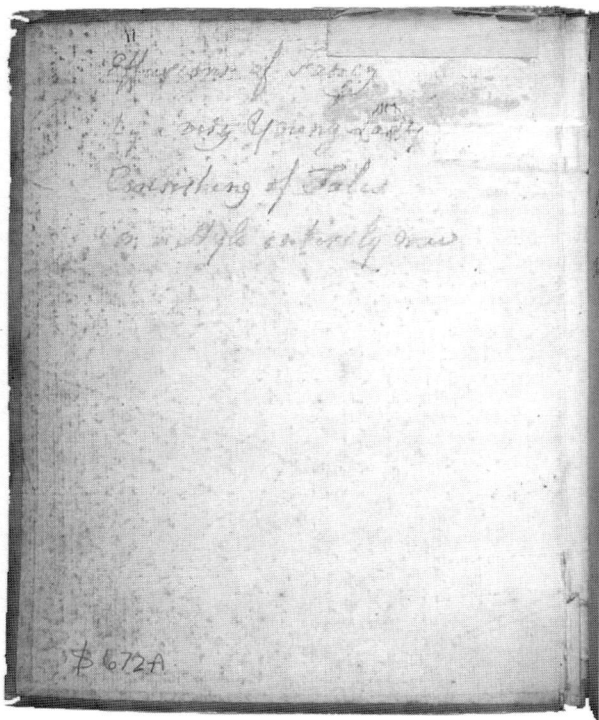

Volume The Third, dedication note from the Reverend George Austen (© *The British Library Board, Add MS 65381, the note in the inside cover*)

Silhouette of the Reverend George Austen presenting Edward to Mr and Mrs Knight. (*Jane Austen's House, JAH337*)

John Ring's Shop c.1904. (*Author's postcard, photographed by Nicky Liddell Photography*)

John Ring account's ledger, entry for writing desk. (*Used with permission of Hampshire Record Office, 8M62-15*)

Jane Austen's writing desk. (© *The British Library, Add MS 86841*)

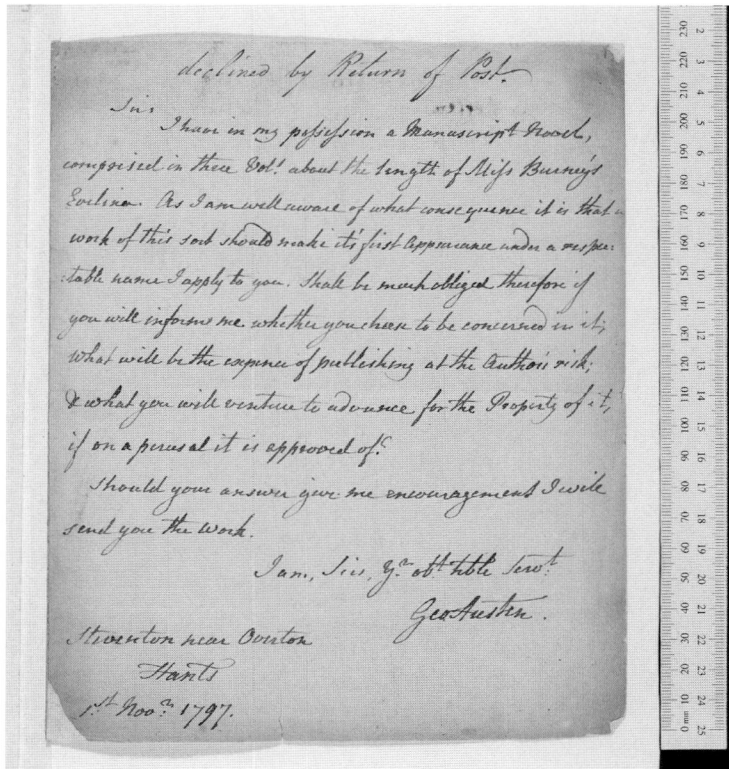

declined by Return of Post.

Sir I have in my possession a Manuscript Novel, comprised in three Vol. about the length of Miss Burney's Evelina. As I am well aware of what consequence it is that a work of this sort should make its first appearance under a respec:table name I apply to you. Shall be much obliged therefore if you will inform me whether you chuse to be concerned in it; what will be the expence of publishing at the Author's risk; & what you will venture to advance for the Property of it, if on a perusal it is approved of?

Should your answer give me encouragement I will send you the work.

I am, Sir, yr. obt. hble Servt.
Geo Austen.

Steventon near Overton
Hants
1st Novr. 1797.

Letter to Cadell and Davies by Reverend George Austen. (*By permission of the President and Fellows of St John's College, Oxford, Ref MS 279*)

Silhouettes of Reverend George and Mrs Cassandra Austen. (*Jane Austen's House, JAH75.1 75.2 LOAN*)

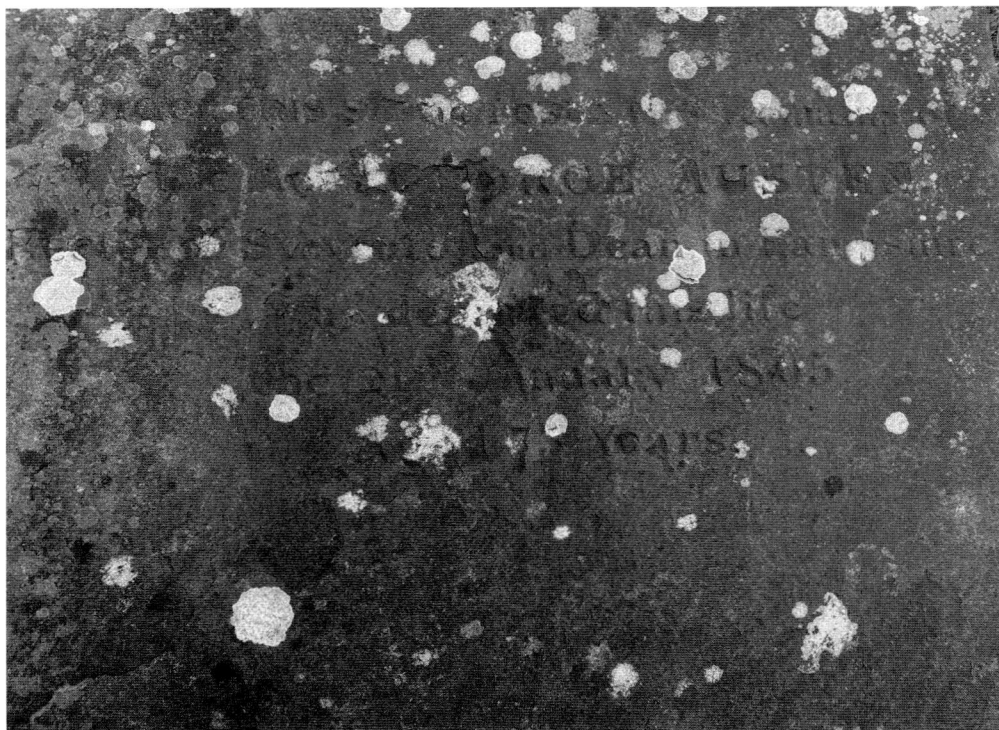

Memorial tombstone to Reverend George Austen, St Swithin's Church, Walcot, Bath. (*Author's own photo, used with permission*)

Jane was able to discover herself amongst the volumes of poetry and prose, essays, journals and letters, travel-guides, sermons and memoirs, she not only expanded her knowledge but was inspired both in regard to her taste and her own creativity. Looking back on her life, she wished she had spent longer in her reading spot and not been in quite so much of a rush to follow her impulse to write. She made a point of advising her young niece Caroline to put off writing until out of her early teens, adding that she wished she had lingered at the reading stage for longer herself.[44] Whether this sort of hindsight was wishful thinking and not necessarily something she would have agreed with had it been raised at the time, it is clear that she believed her reading to be a vital component, an important and irreplaceable requisite for writing at her best.

Chapter Ten

George's Barn

The rectory at Steventon stood within its kitchen gardens and glebe lands of about 2 ½ acres. An extra parcel of land of about half an acre in the nearby Middle Common Field was also credited to the parsonage. In addition, there were the four acres of land that George rented thanks to William Hellier to help supplement his income.[1] It came with a small garden and possibly a tenement; there was also, however, a barn.

The creativity that sprung from George's literate and educated family who enjoyed socialising together more than apart found its outlet in this barn. From a young age, Jane was involved in the family's mutual love of drama and theatricals. In the winter of the mid-1780s, acting became part of their Christmas entertainments at the parsonage.[2] The family, along with accompanying visiting extended family members and a few invited neighbours and friends, set up in the dining room. Reminiscent in some ways of the remodelling of the house that took place in *Mansfield Park*, George's study was notably not touched.[3] However, although they had taken over what was probably one of the larger rooms in their house, it was still a room in a country rector's family home which relied upon parental patience and permission for its use, rather than a wealthy gentleman's grand mansion where a ball or a play might be hosted with relative ease.

As a result of the inconvenience and the tight fit and in response to the family's continued love of acting in the summer months, with George's permission, the Austen children transported their theatricals to his barn.[4] George seemingly had no wariness of any impropriety or lack of decorum connected to acting out plays at home. Certainly, nothing of the kind that initially concerned Edmund Bertram and lay cradled in the heart of Fanny Price (*Mansfield Park*).[5] Having truly caught the acting bug, they painted and erected large screens as scenery. James wrote prologues and epilogues, lopping and cropping scripts, and assigning different younger family members to perform them. According to family memory, Jane was aged 12 to 15 during the period when the passion and desire for performances amongst the family was at its peak; however, other historians have noted that she may well have been observing her family's privately performed amateur dramatics since she was 7 years old.[6] It is thought that in her teens she too took part, even though the subject matter of some of the plays might nowadays seem quite adult and risqué in content. As Jane read aloud so well and her expressive talents were so appreciated and esteemed in the family, she must have acquitted herself very well for one so young. Their French-speaking, glamorous cousin Eliza took on main parts in these amateur productions and Austen family tradition has it that she won the hearts of James and Henry in these moments. However, not all family members wanted to be a part of things, and George's niece Philadelphia Walter decided to stay away from Steventon rather than be forced to take part, even though she was kindly cajoled and entreated through messages from Eliza, now a mother with a 16-month-old son, and her Aunt Cassandra Austen.[7]

One of their earliest plays, *The Rivals*, performed in July 1784, included scenes where the heroine was cajoling her maid to hide her library books in case others saw them and judged them and, by implication, the heroine too harshly. In the play, she instructs her maid to leave out only those titles which might be thought more appropriate and suitable for a young lady. For a young girl who was just venturing into her father's library, this must have been a relatable and hilarious scene for Jane and could have been a topic of conversation in her mind as she made her choices from George's shelves.

However, Jane's enjoyment of the drama and theatre at home was not solely confined to observing others and taking part. She also began writing, adapting her reading into little playlets of her own. When Jane returned from the Abbey House School, never to venture back, and the family had begun to write their own pieces for performance together, George recognised that his younger daughter's ideas and 'effusions' were spilling out of her pen at a greater and greater rate. Lampooning storylines, characters and ideas that she read in the books that she devoured and combining them with her own witty observations of the people that she saw round and about, Jane was beginning to write more sophisticated short stories to accompany her sketches, charades, playlets and poems. Written for her own amusement as well as that of her family and intimate friends, Jane had begun, even at the young age of 12, to loosen herself from any shackles that her local community and even her open-minded parents may have tried to place upon her. George recognised her talent and interest, and he encouraged it. As a parent he saw something to nurture in his child and as a teacher he instinctively felt the opportunity to consolidate and challenge her critical thinking, creativity and natural abilities. He bought Jane three white vellum-bound notebooks, decorated on the cover with a simple tooled geometric margin and which look to have once had edges sprinkled in red. These notebooks are now known collectively as her *Juvenilia*, or youthful writings, because in them Jane made fair copies of her stories and 'scraps', as she called them. She named them *Volume the First*, *Volume the Second* and *Volume the Third*, in line with the traditional format of novels at the time and copied these titles onto their front covers. This feature, in addition to her dedications to friends and family, begging for their patronage and acceptance of each piece, make them feel like home-made yet real little books.

On the inside first page of the second notebook, Jane wrote 'a gift from my father' in Latin ('Ex dono mei Patris'); simple, neat and clear, her penmanship poignantly sits at the top of the page with the contents of her book noted underneath. In the third notebook, which is similar in size but slightly thinner in the number of pages, George wrote a note in the inside cover. Even though it is in pencil, it still sits there to this day, a moving note of encouragement from a proud father: 'Effusions of fancy by a very young lady, consisting of tales in a style entirely new.' In these notebooks, Jane wrote with a freedom that she might not know in quite the same way, ever again. She wrote with passion and let the words and thoughts, which many in the outside world at the time might not have viewed as appropriate for a young parson's daughter, flow onto the pages. Indeed, some who met her around this age thought her precocious. In reality she was quite shy and found a release in writing, in parodying what she had read and highlighting the foibles of adults she observed there. Her notebooks paved a way for her to explore the ideas bouncing around in her head as she read and began to pay close attention to the world around her. They allowed her to communicate thoughts and feelings that she might otherwise never have voiced. These entries were for herself and her family, to be read, performed and discussed within the confines of their intelligent, witty and liberal conversations with invited friends and some of the boarders who were privy to her offerings.

It is entirely possible and quite probable that Jane had submitted her own sketches and plays for family re-enactment. *The Mystery, An Unfinished Comedy* was included in her *Juvenilia* notebooks in *Volume the First*. Dedicated to her father, as we 'watch' the action, we are privy only to snippets of conversation and know not what the advice offered by the protagonists, two parents, could be. Nor do we know the matter to which anything in the piece pertains. The play leaves the audience happily perplexed and confused, which is, of course, a delightful thing for a teenage author to have the power to affect her parents and perhaps also reflected her own adolescent confusion in the face of their own conversations with her, her siblings and other boarders.

Another of these pieces, included in *Volume the First* told a *'moral tale'*, imitating the fable, a style popular at the time and often used in children's literature in order to edify and educate them on a particular point of behaviour, etiquette and manners.[8] Although set in a different county, the protagonist is one Mr Williams, a clergyman whose living amounted to the same as received by George. A witty synopsis of a family of small means, nevertheless contented, thankful and happily resigned to their economic station in life. He too had married on presentation to his living but had a slightly smaller family of 'only' six children. All 'very fine' of course. So far, so funny. There may well even have been an in-joke about the name Williams, and perhaps the missing out of the girls to make six male children. One son is talked of as entering the Royal Academy for Seamen at Portsmouth as Frank recently had and Charles would go on to do. The fictional son had even embarked on his first mission, as Frank had done, although hopefully Frank did not include a giant dog every time he sent a letter home, like the hilarious son in the story. Another of the clergyman's sons had been adopted, not by a local wealthy landowner who might benefit his education and his future, but by an impoverished clergyman, who had no means, no business and nothing worthy to impart to Williams junior. The story ends with the schoolboy antics of this son and the hapless and hopeless lenience of his master. These are musings which we can trace in part to the lives of those at the rectory with an amusing twist that would have entertained them all and most likely made it into a letter or two to the absent Frank at the Royal Naval Academy, and Edward who had just embarked upon a grand tour of Europe.

Although highly entertaining and packed full of punchlines designed with this aim in mind, the absence of his two sons must have been a bittersweet reality for George and any parallels, no matter how funny, would still have given him cause to reflect. Delighted to have forwarded the education and purpose in life of two of his sons, supporting them in the same way that his uncle had provided for him, this was still another separation. In his own childhood and boyhood, he had known the strain of being parted from his father and absent from his closest relations for long periods of time. Having found the loving support of his wife Cassandra, through their sheer hard work and a great deal of entrepreneurship, he had built a secure home life for them all. Now he had to let them go. He had worked hard to cement their futures and at a personal cost to himself. However, unable to keep them all close to hand and to spare them the hardships of seeking a profession, the truth of the matter was that he had to let them go in order to help them find their own future financial security.

Just a few years before, in 1779, when Edward was 12, he had caught the eye of the son and wife of his benefactor, Thomas Brodnax May Knight. Thomas junior and Catherine Knatchbull had no children and were looking to secure an heir for their estates in Kent – Chawton near Alton, and Steventon. Thomas junior's mother, the wife of George's generous benefactor who had presented him with the living at Steventon, was Jane Monk. She was George's second cousin, being the granddaughter of Jane and Stephen Stringer. He was the uncle to whom George's grandmother, Elizabeth Weller, had been forced to give up guardianship of her eldest son John to all those years ago under the terms and conditions of John III's cruel will. Family legend remembers that initially a letter was received from these Knights, asking that Edward accompany them on their family holiday.

Right at the very beginning of the matter, everyone noticed what a struggle this was for George. Having been an orphan himself, he had had to work his way up to security through the benevolence of others and the endeavours of his own education. He had achieved the object of his childhood longing and yearning, his dream and goal of being able to provide for himself and protect and enjoy his immediate family. Cassandra had come into his life and through love and commitment, they had enlarged that vision to include another generation. One which had delighted George but had also presented him with another challenge, that of supplying all their needs too. The decision as to whether to allow Edward to go on holiday with the Knights was not therefore an easy one on so many levels. Initially, ever the schoolmaster, George clung to the obvious threat, that to his son's education. He feared, he said, that Edward could not go because the time out would put him back in terms of learning his Latin. In short, Edward simply could not afford to miss that much schooling. However, Cassandra, with an eye to the practical needs of securing a future for their Ned, who was not as academically minded as James, and perhaps sensing the opportunity as well as the expectation from a family who had been so helpful to the two of them in the past, suggested that she thought George had better agree to their request and let him go. No one else could have swayed George and her opinion ultimately guided him into agreeing. Edward returned after his holiday and family memory served that to all intents and purposes, everything continued as it had done before, even his Latin.[9] Edward did not change at all and neither did his status within the family. However, then, little by little, it had come to be generally accepted amongst the Austen family that Edward would be adopted by the Knights, be educated at their expense and that in becoming their much-longed-for and much-needed heir-in-waiting, his future would be well provided for. When Mr Knight died at the age of 59, he named Edward as his heir following his wife's death. It was expected too, though, that in the event of *his* premature death, this status would be granted in turn to one of Edward's brothers.[10] Wary of last wills and testaments, having grown up knowing the terms of his great-grandfather's demands, George knew how splitting siblings in order for conditions of benevolence to be met had fragmented his father's family, socially and emotionally, and had effectively separated them for ever. George had directly felt the depth of this loss himself as a child, financially and in terms of support when his father had died so prematurely. Wilfully submitting to his own son being adopted in order to benefit from the terms of Thomas Knight's will would have personally been a very difficult decision for George. Even if, in later years, the family themselves treated everything lightly including the changing of Edward's name from starting with an A to a K, and even though such consequences would not come into play for many decades, for George there was much more *personal* history to be overcome in living with his decision.[11]

Perhaps on one level, he feared that in agreeing he had tacitly been the instigator of another separation, that he might lose his son forever, despite the best intentions of ensuring and securing his financial future. On the one hand, this was the pinnacle of all that George had hoped to achieve, an untouchable wealth that could never be shaken from his son, a foot on the highest rungs society had to offer, but yet at such an untold, unknown personal cost to them all. This truly was a double-edged sword. However, ultimately, this was a situation that only Cassandra's supportive words and understanding could have calmed.

On another level it must have felt as if George were casting his son off, making him in some senses into the orphan that George once was. In *Emma*, Jane Fairfax was orphaned and sent to live under the care of her grandmother and aunt. She is rescued from poverty and parental obscurity by a military friend of her father's. Colonel Campbell initially invited young Jane into his home with his wife and daughter. As time passed, he, too, just as Uncle Francis had done for George, decided to take complete responsibility for her education.[12] Her own inheritance and the limited extent of his wealth was not enough to support her into adulthood and so he aimed her training at the chance of gaining a governess position at some stage. However, the role of governess was not at all a profession to be envied and certainly not one at all admired by Jane. Her Miss Fairfax had been rescued but she had also been dealt a fate worse than anything in some young women's minds.

In *The Watsons*, Jane compounds her own feelings within a conversation between two of the Watson sisters. Both loathed the teaching role; one would countenance it in preference to a loveless marriage, but the other, who had witnessed the realities of those living out this station in life at school, vowed she would not submit herself to it at any cost. The outcomes for an orphan like George had never been certain, and if there were any certainty it was that the scales were tipped towards the lower end of life's chances, just as was feared in Jane Fairfax's case. George had worked his own way up, rising due to his uncle's benevolence and his own hard work, intelligence and character. He would not be banishing Edward to a life of difficulty or of any pain or misery, quite the opposite. Still, the idea of turning him out and letting him go into another family would have been quite the change and would have gone against all George's former instincts of protecting and providing for his own family at all costs.

Harriet Smith's (*Emma*) parentage hung over her as she approached her own young adulthood, the concern for her economic wellbeing palpable in Emma's handling of their friendship. Her reputation was protected to a certain extent by her being sent to a respectable school. To be elevated to a parlourmaid, as Jane and Cassandra had been for a short while at the Abbey House School, signified a certain sense of relief in that someone, somewhere was able to provide for her. However, her roots are shrouded in mystery for a time, a sense of suspense is in the air. This atmosphere was one that George would have felt as a cloud above his head moving through the years at Tunbridge School. The realities of his childhood were known, yes, but the risk of slipping back down the scale into poverty and lack of opportunity was all too real. There was a fear that any revelation of Harriet's true father might bring about a downturn in her fortunes or taint her with the reputation of being low-born, thus stunting her social progress. However, she was finally restored by a good match and the revelation that her father only had the sting of 'tradesman' in his tail; due to his good fortune, she would always be provided for in comfort.[13] Jane lets the relief and the contemplation of the alternative outcome linger in the mind of the reader for a while, highlighting the intensity of feelings attached to this fate. In letting Edward go, there was no doubt of his future wealth, and no risk that he might lose it all, but there was the reality of how his true connections might affect him socially.

Adoption, quite common amongst wealthy families at this time, would involve George giving his consent. In giving up his own son, even if only on paper, George would protect Edward's future but at the same time tap into the traumatic feelings he had experienced at the height of his own crisis, all those years ago in the bookshop in London.

Fanny Price (*Mansfield Park*) is also taken away from her childhood home by relations of a wealthier sort. Her parents are very much alive, yet two sisters, her aunts Mrs Norris and Lady Bertram, contrive to bring her to Mansfield Park, outwardly as an act of charity towards their hard-pressed and overstretched sibling. In reality they have more of an eye to their own requirements and begin moulding and pressing young Fanny into a subservient role. Taken away from difficult circumstances of one kind, Fanny is press-ganged into their service, albeit in better surroundings. Their provision comes with strings attached. Fanny quickly became very isolated, separated from her beloved brother William, and placed in the company of cousins with whom she had nothing in common and an uncle whose overbearing nature was a cage all of its own. In effect, her own family had conspired to trap her. Placed in a world that she was totally unused to, ill prepared for and in which she was tied to their whims and needs, Fanny immediately felt great powerful waves of homesickness. These only highlighted her feelings of being such an outsider at her uncle's house. With her female cousins ready to turn on her for not knowing French and because she possessed only two sashes, she had been placed in an unenviable emotional state by her family.[14]

Her mother and father had not made provision at all for her emotional welfare or wellbeing in making such a transition. Their lack of education had a direct impact on their daughter's happiness and their minds had been occupied solely by the practicalities of providing subsistence for their children. This was an echo of the urgent need which pressed down on George's uncles and which they prioritised over every other consideration, the fundamental requirement to find food and shelter for their brothers' orphaned children. George would have felt a similar pang when dropped off at his uncle's front door in London. Essentially trapped with no way to go 'back', he was equally as unprepared for the expectations or experiences of his new 'home'. He too had been powerless, forced to come to terms with feelings of guilt and shame placed on him by the adults in whose care he found himself, all the while coming to terms with his own grief for his father. Even as a child he absorbed the message that publicly he had to be grateful for every scrap of comfort; in some way he felt he had to prove himself worthy of his keep. His fears for Edward, although tamed by the perceived comfort of his new world, would still have had the power to pull trauma to the front of George's mind.

At her wealthy relatives' beck and call, poor Fanny was saved from the immediate distresses that the poverty of her father's house held but very much put upon within her new surroundings. The niche that she fell into in order to fit in was in acting as a glorified lady-in-waiting to her aunts. She had been abandoned into a role by her parents which she might otherwise, in a different set of circumstances, have expected to be paid for. Her parents had made a deal on her behalf which she as a child was powerless to stop. That feeling was one that George himself remembered from the time when he arrived at his Uncle Stephen's home. He too fell into a helper's role in order to find some way to be useful and to avoid the feeling of such an uncomfortable welcome. Fanny's good nature and innately positive personality were all that saved her. Just like George, she had qualities that enabled her to turn what could have been a curse into a blessing. In travelling there for the good of her education, Fanny actually taught her family important lessons. In achieving all that he had, especially if it might culminate in his son becoming part of the established landed gentry, George too had a lesson or two for his Uncle Stephen and stepmother Susanna especially.

George may have worried about what exactly he might be subjecting Edward to. The picture that looked so rosy on the outside, as it did for Fanny Price, could, he knew, be completely different in reality. His was not the hard heart of his Uncle Stephen who, family memory asserted, coldly and reluctantly housed the three poor orphans all those decades ago. George was much more sensitive to the need for this move to improve Edward as a person, to continue his education, to give him a purpose to fulfil in life and an income stream to support him.

The closest reflection we can encounter on what this decision meant personally for George is encapsulated in the characters of Mr Weston (*Emma*) and his only son, Frank. Captain Weston's marriage to a Miss Churchill had caused consternation amongst her wealthy relatives, especially her brother. However, their son was a major means of reconciliation. Upon his mother's death, the elder couple took him under their wing and brought him up at their own expense. We learn that Mr Weston did indeed have 'some scruples' and 'reluctance', but his fatherly heart succumbed to the powerful notion of wanting the best for his son. In comparing the wealth of both families, he concluded that there was no competition. Mr Weston did not count love and affection or his own paternal ties as worthy of the substitution. He could not bring himself to enforce his son's submission to these in the wake of the obvious financial security and opportunities that would await him with his maternal relatives. In some ways, this fortune was only his birth right as his mother's son, but as a father, Captain Weston would have had to consent to laying down his claim.[15] George, just like Weston, would have had no further worries for his son's economic needs but the reality of this choice was a stark and permanent one. Edward, just like Frank, would move from being tacitly and quietly brought up as the chosen heir, to being formally adopted and legally changing his name.

Isabella Woodhouse (*Emma*) voices some of the human emotion surrounding such a choice, and the shock and scandalised dawning of comprehension of such a decision. Giving a child away goes so against the grain of decent, caring parents that to do so is unfathomable to her. Living as she was, this was a luxury point of view which she could afford. But for many in these times, it did happen and many marriages were made for the very same business-like and practical reasons. Isabella held grudges of unease and dislike in regard to those involved in brokering such a decision, but the truth was that she and her children had the protection of Donwell Abbey to fall back on and Captain

Weston, just like George Austen, did not. Her husband viewed the adoption of Frank as a decision free of sentimental ties and sensibilities for Captain Weston, who he saw as someone with such a positive and cheery disposition as would lean into the liberties that this life might bring for them both. However much Captain Weston, like George, was bright and positive in his outlook, he was not laissez-faire nor did he exhibit an easy come, easy go regard for his family. Quite the opposite in fact.

George was most definitely grounded in his roots and his determination to ensure the preservation of his own family unit ran deep. He had a great longing to belong, springing from the fountain of life that was his youth, and yet his drive to survive was even stronger. A pragmatic approach was ultimately the side of the coin which George landed on. In order to keep his family, he had to somehow lose it, at least on one level. He may even have had one eye on the future provision for his daughters and his wife, assured that not only his stocks and shares might pay out for them in his absence but that Edward, as a son and a brother, would not forget his deeper honour and duty to them in the future.

In a reversal of Edward and George's own fate, Miss Emma Watson (*The Watsons*) is returned to the family home, having been brought up by her aunt and uncle, the Turners, and not having had much contact at all, bar the odd letter, with her father or siblings in many years. Upon the death of her uncle and the subsequent second marriage of his widow, her aunt, she is sent back home and is suddenly repatriated, without any money apportioned to her for her own future nor any bequest granted her on the part of the deceased. Having spent her life in the lap of considerable luxury, she was now to be supported at the full expense of her father, an impoverished, elderly man in ill health. She must now await a much bleaker fate than the one she had had in prospect before. Being no longer the sole object of attention for wealthy relations, she instead had to take her place as one of six siblings, including three other daughters all reliant on her father's rather basic estate. How much worse this turn of events would have been for the Austens. In reality they all had hope that Edward's luck would be something of a boon for them all.

So it was that Edward's education took a different turn, and in 1786–1790 he undertook the grand tour of Europe, in preparation for all that awaited him as a gentleman landowner and estate manager. First, he spent time in Switzerland from where he set out for Germany, Amsterdam and Italy.

The reality was that if George had not agreed to his son's adoption, Jane would not have received Edward's invitations to be part of the world of high society of the landed gentry, benefits that would quickly become obvious to them all. When Mr Weston later boasted of Frank, it was still as his son, one he staked his claim to as such even though 'he does not bear my name.'[16] Frank too ultimately declared that he still held dear his biological inheritance from his father; his positivity and outlook something he avowed that he never took for granted and 'which no inheritance of houses or lands can ever equal the value of.'[17] For George, the blessing of Edward was the same in his heart as it had always been. George had helped to secure a future for his family and his son was both his and someone else's – his family had simply expanded. A true lesson, it is only to be lamented that Susanna Kelk Austen could not have had the same openness of heart and mind when she held the power to add to the provision for George and his siblings all those years previously.

At the same time as 19-year-old Edward embarked on his European adventures, Frank enrolled at the Royal Naval Academy and left for Portsmouth. He was 12 years old. Full of George's 'get up and go', Frank had already shown his drive and desire to make things happen in his life. At a very young age he had saved up and bought his own pony to ride about on and then sold it again when he outgrew it.[18] Now he too was about to leave home. As well as physical training, Frank undertook a course of mathematics and amongst other things, he was given further instruction on how to calculate and measure longitude and latitude as well as knowledge about navigation and other skills that would help him once aboard ship. Frank acquitted himself well, completing the course successfully, and just two years later he earned the recommendation of his headmaster that he be accepted into the Royal Navy. The academy leadership recognised the exceptional speed of this accomplishment and took the bold and unusual step in bringing Frank to the particular attention of the Admiralty on his graduation. Sir Henry Martin made the point of commenting specifically on Frank's excellent attitude to study, his focused and determined hard work, and his exceptional standards of behaviour as well as congenial and animated personality. He made it clear in his eloquent assessment of him just how unusual and outstanding a pupil Frank was. These exact qualities could have appeared in any report for George from Tunbridge School or St John's, and mirror the values and abilities demonstrated by him personally throughout his education. George had kept up a timely correspondence with young Frank and had advised and guided him closely throughout his time as a pupil. Having lived alone for extended periods in institutions himself in the past, he had a lot of practical advice to impart. Having done so as a younger boy than his son, he also had a depth of understanding and empathy with which to support Frank should he find himself in any similar situations with friends, masters, boarding life or schoolwork. Like his father before him, Frank stood out from the crowd of his fellow classmates and cohort, and was singled out for glory and success at the end of his time at the academy. George believed that the integrity and reputation which Frank had secured for himself at the academy at such a young age boded well for his future success in regard to his conduct and learning. The proud master, Sir Henry Martin, had taken the liberty of recommending him to the Admiralty, for service not only in the immediate present on a particular ship (having already made the skipper, Captain Smith, aware of young Frank) but also in the future.[19] Once begun, he did not stop in taking the chance to petition for Frank, asking that in due course he be brought to the attention of Commodore Cornwallis who oversaw the promotions of new sailors. The master was quick to point out the educational opportunity that promoting such an able and outstanding pupil could have. Ambitious for his students, the master believed in the influence and example that elevating someone with Frank's qualities would have on other pupils at the academy in the future, an outcome that the proud teacher could see would benefit the navy as a whole and be in all their interests. Frank was assigned to HMS *Perseverance* and was promoted within a year. Within a decade, he was commanding his own ship, HMS *Peterel*.

George had indeed instilled these principles as a priority and was proud to see them displayed in Frank. This was confirmed in a memorandum that he wrote to his son on his first appointment.[20] George's motivation for writing was a fatherly one, showing a keen regard for his son's pastoral welfare and an awareness that his wisdom and guidance could now only be requested or bestowed infrequently. George personally felt the distance in both time and space that was going to separate them and was compelled to offer meaningful support in the form of his memorandum, something for Frank to consult and rely on as straight from his father's heart and mind whenever he should need his advice. Dated the very same month that Henry Martin wrote his noteworthy letter, Frank treasured it and kept it with him on every subsequent mission, guarding it closely for his whole life.

The advice George gave paints a picture for us of what mattered most to him, what he believed was of the utmost importance, the most vital information that he felt obliged to ensure he passed on to his son. It was advice that George himself had learnt to live by, either as he also received it from his Uncle Francis all those years ago, or because he had learnt it first-hand through his own life experience. George's words of wisdom were practical, educational and clear. Focusing on the larger questions in life, rather than the nitty-gritty of his everyday routines and needs, George's words were laced with love and affection and revealed his deep understanding of Frank as a person.

Firstly, George directed his son to his duty to demonstrate his Christian faith day and night to God, his community and himself. In a shared shorthand of understanding, George referred Frank to his own copy of the *Elegant Extracts* which George put great store by and in whose authors he had complete trust. George had guidance for Frank in terms of his behaviour towards what he called the 'three orders of Men'. This advice seems born particularly from his own experience of institutions such as Tunbridge School and St John's College: deference to, and respect for, the authority and wishes of his superiors; helpfulness, empathy and a sense of humour for one's peers; and for all others, compassionate kindness.

As in his own experience at school and university, and in his life as a clergyman, George reminds Frank of the cornerstone of his own 'well-doing': the need to learn and distinguish oneself by one's expertise and knowledge in order to be as 'useful as possible'. Education and hard work were the bedrock of what had helped George progress and they dovetailed with his heartfelt vocation of service to family and one's community, under God.

In all of George's prior training for leadership, sobriety had featured as the foundation of one's responsibilities to oneself and a demand that respect and responsibility took on trust. It was an attribute that George had modelled to his family all his life and one which he was thankful that his son had taken heed of. True to his own character once again, it is not surprising that George also had some thoughts to relay regarding money, most notably the careful, mindful use of earning, keeping and spending it. The precarious nature of his own personal financial situation meant that he could not help but request the 'earliest possible notice' of any expenses that Frank might incur.

The final message that George took the time to impart was so poignant and moving. The man who had known so little of a father himself parted with his own dear son on the following conditions: that he write to them almost continually (including every last detail of his daily life) as George had done at Tunbridge and at St John's. He wanted to leave him with the feeling, the knowledge, the confirmation, that he could not have 'a more disinterested' [impartial/unconditionally loving] and 'warm friend' than his 'truly affectionate father'. How comforting those final words must have been on the long nights away from home on the wide, open sea and how helpful George's specific advice would have seemed, an ever-present counsel in times of indecision or insecurity. It is no wonder that Frank guarded this letter so carefully all his days. Perhaps this was the letter that George wished he had been able to receive from his father; one hopes that he had a similar one from his benevolent Uncle Francis.

With all of these events to contend with, it was no small wonder that the family needed their dramatic entertainments to make the most of their time together and, in the case of 1788, to lift their spirits when their numbers were depleted. That summer George visited his aging and elderly uncle Francis with his wife and daughters. Perhaps he sought the reassurance, comfort and wise counsel from his kind patron and mentor in these unsettling and changing times. In this light, Jane and James' writings were a great support to George as he sent two sons off to make their way in the world and grappled with the pangs and pains of missing them, as well as the twinges of past traumas that loomed large in his own memory.

Jane's love for the Richardson volumes, *Sir Charles Grandison*, spilled over into a version of the play for her own family to perform. She began it just as the family productions were coming to an end. A longing to recapture the fun that they all had together may have stimulated her to put pen to paper. Relying on the fact that it was a family favourite and that everyone who might watch it or take part was as well-versed in its famous plot lines, characters and dialogue as she was, she set about in writing an adaptation that would shrink the lengthy narrative into a play fit for her family of would-be thespians.

When the play was unearthed in the late twentieth century, many believed it to be so poorly written and so far removed from the quality that readers associated with Jane Austen that it should be relinquished as an unworthy addition to her oeuvre. However, it provides a link to the stimulation found and the passion ignited by her love of literature fostered by her father's support. The jokes contained within refer not only to the assumed knowledge of the original text, but also give glimpses into Steventon rectory life. Laughing at themselves through the inclusion of in-jokes and references to shared knowledge add to the idea that Jane intended this little play to be acted out in the same manner as previous family shows. Indeed, Austen scholar Brian Southam believes that it was started but then abandoned for nearly a decade and then 'hurriedly finished', even perhaps as late as the end of 1800. He concurs that this timing in itself makes the argument that if it was ever performed at Steventon, then it would have to have been between the summer of 1799 and what would become their final one of 1801.[21] It is entirely plausible therefore that Jane resurrected and completed her *Grandison, The Happy Man* as an intentional and poignant piece of family entertainment. Perfectly timed to pull at their heartstrings, it was full of reminiscences of shared jokes and Austen family conversational references. She may very well have intended to stir up a little family nostalgia around a novel that the whole family knew and had shared together as they had once shared many others. This was the perfect piece to parody at this point, for Austen family old times' sake. Acting it out together might well have offered the opportunity for one more final rectory performance with family around. It was a fitting entertainment, a tribute to times gone by, at this, the exact moment when her father George's time as rector, and family life as they knew it at the parsonage, was about to draw to a close forever.

The piece shows a true father-daughter understanding and a relationship with amiable humour at its heart. Act One, Scene One, we are told, takes place in the 'afternoon', perhaps a little reference that the spirit of the scene that follows could have been a typical afternoon at home in George Austen's rectory. Mr Reeves, the father of the family, arrives home and stumbles across a delivery of millinery (perhaps a reference to George's sister Philadelphia's apprenticeship training in Covent Garden). He happily yet grumpily celebrates with himself at having successfully diverted the arrival and inconvenient deposit of so many dresses, accessories, packaging and boxes from his own protected space 'for once'. He sounds off a little to himself about avoiding such interruptions and despairs at the recollection that they had recently nearly impinged upon his very own study! George's personal space may over the years have grown in celebrity amongst the family and perhaps the protection of his study was the stuff of family legend. There may even have been a catchphrase or two of his bandied about the house in regard to this room of his own. Southam, in his introduction to an edition of Jane Austen's *Grandison*, concurs, especially, he says, as this scene was not part of the original work. He even suggests that perhaps there was some truth in the *Mansfield Park* scene that included Sir Thomas Bertram's study being gate-crashed and turned upside down in his absence.[22] Oh, the horror of that thought.

The play captures other humorous snatches of George's character and personality. It would be interesting to know who played the part of their father and just how they exaggerated and hammed up his foibles and mannerisms. In Act One, Scene Two, we see Mr Reeves bossing young messengers about. Three of them are coming and going, a William, a Thomas and a John, all sent off on missions with his orders ringing in their ears, his hastily written notes clutched in their hands. This could easily have been George with his bailiff and farm hands.

In Act Two, the clergy too come in for some ridicule. James was now ordained and had taken on roles as deacon and curate, but perhaps the poor clergyman drafted in by Sir Hargrave Pollexfen to conduct his marriage to Miss Byron was aimed more in spirit and caricature at the ageing George. Miss Byron wants none of his 'dearly beloveds' and treats his Common Prayer Book with exasperated contempt, once even knocking it out of his hands and subsequently throwing it into the fire. The clergyman is left lamenting 'my poor book' and demanding a replacement. Perhaps George's 'prayer book' and his 'dearly beloveds' were the perfect excuse for a little lovingly aimed lampooning for old times' sake.

Chapter Eleven
Jane's Effusions

Meanwhile, the greatest gift that George gave to Jane around this time was time itself. Once her chores such as sewing, mending or errands in the village were done and all morning visits to the rectory were complete, Jane's time was mostly her own. As the daughter of a clergyman and one with extra streams of income, she would not have had to work as someone else's maid or home help and was not to be trained as a dreaded governess. When her own schooldays were finally behind her and she had no masters to contend with, she could continue to develop her own strand and style of educating herself. Jane's future was expected to include marriage, to someone wealthy enough to provide for her and thus her chores and household training were the only draw on her time, apart from the pursuit of certain accomplishments. The rest of the time Jane could indulge her creative fantasies, trying them out on Cassandra and her friend Martha up in the 'dressing room'. She could also roam free. Taking long walks around the village and up and out to others surrounding the environs of Steventon, Jane could wander through fields and country lanes, alongside the hedgerows and over the rolling chalky hills. She enjoyed walking out in all weathers, even black frosts and soggy days in her boots or pattens (a metal shoe that fitted over a boot to give a walker extra grip on the muddy paths). Jane walked in all seasons and grew to know the flora and fauna, her father's sheep and local cattle that she passed on her daily jaunts. She could wander through the wheat fields after harvest and alongside the barley as it grew. Much research has been done in more recent times that has proved the value of walking in nature for one's mental health and wellbeing. As Jane meandered along familiar routes, she would also have had time for her creative juices to flow. As she clambered over a stile or went up and over a rolling ridge, she might even have remembered ideas that had flourished in that spot before. Mr Willoughby (*Sense and Sensibility*) might have met her in her mind as she crested a familiar hill. Mr Darcy (*Pride and Prejudice*) might well have been conjured up alongside the memory of the marriage register as she crossed over and behind St Nicholas' Church. His rival for Elizabeth Bennet's affections, Mr Wickham, might have sprung to mind as she crossed a stream or sat under a particular tree and returned to meet her there again and again, each time she revisited the same spot. The gift of time to wander and ponder and to glean the treasures of her mind was the greatest benefit that Jane gained from her father's provision for her. For twenty-five years, she could follow the familiar trails to her head and heart's content. She knew the local routes and roads like the back of her hand, and with the beauty and benign friendship of the fields she could shut off from worries and cares and slip seamlessly back into the surroundings of her imagination. In her book *Wanderers: A History Of Women Walking*, Kerri Andrews tells of other authors who did just the same, by the shores of Lake Windermere and in the mountains around them. One of Jane's favourite books, *Mrs Grant's Letters*, was a collection of correspondence written to communicate such a life in the Scottish Highlands to friends. Jane could relate to communing with one's environment, and the descriptions of the landscape and all of life lived within the surroundings echoed Jane's experience, albeit in the chalky hills of Hampshire. Jane developed the stamina to walk for hours, perfect for a writer who had to unravel the conundrums of an evolving plot line or figure out how Mr So and So might come to meet Miss X. If things were not coming together in her ideas, a plot walk would soon sort that out. Walking gave her the chance to mull over her observations and to make others too. Equally if the real world was encroaching too far on her imagination, escaping to the fresh air and comforting views would sooth any agitations and free her mind to focus on her 'darling children' once again.[1]

In around 1794, Jane had begun to develop her writing into longer and longer pieces. She moved on from writing snippets and short stories to more detailed, chaptered novellas and novels. On Friday 5 December of that year, George headed for John Ring's shop in Basingstoke. As we know he was not someone to buy spontaneously or gratuitously, and his purchase for Jane seems all the more intended and special as a result. On the previous Wednesday, he had endorsed a payment of £29 from C. Hoare & Co. Bank to Ring's account and he had now set out to collect something very special, a gift for Jane's upcoming nineteenth birthday, just eleven days ahead.[2] The small mahogany writing slope-type desk, with a long drawer included and complete with a glass ink stand, held so much tender meaning.[3] In this simple purchase, George touchingly acknowledged his understanding and approval, and no doubt his pride, in Jane's industriousness and her emerging ability. In gifting her something so personal, he signalled his support and encouragement for her writing, for her 'effusions of fancy' as he called them. His teaching business was going well and his heart could not resist spending their happily timed wealth to encourage his daughter in the pursuit of her talents. How grateful we all are that he did so.

From Jane's pen, treasures soon began to emerge. In 1794 she wrote *Lady Susan*, the dramatic tale of a self-absorbed mother who plots and schemes for her own advancement at the expense of her daughter's happiness.[4] Lady Susan shared some characteristics with Lady Craven, her best friend Martha's cruel grandmother of whom Jane had learnt so much when they were both cocooned together up in Jane and Cassandra's private rooms. The story combines the sharp wit and way with words of the protagonist with her sore lack of social morals and any sign of an empathic maternal streak. The following year Jane began her epistolary novel *Elinor and Marianne* with the two sisters revealing their story in the form of letters. Just two years after the arrival of her writing slope, the earliest signs of Mr Darcy and Elizabeth Bennet took to the page as Jane began to write her preliminary draft of *First Impressions*.

George had paved the way for Jane to follow her imagination. Firstly, he had provided the racks of reading material in his study and the time spent together in conversation about them. Next, he had given the notebooks and combined them with a personalised physical space in the house, just as he enjoyed (or tried to) in his study. He also enabled her to have time in which to enjoy nurturing and crafting her stories, and now he had gifted her the writing slope. George had both kindled and recognised Jane's spark and passions, and his pragmatic and practical investments in support of her reading and writing had acted as a catalyst and bellows to the fire of her talent. It is known that Jane read out her ideas and work to the family, for their entertainment and enjoyment. Once they were in their completed form, she also enjoyed giving her characters voices. She read them in the way she had learnt from her father, seeking the quality of reading that his scholarly background could foster, as well as adding her own tweak and, many think, her mother's wit. It is also probable that George's teaching talents helped Jane along the way. Accustomed as he was to marking and correcting, in his case the Latin grammar and translations of the boys he taught, he may well not have been able to help himself from making suggestions. Jane sought information, advice and the opinions of others to assist her with her writing and for her own enjoyment of an idea. As she and George were in the habit of discussing their reading together, it is entirely probable that she mulled over an idea, or a word or phrase, with him too and that she would have asked his opinions. In later years she kept lists of all that family, friends and neighbours thought of her characters; how she must have longed to have shared her later creations with her father.

Within three years George was so impressed with the quality of Jane's work that he undertook to try and get it published on her behalf.[5] George was very proactive in support of his children's ambitions and careers, famously so amongst his family. He was often penning letters to those whom he felt might be able to bring a little of their influence to bear on his sons' careers in particular. Recently George had written to their family friend Warren Hastings to thank him for his support with attempting to put in a good word for his son, in this case, quite probably Charles who had just completed his course with the Royal Naval Academy.[6] George showed an in-depth knowledge of, and an interest in, the likely decision-makers at the Admiralty. He was even so bold as to suggest ideas and strategies that he had in mind, sharing his thoughts with his well-connected friend. He made his requests quite politely and eloquently, yet openly and almost pointedly all the same. In addition, he was not afraid of initiating an approach, or contacting admirals directly and repeatedly as the occasion or need arose. He was instrumental in the process of promoting his sons' chances, involving himself in all the details of each step, almost chivvying and nudging the decision-making as much as he could and lining up a selection of helpers to put in a good word on their behalf. He sent off letters that ensured communication to and with all levels of people involved in the process of promotions. He made sure that, as well as sending out his own messages, he was in a position to hear back in a timely manner too. What is more, George was successful, enabling his sons to climb the career ladder and secure their next appointments. His intervention along the way got them moved into better situations and onto better ships. He truly helped to speed up promotional proceedings.

Unfortunately, according to later generations of the family, in the case of George's letter to the publisher Cadell and Davies, on behalf of his daughter, his approach was, and would still be, considered quite naïve. They felt that George's actions and wording showed him up as uninformed and quite outside the etiquette needed to be successful in his request. Younger generations thought the letter tactless and discourteous, perhaps a little in line with Mr Collins approaching Mr Darcy unintroduced (*Pride and Prejudice*). In George's defence he was most likely emboldened by his experience of living and working in his Uncle Stephen's shop. Although he was bold in his communications, he did have some understanding of publishing at the time in choosing to write to Cadell and Davies. Thomas Cadell senior had a business in the Strand and was well known for paying generously and representing authors of quality and renown. He had published Johnson as well as Frances Burney. Thomas junior, on taking over, had continued to publish Burney, including Jane's beloved *Camilla* and he also published Gothic novels by Ann Radcliffe. Not all publishers were open to supporting women writers. George had done his homework. Unfortunately, he overlooked the fact that he may have been more familiar with the publisher, their business and their reputation than Cadell was of George's inside knowledge and family publishing credentials. Cadell senior may well have known Stephen Austen as part of the publishing circle in the area, however, Stephen had died a generation before Thomas junior became involved in the business; the letter therefore came unsolicited and quite out of the blue, without any context or introduction from a mutual connection.

St John's College, Oxford, has the letter in its archive; from it we can deduce George's earnest and sincere request, his endearing efforts to promote his daughter's work and yet some ignorance of the process for submissions and applications. George's letter revealed his knowledge of both the esteemed reputation and the works that Cadell and Davies were publishing. He asked relevant and pertinent questions as to the logistics of payment and risk, but all without sending them any of the manuscript. His effusions of praise and his complete belief in the quality of Jane's work to compare it with such other famous and well-received novels showed his father's heart for his daughter as well as his scholarly instinct. In acting with such feeling, George showed his determination to honour his own commitment to his daughter's cause. He wrote the letter on Wednesday 1 November. The rejection was received back at the rectory by return of post.

George's 'bright and hopeful' personality, the same that had helped him throughout his own education and career-building stages, had knocked on the door of opportunity on Jane's behalf.[7] Jane remained undeterred and, encouraged by her father's faith in her and her own creative compulsions she pressed on altering and renaming *Elinor and Marianne* as *Sense and Sensibility* and beginning *Susan* (later to be named *Northanger Abbey*).

George was a reliable touchstone for many of his family, friends and community. His serious and sensible intelligent mind, combined with his open friendliness, warmth, sense of humour and convictions of his Christian duty, made him reliable, respected and approachable in equal measure. His support for his children's prospects was steadfast even when times were difficult. Equally he supported other close family members too. When his dear sister Philadelphia died of breast cancer in London, he took care to look out for his niece Eliza, taking her in at the family rectory – something that she herself valued so dearly. He was beloved to her, her handsome and charming uncle, her closest living connection to the mother she had lost and someone who had always had her best interests at heart.[8] When her husband, Jean Capot de Feuillide, whom George had been so against her marrying, was later guillotined in France, it was George and his family whom she relied on for support. For many years, up until she reached the age of 35, George was actively involved in overseeing the money held in trust for her, ensuring that it was suitably protected and released for use in her best interests.[9]

George was a useful confidante in surprising ways too. Getting time alone with anyone for a private conversation at the parsonage was never easy; in fact, when Jane dined alone with her father one time, she found the whole experience so strange that she considered it noteworthy of inclusion in her correspondence with her sister.[10] When Jane was in her early twenties, she had taken an interest in a certain Tom Lefroy, the nephew of her friend, Madam Lefroy. When her friend, the wife of the vicar at Ashe, visited, Jane was on tenterhooks, desperate to get her alone and hear more of him. She was anxious to hear any news of him at all, but was constrained by etiquette, her pride and shyness, as well as Madam Lefroy's silence on the matter. It was her father who stepped in to offer her some relief. Gently enquiring after the young man to their visitor, he managed to procure a little nugget of longed-for information for her. In this case, her potential beau had abandoned Hampshire altogether with a little nudging by his aunt and was headed back to Ireland to his career and his own good prospects. The tender-heartedness of her father's actions, though, was not lost on Jane and remained with her.[11] She allowed a similar sentiment to flow from her pen straight to the heart of Elinor Dashwood (*Sense and Sensibility*), whose own mother makes a similar enquiry on her behalf. As Elinor sits stock still, paralysed with anticipation and feeling, her mother gently probes their servant for news regarding the object of Elinor's affection, Mr Ferrars. As the narrator sensitively notes, 'Elinor had the benefit of the information without the exertion of seeking it.'[12]

For all her gentle teasing of her father in her letters to her sister, it is in a letter to one of her literary contacts later in life that we see glimpses of her true affection and admiration for him. Jane had been invited to visit the Prince Regent's home to see his library. She was shown around the sumptuous and flamboyant residence by the Prince of Wales's librarian, former Naval and Domestic Chaplain the Reverend James Stanier Clarke. Clarke had also attended Tunbridge School in his youth. He was bent on coaxing Jane to write a novel that reflected the life and times of a chaplain whose biography ran along very similar lines to his own. In putting Clarke off, Jane chose her words with care, trying to hide her biting opinions in humour and aiming to show as much tact as possible in declining his dubious offer. In reading between the lines, it is obvious with our hindsight and knowledge of her personal letters to realise that she was being ironic and that her underlying tone was one of cutting disgust. However, in her comments about capturing the 'Good, the Enthusiastic and the Literary' of the clergy, she was reflecting her experience of her own dear father, and her brothers who followed in his footsteps.[13] In focusing on the need to depict the quality of the topics of conversation of such an honourable clergyman as the one suggested by Clarke in any novel, she was harking back to and promoting the qualities her father exhibited. She highlighted the personal integrity that his gentlemanly education both confirmed in him and conferred upon him. An education, Jane was quick to point out, that in being born a woman she had never herself received and therefore felt self-deprecatingly inadequate at conveying in any such novel, with her tongue perhaps planted in her cheek.

When Jane embarked Marianne (*Sense & Sensibility*) on the process of healing and restoration after her abandonment by Mr Willoughby for a woman of greater fortune, it was to the qualities so liberally found in Jane's own father that she anchored herself: religion, reason and employment. For all her giggling and eye-rolling at her father's involvement in their lives, Jane knew that his example and integrity were the bedrock of their own flourishing. She blamed Mr Collins' odious lack of tact and education on the fact that he had not been as lucky as she and her siblings. He had suffered under the upbringing of an 'illiterate and miserly father', the very opposite to what she had experienced and with a correspondingly different outcome.[14]

Jane correlated her own character and success in life directly with her father's qualities and vision, shining a spotlight in her novels and stories on what it might have been like to live under the auspices of the opposite to her father. In *Mansfield Park*, Sir Thomas, oblivious to any harm that might arise to Fanny, and heedless of his own fatherly inadequacies, but conscious nonetheless of the impact a poor paternally-controlled environment could have on a child, sent her back to her father's house. The educational experiment that he constructed was designed to enlighten Fanny to the benefits of conforming to his wishes and marrying Mr Crawford in order to escape a bleak future.[15] In Mr Bennet (*Pride and Prejudice*), who loved nothing more than to lose himself within the walls and books of his own study, Jane created a father who could give embarrassing speeches and tread heavily in social situations as sometimes George's letter-writing and interrupting of private conversations at home was interpreted.[16]

Peculiarities and flaws are a constant feature in Jane's depiction of fathers in her works. This added to the complexity and depth of each individual character, but it also gave Jane the opportunity to explore the politics of those who held such power over their family's destiny. Fathers generally held a powerful position within eighteenth-century society. Head of the family unit which underpinned the order and framework of Christian society, they held sway at home and influenced the atmosphere within and the reputation of their family abroad for the good, or bad, of all concerned. Edmund Bertram (*Mansfield Park*) was convinced to speak to Fanny about Mr Crawford's proposal against his own instinct and judgement but in favour of the persuasion of his father.[17]

Sir Thomas himself spoke to Fanny of the duty that a daughter, whom she was not, would owe him in her stead.[18] Lizzy Bennet (*Pride and Prejudice*) was entreated not to disappoint her own father in any way by her conduct, be that in word or deed, as was her daughterly duty, and it was a warning that she took very seriously.[19] In Jane's day it was a truth universally acknowledged that one must not invoke shame upon one's father, or risk isolating themselves and their family from their community and consigning them to the realms of everyone's disgust and contempt.

Having a scholarly, fair-minded and thoughtful father of such high social standing in their community, Jane and her siblings felt sincerely compelled to honour him with their own behaviour and good manners at all times, especially publicly. With such a generous and intelligent community-minded father who was measured and fair in his judgements, 'respectful forbearance', as Emma Woodhouse (*Emma*) would put it, was a natural urge as well as an obvious duty to fulfil, but nevertheless society expected it.[20] A lack of reverence for her father was something Jane could not tolerate in others and her letters did not hold back in her well-crafted criticism of those who failed him in any way. Just like Emma's reticence with Mr John Knightley, and Lady Russell's (*Persuasion*) with the younger Mr Elliot, this was a trait that Jane could not overlook or completely forgive. The children were brought up with a healthy respect for discipline which Jane herself lamented when she saw a lack of it in the younger generation. When Tom Bertram (*Mansfield Park*) was finally reformed by his life's events, his humility seemed only restored to him when he eventually showed the due deference and service owed to his father. Jane used poor filial behaviour as an appalling mirror to the low character, morals and respectability of Fanny Price's father, when his own children shouted and fought in his presence with total disregard for his opinion.[21] Oblivious of him as they were, their actions incurred only cursory attempts at control. The boys avoided any sort of consequences from their father and at no point did they show any respectful regard for him.

However, duty of care worked both ways and fathers in Jane's novels are shown up for who they are and for the place they hold in Jane's esteem by the way that they steward their responsibilities. Their behaviour as custodians of the care of their offspring shows their true calibre as people and defines their virtue, or lack of it. Their day-to-day social manners towards others, such as General Tilney (*Northanger Abbey*) snubbing Catherine Morland, might be revealed or something altogether more detrimental, their treatment of their own children. Mr Price's coarseness was highlighted in his total lack of care or interest in his children's behaviour. His humiliation was confirmed by his own base habits, his total submission to his natural urges without any sign of awareness or restraint, and his lack of empathy for his daughter. A crude and crass man, he was revealed as an embarrassment to his daughter, a taint on her and a tarnish on the reputation of his whole family. In a true measure of the impact of her father's leadership, when Fanny accidentally calls Mansfield Park her home, she is the only one who feels any shame in her betraying thoughts. Her father and mother have no sense of shock – they are insensible to any ties Fanny ought to be expressing towards their home. As they never really put much thought into creating one, they are oblivious to her lack of association to it.[22] They have, it is clear, never prioritised their children's happiness and wellbeing. Like General Tilney, they seem to have no measure in their approach. If Mr Price does try to restrain his children's behaviours, it is with loud rebuffs and if he does refer to his daughter in conversation, it is in an offensive manner. General Tilney too liked the sound of his own voice so much that he let his words run away with him so that he caused his children to withdraw emotionally.[23] Sir Thomas Bertram limited his relationship with his daughters and Fanny by his intense and overbearing manner with them, which was laid down so much as a habit that simply being with him could bring back fearful memories and sensations.[24] Sir Walter Elliot (*Persuasion*) degraded and maligned his daughter Anne in front of her sister and others with mean ways and cruel words. He favoured one daughter at the expense of the other and showed himself to be shallow and unkind, unfit for fatherly affection.[25]

In all these cases, freedom from one's father was the optimal condition; the preference for the home and company of another was something they could not deny and escaping his presence was an aim always uppermost in each child's mind even as an adult. A shame that Fanny Price feels guilty in admitting to herself, even in the secrecy and quiet of her own thoughts. She feels the full horror of such a truth.

For a father worth his weight, his word was decisive in any matter. When Mr Collins tried to keep Lizzy at Huntsford for longer than she desired, it was her father's name that she invoked, his demand on her that she aimed as the arrow of fire to quench Mr Collins' bidding. His remark that 'Daughters are never of so much consequence to a father' may well have been strictly true economically for many at the time, but the words themselves also hark back to the humour of the Austen family theatricals and Jane's youthful playlets and could double as an in-joke at her father's expense.[26] With the wonderful playfulness of the banter which flowed around the dinner table at Steventon, there was ample opportunity to share thoughts and opinions and to reveal each other's strengths and weaknesses. Such an open way of living let education and learning flow and for each of the Austen siblings to be equipped by their father and mother. Their true education, of their whole mind, spirit and soul, was therefore touched by their influence. George and Cassandra could see and know just where their children were in their own personal, social and intellectual development. In total opposition to the want and lack of nurturing that the Bertram children received, especially the daughters, the Austen siblings were showered with their parents' own particular brand of attention and affection, and George's anxious and generous supply of support to his children was never wanting. George took his parenting responsibilities, like all his others, very seriously. He took them to heart. All his children were valued as individuals, as people in their own right. Their pleasures, their education and their futures were all equally of 'consequence' to him as he and his siblings were to their late father and as he, in turn, was to their grandmother before them.

George had proved himself to have simple, yet tasteful, interests, and like Edmund Bertram and, according to her brother Henry, Jane herself, his opinions were 'unbending.'[27] His work ethic, his belief in education and his experiences with the leadership at Oxford University, showed that his principles were always at their most visible in times of trouble. A man of principle, his charm, like that of the epic hero, lay in his 'sincerity, steadfastness and integrity'.[28] A hard-working scholar who had had to prove himself time and time again in order to stand superior to his peers, working harder than many due to his difficult start in life. Now, as a teacher and a parent, he too modelled high expectations to his children.

Although generous it is unlikely that he would have been as lenient as the doting aunt who acted in a mother's stead for the wily, intelligent and wilful Miss Crawford (Mansfield Park). Discipline was linked to achievement and usefulness to others as one's duty. Indulging every capricious and selfish whim of a child was not viewed as a positive parenting trait in a father at the time nor by George Austen himself. When we learn that Emma is over-indulged by Mr Woodhouse, this is viewed as preceding, pre-empting and even predicting a most negative impact upon her character at her father's hands.

Mr Darcy lamented the lack of attention to the education of his temperament by his father in particular.[29] Lady Susan Vernon implicates her dead husband's terrible parenting skills as the reason for her daughter Frederica's 'spoilt' behaviours in later life, although in this case we are not so confident in the truth of her narration.[30] Mr Bennet comes to see the errors he has made in his parenting, his denial and ignorance of the potential consequences of indulging a child in their chosen behaviours comes back to haunt him and he is left a shell of his former self for a long while.[31] The Bertram sisters (Mansfield Park) suffered the same neglect, having had knowledge but no awareness of the impact of their lifestyle on others and no development of emotional intelligence through daily practice of doing their duty to those around them. Sir Thomas also comes to the awful realisation of his part in their frailties and he repents at leisure the opportunities that he missed. Both men take the time to grieve the loss that they themselves caused through their lack of foresight, forward planning and commitment to their duty.

Some of Jane's fictional fathers, like Mr Woodhouse, are protected from their own weaknesses, their own lack of awareness of life for their daughters, by the strength of the very same. Others, like Mr Price, are too given over to their ways, oblivious of the impact of their selfishness, with disastrous consequences for those left in their care.

However, George was quite the opposite. Even with a penchant for the quiet of his study, and the respectful adherence to that by his household, nothing impeded him in engaging with his family. He might well have been like Mr Woodhouse with the younger generations, enjoying his time both with and without them, and he too might have thanked the maid who knew just how to shut a door quietly.[32] Certainly, his son Frank in his older age did not suffer noisy and boisterous behaviour around the house, perhaps a seed sown in his own childhood. However, with his scholarly traits, George did not miss out any of their education, of mind or habits. With an attention to detail, both innate and nurtured through his teaching experience and his wife's influence, George managed to navigate the rocky road of parenting, instilling necessary discipline and yet encouraging play and exploration too. The children were expected to be fit in mind and body, and they found plenty of time available to them for outdoor activities. Expressing oneself artistically and musically was afforded the family in no small part down to George's income and outlook. Sharing oneself, through duty, camaraderie and conversation was the embedded culture of the parsonage community.

Jane could have genuinely fulfilling conversations with her father, whether or not they had a book in hand. As a 'man of sense and education', just like her creation Mr Watson (*The Watsons*), she enjoyed his company very much.[33] Their discussions could be 'rational or playful', of the type that Emma, for example, was denied by her own sweet papa.[34] Mr Woodhouse, forever fretting and worrying, regretting separations and longing for the security of his habits and home had a very different 'life' to George. Being orphaned at a young age, this type of temperament could have crept up on George easily, and the anxiety of feeling abandoned and unsure could have traumatised him into inactivity and depression, leaving him with bouts of sadness and a craving for secure solitude. However, it did not. George found solace in activity and caught the love of learning. His antidote was education, engaging him in the thrill of thought and the pursuit of knowledge. His Christian faith, fanned by the routines and enthusiasm of the institutions around him, grounded him and gave him a structure and a purpose. The fact that he made such choices and escaped the grip of his beginnings is a credit to his extended family, himself and his relationship with his stepbrother and his sisters. His underlying disposition, calm gentlemanly manners and way of dealing with hardship were qualities which Jane admired, and there are elements of his character which made a deep impression on her, forming and shaping for her the fundamentals of goodness of person which no amount of reading Fordyce's *Sermons* could convey more effectively. The scholarly Mr Howard in *The Watsons* exemplified this 'quietly cheerful, gentlemanlike air'.[35] Jane once wrote of Mr Digweed, who occupied Steventon Manor, that 'handsome is as handsome does', calling out his lack of handsome behaviour as plain as the want of it on his face.[36] With her father, his good nature really was the beauty she beheld within him, that then showed up in his outward features – a trait that she further attributed to the worthy Mr Howard.

The legacy of George's decision to leave behind his fellowship in order to marry and have a family life of his own was the silver lining, the pot of gold at the end of the rainbow that he craved and yet had never really experienced for very long himself. His children's witty ripostes and gentle teasing were a wonderful consequence of such unexpected and unexperienced relationships. This aspect of their familial culture was something that Jane held dear and an opportunity to put 'pun to paper' about her father was something she never missed. Her hero, one whom no one could have predicted to be one in his childhood, was all the better in her eyes for being able to take the jokes she and the family liked to aim at him. So good was he that Jane gave Catherine Morland (*Northanger Abbey*) a similar father, only with some pointed differences which once again would have hit the family's funny bone. A clergyman, yes, and very respectable with some independent means and two satisfactory if not 'good' livings; so far, so George, but an ugly man, with an unfortunate name, who thankfully did not take to locking up his daughters, made the perfect conditions for a little humorous comparison with their father. Sir Walter Elliot, on the other hand, had all George's handsome features and fine-looking qualities, but vanity to such an extent as to make any personal interest in one's own appearance, as in George's case, a great opportunity for comic exaggeration. As a gentleman who had been brought up under the influence of the Skinners' Company and his college, as well as his profession in the Church, to find all gratuitous dress and foppery of physical appearance vulgar, modesty was very much George's modus operandi. Any hint of excess in this area was a chance to send him up rather than put him down.

Taking care of their father was the family's way of showing their respect and love for him. For all the teasing and the ribbing, showing a true kindness to their father was George's finest treasure. Jane underlined this in her novels. Emma sought daily to achieve and contrive her father's happiness and to encourage him out of himself in every moment. Anne Elliot (*Persuasion*), for all her maltreatment and neglect by her father, sought to protect him from others who might do him wrong, influence him to his detriment or swindle him out of his possessions. She always hoped that he might change for the better and was quick to think well of him for any chink of respectability that she glimpsed in him.

The Austen family rallied whenever there was need and future generations knew to take their place in supporting their fathers, just like Edmund Bertram who, thoughtfully and stoically, put off his own plans in order to stay and be company for his father and mother when everyone else was leaving them. When two of George's sons, Edward and later Frank, became widowers their grown-up daughters stepped into the breach, acting as hostesses at social occasions on their fathers' behalf and taking care of their siblings, showing them as much sympathy and support as they could in the absence of their mothers until such a time as their fathers remarried or outgrew their need for them. Emma, of course, kept her promise to never leave her father, even upon her own marriage. Jane later attested that Mr and Mrs Knightley had to reside at Hartfield for the first two whole years of their married life as the fretful and anxious Mr Woodhouse saw out the last of his days. Such a dutiful daughter to the end, she indulged his needs as he had so often indulged hers.[37]

Chapter Twelve

A New Chapter

One way in which a daughter might expect to rely upon a father in later life was in regard to financial provision for her future. Her education might have been intended to fit her up and equip her for her future life, be that as a housemaid or helper, a governess, or as in Jane and Cassandra's cases, for marriage. A daughter might need a dowry if she were to marry into the higher echelons of society, or she may be entitled to a 'daughter's share', that which Mr Musgrove (*Persuasion*) understood as only fair for his own sisters.[1]

If a daughter were to remain single, then a father would need to have put sufficient wealth aside to provide for her; if this were not possible, then like the Watson sisters (*The Watsons*), a match would have to be found. In *Love and Freindship*, the very first story that Jane copied into her *Volume the Second*, she has one female friend ironically state to the other that at the age of 55, the time had now finally arrived when she was free from any draw on her by a suitor, or any expectations upon her from an 'obstinate' father.[2] The push and pull on a woman in Jane's social class was real. There was not always much choice in any matter, and life as a lady was a succession of vulnerabilities. In the fictional biography of a life of love and adventure that ensues, the teenage Jane enjoys her hilarious rebellious finger-pointing at fathers everywhere. This story, when read to the family, would have had them all exclaiming and laughing. After all, what teenager hasn't maligned their father to a friend, or ranted at them with a diatribe of impassioned but flimsy bravery about how they would never do what their father advised them to do. In the very opposite of the social rules of Jane's world, she has her hero's sister agree that he was not in the habit of adding to the 'satisfaction' of his father and the hero celebrate with glee his opportunity to arouse his father's 'displeasure'.

In reality, of course, in order to have any sort of future happiness, a young woman would need a father's complete support and her connection to him was a lifeline that one hoped was a strong one. The story reveals another secret marriage and the newly-weds' joyful aspiration to forever be separated, 'free' from their fathers. This was a fantasy far removed from Jane's real world and, excited by her reading matter, it was an escape from reality, somewhere she could really let her creative musings rip. The danger of exposing herself to this sort of real life was so great, the ideas so offensive to her own world view, that they totally suited a story that was aiming to create a sense of the ridiculous. They raised an eyebrow and a sort of exasperated smile; the ludicrous nature of such an hilarious exaggeration of choice was on a par with a line Jane wrote at the time in *A Letter From A Young Lady* about an overwrought girl named Anna who declared, 'I murdered my father at a very early period of my Life.'[3] Yet the ties and expectations, the authority of a parent, even in regard to matters of the heart, were real enough even to the young Jane's understanding.

Someone in their fifties was ripe to be construed as old in Jane's eyes. The thought of a woman gaining her freedom by that age seemed a tempting dream, perhaps a merciful and well-deserved release. Equally thought-provoking though was the image of a father of that age who had released and discharged himself of all responsibility. In her short story *Lesley Castle*, Jane describes one 57-year-old father gadding about in the city, spending all his money on good times whilst his family, specifically his daughters, languished at home.[4] If a daughter had to submit to a father's will, it was also expected that a father would consider his daughter's future happiness and security his duty and primary responsibility.

In *Pride and Prejudice*, we see Mrs Bennet's glee that her husband should take up his duty to his daughter and visit the wealthy incomer Mr Bingley as immediately as possible upon his arrival in the village. She was well aware of the necessity to find a husband, and a 'suitable' one at that, for all of her daughters. Society's norms and rules surrounding the paying of visits and showing one's respects to visitors and neighbours, especially to those of an elevated social standing had an underlying edge if one had grown-up daughters about to come of age. Mrs Bennet felt the strain of it all and particularly at her age. As she got older the effort required was only matched by the intensifying of need. Time and energy could feel like they were running out and so much of both was required for the process. Of course, a parent could also compel a daughter into marriage and Mrs Bennet's exasperation at the thought of letting a suitor, even if it was Mr Collins, pass her daughters by was anathema to her. For her the threat of being left destitute and penniless overcame any other scruple and trumped any other consideration. For Elizabeth, the daughter in question, however, the match was unconscionable. That she was saved in her father's safe study, by the triumph of his own good sense, a happy escape from such an uncomfortable situation, cannot have been an accident. Surely Jane picked that location on purpose, for who would not rather sit safely in the bosom of those beloved bookshelves back at Steventon, safe and sound, away from any threat to one's freedoms and true passions in the sure and certain confidence that a kind and capable father was nearby.

In December 1791 Edward had married Miss Elizabeth Brydges and moved to their home in Kent. The following spring in March 1792, James married his first wife, Anne Mathew, and moved into the parsonage at Deane. There was most definitely something in the water at the time as that same year, Cassandra became engaged to one of George's former pupils, the Reverend Tom Fowle. Son of the clerical Fowle family at nearby Kintbury, George had also taught his elder brother, Fulwar-Craven Fowle, and all of the young men had simultaneously attended St John's College, Oxford, for a period of time. Tom was a match the family wholeheartedly approved of. The happiness with the match was, importantly, reciprocated by the groom-to-be's family too. George, like Mr Lucas (*Pride and Prejudice*), may well have visited friends and neighbours of social standing to make the announcement and share the happy news.[5] The Reverend Tom Fowle had already received some paid positions as a curate; as a profession was necessary, neither side of their family being able to offer them the possibility of living by independent means, he was waiting for that elusive 'living' that carried with it a more realistic salary. Cassandra had been expected by the family to marry and move to Shropshire, with no doubt an immediate visit from George and Cassandra planned in their minds, as Mr Lucas did too, to ascertain that all was well.[6] In this regard of happy expectation, the Austens were doing what they could to foster the excited anticipation of a future wedding. Like Mr and Mrs Morland (*Northanger Abbey*) and Musgrove (*Persuasion*), they were supporting their child's wedding wishes and, no doubt convinced of his personality and prospects, were not needling or begrudging the happy couple in any way by harbouring any other ambitions. No such hopes had been defined for Jane, and her mother expressed exasperation in a family letter that Jane would end up 'Lord knows where.'[7] Her sister being married to such a respected member of his new community would have done Jane's reputation only good in regard to her potential suitors. There was to be no shame or tarnish of the sort of behaviours demonstrated by Lydia Bennet (*Pride and Prejudice*) when following her affections.[8] In the meantime, Tom took one final bridging job, as personal chaplain to his relative Lord Craven on his voyage to the West Indies. However, five long years of waiting ended in heartbreak when Tom died on board ship in 1797, just at the very time he was expected to return. The outpouring of support from her own family and the Fowles in Kintbury would have been echoed in the compassion of her neighbours, but George's reputation as a safe port in a storm would have rendered his care of particular importance to his eldest daughter at this time. The family's Christian faith was the anchor for their collective souls and, in his position as both head of their household and of their local spiritual community, George would have been a tower of strength to run to for shelter at this truly difficult time. He would have directed Cassandra to look for consolation in the scriptures and in her faith, as well as in her family.

In *Pride and Prejudice*, Mr Bennet seems to have become trapped inside a marriage, finding himself a father to so many daughters. Whilst of his own making, his choice brought with it consequences that a little more foresight might have avoided. He was attracted by the vivacious beauty and wit of a young woman who, in reality, could not match him for intellect or conversation. The signs that they are ill-suited are hinted at and alluded to.[9] Mr Bennet has to take the rough with the smooth and make the best of his situation. However, in lacking the will to educate and foster the conditions that might help his wife to grow, or to discipline his daughters in the present and, most egregiously, to plan effectively for their lives in the future, he too is flawed. Love is blind and both parents have to find a way forward in their married life together to somehow fulfil their duty to provide for their offspring. In the eyes of the outside world, however, the greater responsibility for one's children's future provision lay with the father as the deemed head of their household. The effect on Mr Bennet when he is presented with the results of his failures is catastrophic, both in terms of the potential damage to his daughters' reputations and his own self-respect.[10] James Austen, who had become a widower with a young child just three years into his own first marriage, knew these responsibilities full well. His family had been a godsend in helping him to care for his young daughter Anna, just as George's father William had experienced on the death of Rebecca.

Five years after his marriage to *his* Elizabeth, in 1797, Edward moved into Godmersham Park, the house that internally is said to have echoed Sotherton in *Mansfield Park* and externally the beautiful, picturesque grounds of Pemberley in *Pride and Prejudice*. The Austen family's attachment to one another had proved deeper than any piece of paper and any change of initial could alter. The values which George and Cassandra had instilled in their son remained and their bond was as strong as one could hope for with respect shown, as was due, on all sides. The qualities that Edward displayed, which so suited him in his rank and role in society, were linked to the upbringing and education provided by his father who commanded all due respect as a result.

Jane and Cassandra still sewed garments for their brother and Cassandra spent many weeks in his home caring for his children and assisting his wife, especially around the time of her confinements of which there were to be eleven. Mrs Edward Austen, later Knight, definitely held a preference for young Cassandra rather than Jane; however, the family was able to visit and Jane found a way to survive by hiding away with their governess, her friend Anne Sharpe, or burying herself with a good book and a good idea along with her father in the well-stocked library. George took great delight in extending his letter-writing habits to include his son, sending messages via his children's communications too, and taking much interest in their fresh common ground of raising livestock and producing crops.

The same year that Edward moved into his large estate, his widower brother James remarried. His new bride, Mary Lloyd, was the sister of Jane's best friend Martha and Eliza Fowle, who had married one of George's former pupils, James's friend and her cousin, Fulwar-Craven Fowle of Kintbury. By the end of the year, Henry had also married, to a different yet familiar Eliza, their elegant cousin Eliza de Feuillide.

With everyone so settled, and after nearly forty years as the rector of Steventon, George began to seriously consider retiring. His son Frank later wrote in his *Memoir* that the timing was all to do with George's age and state of health. At nearly 70, it was said that he himself felt he could no longer carry out the role to his own satisfaction and high standards.[11] In the late winter of 1800, Mrs Austen was also unwell. The couple considered going to Bath, a city that was known for its health benefits. A spa town, it had long been a resort favoured by the middling classes as a place for relaxation and restoration. Not only would they be able to gain health benefits from drinking the waters there, but they would also be local to increasingly recommended sea-bathing resorts. In contemporary 'scientific' reports, medical practitioners had been prescribing the seaside, not in the height of summer when the warm weather naturally inclined one to be in the sea, but in the coldest winter months – and very early in the morning at that.[12] As the winter weather rolled in, the final decision to prioritise their health and expose themselves to some of these advantages was made. In late November, Jane returned from a visit to her friend Martha Lloyd to the astonishing news that 'it was all settled' and arranged and that the family would be moving to Bath.[13] Family memoir says that this was a huge surprise, so shocking that Mary (Lloyd) Austen, who was present, later told her own daughter that Jane took it badly, perhaps even fainting away practically on the doorstep. It had not been discussed with any member of either the immediate or extended family. Everything was felt to have been done rather quickly with George hastening to affect his decision in what the others came to feel was somewhat of a habit with him, one of his ways and quite typical of his approach to life.[14] He took such quick action that Cassandra's brother James Leigh-Perrot and his wife, who, as regular residents of the city and such close friends and relations of both, might have been able to offer helpful advice in the decision-making, knew nothing about it either. As a result of being kept out of the loop, they were not able to comment or confer with the Austens until the middle of the following January. George preferred, as usual, to trust his own judgement and make the decision based upon his own gut feelings. This truly stemmed not from a capricious nature but from the self-preservation instincts instilled and nurtured in his childhood when he only had his own wits to count on. George was also more confident in his own judgement, surer of his own wisdom than his brother's and particularly his sister-in-law's.

The summer before, Mrs Leigh-Perrot had been accused of theft. Whilst out shopping in Bath, she had visited a shop and bought some black lace. On leaving the shop, she was accused of stealing a card of white lace, it being found wrapped up in her parcel. The trial had not taken place until spring 1800 with Mrs Leigh-Perrot's time in between spent in Ilchester prison, where her husband James had chosen to reside with her. Their lodgings were not a cell but in the jailor's house, still Mrs Austen and George had thought it right to give them help and support by offering Jane and her sister's assistance.[15] This had been declined, but it was not until eight months after the accusation that Mrs Leigh-Perrot was finally acquitted and the threat of deportation to Australia removed.

To the outside world of extended family, as it was for the nuclear one, the decision to move to Bath did seem to come out of the blue. For George, though, always measuring the meaning in his actions, and with a careful eye on preserving and protecting his family's interests, this was not such an impromptu 'whim' as the family famed him for. George did believe in his own decision-making and he was a man who stuck firmly to his own principles. If he was about to undertake what seemed on the outside such a huge revolutionary step, it would have been down to the weighed and measured evolutionary development of his innermost thoughts. For an ageing husband, brother, uncle, father, grandfather, clergyman and farmer, there was much to consider privately away from the prying eyes of his close-knit community. With all that responsibility, George is unlikely to have been acting flippantly, even if he did respond quickly to his gut instinct. In any event the change came as a surprise to all George's children, not just Jane, and they all vowed to come back and visit for one last time.

Perhaps the possibility of James, his eldest son, taking over made this an easier decision for George's conscience. Passing on the opportunity of the curacy to his son and providing for him in this way, ensuring a better home and a better way of life for him and his family, might well have been a 'push' factor in George reaching the decision to retire. With all the contacts and connections they had established over the past four decades, they, too, like good Dr Shirley (*Persuasion*), would have been told if James did not live up to expectations. Surely Miss Musgrove and Mr Hayter (*Persuasion*) in their imagined world would have rejoiced in the changing of the guard as Mary and James Austen certainly did in their real one.

The prospects of increasing their social circle in Bath and having the time to do so, perhaps in their daughters' best interests, might well have been a 'pull' factor affecting George's decision. With James Leigh-Perrot and his wife residing there when they were not at their Scarlets estate in Berkshire, it would mean they had some means of introduction. Some fathers schooled their children for marriage, such as the soon-to-be orphaned Louisa Burton (*Lesley Castle*), knowing that this was the only pathway for their future keep.[16] The Austens had encouraged their daughters' accomplishments but had never insisted on bringing them 'out' into society, nor had they been in the habit of overtly arranging suitors for them amongst their acquaintances. However, a period of time in Bath, which in former times had been the centre of life for high society, might well have informed their minds, sparking as an idea. Bath as a place held happy memories for them. Cassandra's brother and his wife had a home there which they had visited for happy holidays in the past. George and Cassandra had married there and therefore had an emotional tie from their pre-parenting days. The allure of Bath was compelling but other factors may have operated in tandem with the senior Austens' nostalgia, when it came to making their decision. The turn of events in agriculture at the time were equally making the farming life more of a strain. Crop returns were still unpredictable, and considerable investment in advancing technology was required as developments in techniques and approaches to farming began to progress. Agricultural workers too were gaining more awareness of and confidence in claiming their rights. The price of crops had gone up exponentially with the shortage of wheat due to the war in France and the cost of staple foodstuffs for citizens had risen too. With increasing resentment amongst the countryside from parishioners required to give their tithe to the parish priest, this was a stressful time.

Any hints of ill health when balanced against the obvious need for resilience and perseverance as a farmer and priest, and the high energy levels required to accomplish this, just to stand still must have weighed heavy on George. James was ready and waiting in the wings, well qualified to take over the curacy of St Nicholas' and his socially ambitious wife Mary was more than willing to upgrade from Deane Parsonage to Steventon Rectory. George junior was boarded out to a family in the village of Monk Sherborne who cared for his particular needs alongside another relative, Cassandra Austen's younger brother, Thomas Leigh. George junior's upkeep was paid for by his parents and, later, his brothers. Edward was now happily settled with his already growing family of seven children at his estate in Godmersham, Kent. Frank and Charles were engrossed in their naval careers. Their only true dependants were Cassandra and Jane.

With all of his roles, the chance to sit at his own ease as a 'bon vivant' and do nothing but eat, 'read the newspaper, watch the weather and quarrel with his wife', as Jane's Miss Crawford (*Mansfield Park*) observed was the way of clergymen must have seemed like quite a fine ideal indeed, a really tempting yet hilarious dream, quite the opposite of his own experience of a busy and committed working life.[17] His was more akin to the life reflected in the mirror of Jane's Dr Shirley, the rector of Uppercross in *Persuasion*. He, too, like George, had been in the role 'zealously discharging all the duties of his office' for approximately forty years.[18] There is an eagerness prompted by love behind Charles and Miss Musgrove's desire for him to retire and hand over the reins to a curate on his behalf. They, snapping like puppy dogs at his heels, viewed the incumbent as growing old and infirm, perhaps approaching 70 and unable to carry out his duties to the level he once could. It is possible that George sensed some of his children and his parishioners had noticed and commented upon things similarly.

George, like his counterpart, the Reverend Lefroy at Ashe, may also have become increasingly fatigued at the end of a Sunday service in two churches. Miss Musgrove's petitioning of Anne for her views might well have echoed familial conversations, or worse, those they heard whispered about the village. Was George's retirement a taboo subject which could not be directly countered with him? Family legend runs that he was apt to act on a whim, or to take prompt action as soon as he had reached a decision. But did he too need time to come to a realisation that leaving his parish to the charge of someone else was a possibility and a desirable one at that? Did the family believe that George was stubbornly clinging on to his post despite a decline in his health? Had George begun to realise this too and to think of all the other things he might now enjoy at the same time as taking care of his health? Or did George find the thought of handing over his duties to someone else emotionally hard on account of his passion and commitment, and his conscientious undertaking of the role for all of his working life?

Once the decision had been made, there was much to be done both in looking for and setting up a new home and winding down George's business and church interests at Steventon and Deane. Jane, revived from the shock and with her customary use of humour to brush off any other feelings, wrote to her sister Cassandra at Godmersham that she was growing tired of the poor quality of balls in the area anyway.[19] She and Martha threw themselves into the important matter of taking care of George and the family's books. With over 500 volumes they were going to sell as many of them as they could in order not to have the expense of transporting and housing them in Bath. Jane was hopeful to get good prices, especially for her own collection, perhaps even from her brother James, but she was a scholar of George's catalogue with personal expertise on the value of his treasure trove so she was hugely biased in their favour. James was already to receive all of George's art donated by wealthy parents and friends as well as all his miscellaneous papers and manuscripts. Jane felt that, on reflection, James was far too eager to agree to his father's donations and that he should pay for the privilege, hence her hopes for the bulging stacks of books.

A lot of the furniture that had been so heartily welcomed only a year before was now to be sold; the difficulty and expense of transporting it was considered higher than finding something similar once there, although probably not as bespoke or fancy. George's beloved Pembroke table was added to the list for valuing and auctioning, and the only pieces intended to make it out with them were their beds. Mr Bayle, who had provided most of the furniture purchased in recent years, came back out to give an evaluation of its worth. The family were hopeful that they would make a lot of the money back, but in the end they, and especially Jane, were a little disappointed by the initial valuations. The sale was eventually overseen by a completely different auctioneer from Newbury.[20]

James was to take over as curate at Steventon and would be moving into the rectory, a decision welcomed by everyone locally. This now meant that there would be a vacancy for a curate at Deane which George had to ensure was fully covered before he left. The whole family were anxious that this should be settled well. George himself would have been looking for someone in whose integrity he could trust. In living so far away from the village, his own reputation would now be on the line if a substandard curate was appointed in his absence. He originally thought of Peter Debary, from a family known through friends and contacts whose father, Peter Debary senior, was the Reverend at Hurstbourne Tarrant where Jane's best friend Martha was living. However, he turned George down, citing the locality of the position as too rural and too distant from London in particular. Jane was quite put out and compared this Peter to the disciple Peter who denied his connection to Christ in a cowardly act of betrayal that he deeply regretted. She was disgruntled at his rejection of the place and annoyed that they now had to continue their search.[21] Out of deference to the residents of the Steventon manor house, the respected Digweed family, George next offered the post to their son James. Jane, though, did not put much store by this decision and believed from the outset that the post was too small for him, both in its rurality and salary. Unsurprisingly to her, he turned the position down too and it finally fell to the future son-in-law of Jane's beloved Madam Lefroy. Henry Rice was already curate in his father-in-law's church at Ashe and the curacy of Deane would no doubt have helped him to finally marry his betrothed, Jemima-Lucy Lefroy.

In regard to the farm, firstly the lease had to be sold on to a farmer who would work the land for the remainder of George's tenure. Mr James Holder, currently renting the Ashe Park estate, was very interested in acquiring the farm for the rest of its lease. Local squire John Harwood of Deane House and Farmer Twitchen had also expressed an interest. The Austens' livestock needed to be sold or rehoused; James took two of the mares and the Lefroys at Ashe bought one of their cows, which sadly for them did not live for much longer past the purchase date.[22] The Austens' hopes were more decidedly fixed than ever before on the prices they could get for this, their last 'harvest' of bacon, hay and hops.

George's bailiff, John Bond, needed to be found another situation too. Jane's sister Cassandra felt compassion for him at his change of circumstance, for he lived in a home tied to the farm and his job. A change of employment would mean a change of address. However, Jane grew exasperated with him reporting that he was quite full of his own worth and a little disdainful of the post he was leaving anyway. Bravado at a difficult time is understandable, but Jane did not care for his attitude.[23] In the end James Holder won out and took John, (who had, in fact, received other offers) as per his contract with George.[24] Over the course of the next seven months, three large payments were made to George, adding a welcome boost to their coffers.[25] In this way George took great care to ensure that those in his employ were provided for just like Emma Woodhouse (*Emma*) admired and flattered her father for taking the pains to do.[26]

Finding a new, permanent home for the Austens was no small matter. The place had to accommodate them all comfortably and, more importantly for George's wife Cassandra, it had to be in the 'right' part of the city. All of which had to match the money that they had available in their budget for the rent. Initial choices included support for properties on Westgate Buildings, Charles Street, Laura Place, Gay Street, Pulteney Street, Chapel Row leading to Prince's Street, Queen Square and Sydney Place, and latterly Seymour Street and Green Park Buildings. There was a definite disdain for others not so blessed with a position on the outskirts of the town or with access to the green spaces they had been so used to enjoying in Steventon, such as Trim Street, Axford Buildings and New King Street.[27] All of these were hotly debated and endlessly discussed within the family with each one's popularity waxing and waning over time. George and Cassandra seemed almost giddy from the decision-making and had differing views. This was even harder than choosing furniture! With every delay between letter and answer from Jane to Cassandra, another objection or suggestion was raised with both parties changing their mind and favouring different options as all was mulled over. Positive features in a house's favour for the countryside Austens included the appearance of the house from the outside, its age (preferably newer rather than older), its opening on to a broad rather than narrow street, and with some sort of green field, park or gardens nearby.[28] It was clear from the start, however, that being able to afford their ideal home was going to be a hugely influential factor in their choice. They soon had to drop some preferences in favour of a more realistic outlook. George relaxed his initial strict guidelines and began to develop ideas and aspirations for their next abode.[29] He grew quite excited and became more involved in their search. He still, however, made a careful point to never go beyond his means. A few of the streets had to be ruled out altogether, or at least only a few particular houses in less attractive positions on those streets were allowed onto their wish list.

In May 1801 Jane and her mother went ahead of the party to Bath, with George and Cassandra planning to follow a few weeks later (George had some business in London). As Mrs Austen had been unwell over the winter, they were initially taken under the wing of her brother and sister at their home in The Paragon. Their knowledge as residents of the city had been called upon, although not necessarily heeded, throughout the accommodation decision-making process.

Not long after George finally arrived with Cassandra, the family embarked on a long-awaited holiday. Jane herself had been won over to Bath by the prospect of the proximity to the sea and to Wales, and hoped with all her heart that they would now spend summers not visiting relations in Kent or Yorkshire but instead enjoying coastal delights together.[30] Family members also remembered these plans and associated them strongly with their memories of George's retirement. George had certainly talked up these schemes and given Jane the first hope of them. The year they arrived, Jane had in her heart that her parents' plans to visit an ex-pupil in Colyton were going to be combined with a visit to Sidmouth in Devon, a village that would become very popular as a holiday resort just like Sanditon began to grow and expand.[31] Happily, for her, no sooner had George arrived in Bath than the family set off in search of their holiday.

In those days, travel was always an issue where young ladies were concerned. Not only in regard to summer plans, such as Lydia Bennet being inspired by the movements of the militia and setting her heart on staying at Brighton, but also in everyday life.[32] Jane and Cassandra were, as were most, at the whim and mercy of their father or perhaps one of their older brothers if they ever wanted to travel anywhere. When Mrs Clay set her mind on Sir Walter Elliot at Kellynch Hall, she had to rely upon her own father to get her there.[33] If the

Austen sisters made it to their brother Edward, another relative or a friend's house, travelling back or onward by a particular date was never a certainty. The women had to wait for their father's plans to be confirmed or to change or coincide with their wishes. On one occasion, when she stayed with Edward at Rowlings, his home in Kent, Jane joked in a letter to her sister that she was just like Camilla in her favourite story, abandoned at Mr Dubster's summer house with no means of escape. Although she confessed herself to be happy to be visiting, her hopes for being home within the month were not spoken in jest.[34] Consequently, Jane became adept at planning and scheming, working out all sorts of complicated ways in order to be able to visit friends or have them visit her. One such time when she was the grand old age of twenty-one and in the middle of making one of these arrangements, she joked of herself as the prodigal daughter and hoped that her father would fetch her rather than abandon her to wanderings around London.[35] This was a joke that made light of the waiting and planning but revealed nonetheless that roaming free around Steventon was one thing but spontaneously travelling around the county or into another city alone was completely different.

In her early twenties, Jane was journeying through Kent with both her parents. Travelling alone with them was a matter of some exertion to Jane. They had their foibles and settled routines, and taking public transport with them for longer journeys always required a certain degree of patience on her part. In these situations, Jane was mostly concerned at how her mother's nerves and health would be affected because she often had needs that were exaggerated by a long journey shut up in a carriage. When George arrived anywhere, he liked to retreat into a book. On one occasion at Dartford, he left Jane to share a bedroom with her mother. Whether this was because he feared for her safety, a young woman in a room on her own, or if he just wanted to embrace the opportunity for some peace and quiet, Jane left that up to her sister to decide.[36]

There had been a time in Steventon around 1784 when George had kept a carriage himself. Later, when taxes were levied upon possessing a carriage for private rather than farming use, not to mention the fact that the cost of sparing two horses to pull it became an unjustifiable expense, George decided to lay it down. There is very convincing evidence that this may well have coincided with a particular tax due in 1798 on private crests and family heraldic arms painted onto the carriage. Vick, in his report to the Jane Austen Society, confirms that driving a carriage without this type of signage would have been unheard of in the locality, either because it signalled to others that George was not worthy enough to have a family crest or that he had removed it in order to avoid paying the tax.[37] George did have the Austen family crest and Le Faye has established it was even published in a road book known as *The*

Western Circuit.[38] The book gave accounts of the six south-western counties of England and may well have been one that George perused whilst planning his visits and retirement. He was a subscriber and it must have been most satisfying for him to see himself listed as gentry for the area. Although he was not a baronet, the publication mentioned the great and the good of the local hierarchy, including a mention of his own rectory, and he may well have had the book out often enough to have attracted a little teasing now and again from his family. The law allowed for the carriage to be retired from the road without further expense.[39] It would seem that this timing coincided exactly with 67-year-old George's priorities for his money.

Having the chance to be wrapped up warm in a carriage and taken comfortably to a ball with two strong horses making lighter work of the rough roads rather than a single steed was something which Jane, like Miss Watson transported by her friends the Edwards, had once enjoyed.[40] When the carriage was taken out of use, Jane joked that the balls had gone downhill of late anyway so all in all everything was well timed.[41]

The summer vacations meant just as much then as they do now: a chance to get away from the normal stresses and strains of life and swap them for a different set. The opportunity to travel some distance made the whole adventure extra exciting, and undertaking a journey of any sort was a novelty in itself for Jane and Cassandra and even George. Many years later, James's daughter Caroline remembered that her Aunt Cassandra believed most passionately in the distinct probability that a romantic connection had been made between Jane and a dashingly suitable young man whilst on their holidays in Devonshire. Jane, it was revealed, had met a very charming man and the two of them had seemed very interested in one another. They had arranged to meet again, leaving each other with a strong impression of just how much such a promise meant to each of them. Tragically, the young man died not long after and along with his death went Jane's holiday romance hopes.[42] The following year, the Austens visited Dawlish and Wales as per George's previous plans.

Jane was not to find herself mired in matters of the heart for many more years. In December 1802 when a suitor appeared who would have been most eligible in every way, all should have been perfectly well. He was wealthy due to private means, local to the neighbourhood where she grew up, respected by all in the community and personally known to Jane through the network of her friends, his sisters. Harris Bigg-Wither, heir to his family fortune and inhabitant of the Manydown estate, home to his family for generations, had everything going for him. With the exception, as Jane's nephew would later point out, of the ability to invoke the tenderness necessary to 'touch her heart'.[43] How she would have perhaps wished for the 'paternal kindness,' the unusually delicate touch displayed by Sir Thomas Bertram (*Mansfield Park*) who took the step of ensuring that his daughter, who had become betrothed in his absence, was completely at ease with her situation. He was willing to step in and publicly and privately free her from her commitments, to throw all advantage and convenience to the wind in order to preserve her happiness.[44] Jane did not feel trapped into a marriage by her father's wishes, although she might well have felt the compulsion to marry brought on by a fear of poverty and what she might then be able to provide for her loved ones. When Sir Thomas reprimands Fanny for not accepting Mr Crawford's proposal, he forcefully recounts the lack of empathy Fanny's refusal shows for her family. He layers on the guilt in the hope that he will achieve her acceptance.[45] What a weight this feels for poor Fanny and would have been an accusation to strike at the heart of a respectful and family-loving woman like Jane. She had never felt repelled by a formidable father or by the company of her immediate family, there was no impulse to escape their hold over her as there was for the Misses Bertram with their Mr Rushworth and Mr Yates. Therefore, when Jane freed herself from an engagement, accepting Bigg-Wither in the evening and then declining his offer the next morning, how she must have wished for the protection and comfort of her father to be right there, right now. In a society where, for the large part, only men had educational and professional opportunities, choosing to stay single was a luxury few women, especially those without the patronage of a wealthy father, could countenance. In her heart, it was her father George, who, with his scholarly leanings and the understanding built up between them in all their long conversations, would have understood her the best and confirmed her convictions. It would have been very clear for her that in one meeting with him on the subject, she might have had her instinct affirmed and accepted in a way that no one else could. In returning to him, to his compassion and the comfort of his study, she might have relied on a quick restoration to herself, to her normal levels of wellbeing.

When Jane contrived Maria Bertram's storyline sometime later, how she must have felt the power of her own words on the page and relived all the sensations of the pain of 'rupture' and 'reproach' that her solitary decision entailed and how the comforting knowledge of her father's understanding of her had bolstered her.[46] The most compelling indication of fatherly solidarity is surmised from Mr Bennet's reaction when cuckolded by his wife into forcing his Lizzy to marry Mr Collins. Barely stirring from behind a book in his study, he calmly emphasises the real choice Lizzy faces with his deadpan, droll delivery of the immortal words, 'Your mother will never see you again if you do *not* marry Mr Collins, and I will never see you again if you *do*.'[47]

Of course, it was a hope, if not an expectation, that the social circle of acquaintances kept by a mother and father might bring some satisfaction and happiness to their children, especially their daughters. It would be a happy ending indeed for both families if a mutually beneficial match could be made amongst people of one's own social level and respectability. Though nothing could be worse than 'Parental Tyranny' such as that exemplified in General Tilney (Northanger Abbey), a set of schemes and plots set upon by a father and/or mother in order to lure in a lucrative 'catch'.[48] Parental consent was so strongly desirable, the practical support in regard to finance and payments a necessity for most young couples. No one wanted a match to fail and to have to return home, as Mrs Clay does in Persuasion after an 'unprosperous' marriage, so an engagement was not sought at too young an age.[49]

However, from twenty-one onwards, the clock began to tick on the marriage prospects of a young woman and the expectation of a young man's enquiry for a father's consent was at its height. Of course, both a father and a daughter may have dreaded this moment in equal measure. In the case of Lady Susan, the prospect of her union with Reginald filled his sister with great anger and fear. She was gripped with apprehension at the thought of her father finding out and alarmed at what might happen to his health upon hearing of her intentions. When he himself warns his son of the consequences for their relationship should he marry Lady Vernon, it is his disappointment in his child's integrity and decision-making that he leads with.[50] Losing the respect of one's father over a marriage choice was considered a huge fall from grace. It was a situation that Jane used for comic effect in her Juvenilia; nevertheless, in real life, to take the courage of one's own convictions over and above the opinion of one's father was riddled with risk. An objectionable marriage, especially for an heir or heiress, could damage not only the bride or groom but a whole family's reputation. An injudicious match could lose them all vital respect and lucrative connections, their very standing in society could be at risk. Should a fracture in the filial relationship occur, such a separation would have dire repercussions for the whole family, including any siblings. It was a very serious matter. The father/child relationship was so important to one's place in the eighteenth-century world that jeopardising it was foolish, and gambling with a father's favour or good name was inviting calamity. As George knew all too well, one's choice of marriage partner carried huge consequences. His stepmother Susanna had withheld everything from him and his siblings on his father's death. When Sir Walter Elliot's (Persuasion) family try to protect him from falling into an unwise union, it is the ensuing administration of his fortune in the eyes of the law and the ramifications for themselves that they are mindful of.[51]

In 1803 the Austens travelled to a place further along the coast from Devon and a little nearer to Bath, Lyme Regis. Jane was at once recovering from her ordeal of Harris Bigg-Wither's proposal at Manydown and celebrating her first-ever publishing deal. Lucy Worsley believes that this was once again the work of George Austen.[52] Her belief is that he sought out the same publisher in Bath who had published pamphlets about Mrs Leigh-Perrot's trial in 1800, who also happened to have connections with a publisher in London – Crosby. George's confidence in approaching a publisher personally rings true with his boyhood experience and knowledge, and the evidence of his efforts to support his daughter in the past. His motivation is matched by his confidence in the expectation that this is how things were done. Cheering up his daughter by focusing on promoting her writing doubled down on his acceptance of her refusal of Bigg-Wither. *Susan*, that we have come to know as *Northanger Abbey*, was successfully sold as a novel in two volumes for £10 on the stipulation that it would be published as soon as possible.[53]

That summer of 1803, Jane's thoughts were happy and hopeful for her book. She had enjoyed a season of seaside delights including a family visit to her brother Frank in Ramsgate. Now, getting out amongst the rugged Jurassic coast and surrounding countryside of Lyme that autumn, Jane and her sister could once again enjoy the delights of roaming free as they had at Steventon, only this time with the added bonus of the sea breezes. It was not their familiar Hampshire haunts, but in some ways, it was something better, something new and unique, freeing and exciting. It was a new view of nature, a chance for Jane to spread her wings and discover somewhere different. The following summer of 1804, they returned to Lyme once again, this time enjoying their 'rambles' with Henry and his new wife, their cousin Eliza de Feuillide, who had made plans to come with them as they too enjoyed the seaside and had already visited Weymouth with Cassandra.[54] These were the seeds of a special relationship with Lyme; sewn deep into Jane's heart, they took root and blossomed.

However, Lyme, like the now slightly less fashionable Bath, was a resort for those of the middling sort who were looking for a cheaper getaway. This was reflected in the quality of their accommodation, which was considered dirty and below their normal standard of living. Their lodgings, though very affordable, were just about verging on the acceptable. Their time here was made somewhat more pleasant as they were looked after by two servants, James and Jenny. In actuality, George and his family all spent as much time out and about as they could rather than being cooped up indoors. In the daytime Jane herself was taken out for bathing. Wheeled down inside a little bathing hut, available to hire on the beach, she was then held and supported in the water to experience the stimulation of the sea. In the mid-September climate Jane enjoyed herself, staying in a little too long and wearing herself out for the rest of the day.[55] This opportunity would have been on offer to the whole family and the effects available for each one's pleasure. In Lyme, there were evening entertainments too. Jane became very familiar with society there, making some tentative friendships and noticing all the arrangements and activity of those about her. Her father and mother ventured out with her to the summer and autumn balls. Jane wrote of an evening where George managed to hold out quite happily for a whole hour and a half, finally retiring at 9.30.[56] At Lyme the assembly rooms also connected to rooms for card-playing which Jane's mother enjoyed and was happily successful at. There were also opportunities for reading, including local and London newspapers and even a little library. Although it was not as well stocked as George's own back in Hampshire, it did offer some supplementary reading materials and the chance for stimulation in conversation with the librarian and other visitors who enjoyed reading novels. Jane was also able to pick up copies for herself and enjoyed sharing her love of reading by supporting that of her servants too. These additional entertainments meant that each member of the family had a bright spot at Lyme offering stimulation and relief, all with the backdrop of the picturesque views and the abundance of nature.

When the Austens settled into their Bath home after their first summer season of holidays, their new routines felt like a new lease of life. Family members recalled how much George and Cassandra enjoyed the atmosphere of the place and how they soaked up the happy differences to their working, countryside life. They had hoped to take a cook and some housemaids with them if their finances could stretch to it. No doubt this help contributed to how much they appreciated the new-found rest and relaxation that contrasted so obviously with the busy nature of their working days. Retirement, it seemed, suited them well and was always considered the 'short Holyday' of their lives together.[57] Their strength was badly needed that autumn to support Eliza once again, when her son, their great-nephew, 15-year-old Hastings De Feuillide, who had always been a vulnerable child when it came to his health, died.

The health of both the senior Austens was improved by their stints by the sea and George could still turn heads when out and about, his stature and good looks having stayed with him into older age. To mark his retirement George had his miniature painted, in which his curls of silvery white hair sat neatly above his ears, and his clear complexion and handsome features, including his dark eyes and strong long nose, were on show.[58] He looked both elegant and stylish, highly respectable yet with a small smile tugging at the corners of his mouth, and gentle too. It is easy to imagine how distinguished a figure he looked when walking along the streets of the city. Feeling buoyed up by their change in circumstance and in celebration of this new chapter in their lives, George and Cassandra also had their silhouettes taken. They were happy indeed in their decision and perhaps they felt it had been a long time coming.

Chapter Thirteen

A New Reality

With retirement, as would be anticipated, although not necessarily understood, finances took another distinct turn. For the first couple of years, when the monies from the sale of furniture, agricultural tools and the final benefits of the farm amalgamated with large pay-outs from dividends, everything was buoyant. However, within two years, George's income stream had dramatically narrowed. Now his only sources were his share of the salary and tithes from Deane and Steventon, his regular dividends on stocks and shares that he had diligently paid into for decades, and a small monthly allowance from his pension fund, the Hand in Hand society.[1] Times had most definitely changed and still the Austen family had not yet bought themselves a permanent home; they were renting and, as such, remained at the whim of landlords and their rental prices.

The long-term prospects of such a lifestyle seem more short-term in their planning. George may have had it in mind when they left to buy somewhere as his brother and sister-in-law later did. However, one wonders if George thought that the city would be cheaper than in reality it turned out to be. Certainly, food prices in Bath caught their eye and purchasing fruit and vegetables such as cucumbers, which they had grown and enjoyed in abundance at home, was surely a reversal of fortunes of sorts. Produce whose availability they had almost come to take for granted as part of their store cupboard and pantry was now a luxury. The Austens did the reversal of what many do today, living and working in the city and then retiring to the countryside. They left the country idyll, a favourable income, friends and security for the bright lights of the city. It would have been possible to rent another small home from Mr Digweed back at Steventon or even from their son Edward, who was now the owner of the parish after all.

To move lock, stock and barrel to Bath might then seem more likely to have been viewed by George as a temporary adventure. Perhaps he had truly hoped that he and Cassandra would themselves have been quickly reinvigorated, refreshed and restored by the health benefits of their proximity to healing waters and experienced a much-needed return to full strength. This being so, his expectations may well have been that he would then have been able to focus all his energy on his hopes for 'the girls', as he called them, and that they in turn would have subsequently quite naturally and easily found futures for themselves in Bath. His long-term plans may have involved himself and Cassandra seeing out their days at Godmersham or in Hampshire under the care of his son Edward. The marriage proposal in Hampshire by Harris Bigg-Wither to Jane, just eighteen months after they had enacted their retirement plans, must have added expectation to his hopes and even though she had refused this offer, it left open encouragement for the possibility that another suitor may still yet come forward.

The reality, however, was very different. To hope that their funds would sustain a lifestyle that was always at the mercy of a rental contract seems to have invited uncertainty and agitation at a time of life when George might otherwise have wanted to wind down. The anticipation and joy at living in the city also began to wane. Initially Jane had been able to overcome her grief at the prospect of leaving behind her home and the place that had helped shape her from child to woman, in part because of the novelty and excitement that Bath offered. The tantalising prospect of change and growth had piqued Jane's imagination and the opportunities to have a wider social life with a very different set had shone brightly before her. However, even if the words were written in order to protect Jane's image and modesty, later generations pointed out that although she did indeed socialise, it was in a modest, understated way and mainly with female company.[2] These were more muted soirées, more subdued in tone. The frivolous air of light-hearted jollity which permeated the balls amongst eligible peers in Hampshire had gone. As Jane spent more of her time under the guidance and restrictions of her parent's routines, however, she grew bored and frustrated. With the loss of places of escape and recovery, such as her father's library, her pianoforte and the chance for long relieving walks, the time and energy she had channelled into her writing diminished and her creativity slowed. The needs of the two generations were so divergent, and life, especially out of season, held different levels of stimulation and interest. The same feelings of disappointment may well have begun to rub off on George too although the hard-working and long-suffering vicar's wife Cassandra may have had dreams enough for the both of them.

The slide in George's fortunes can be traced through their accommodation. The family first took up residence at 4 Sydney Place overlooking the pleasure gardens in which lay hidden a thrilling labyrinth. Of an evening, it was quite the thing to wander around the flowers and paths and pause on the little bridges there. There were, on occasion, even fireworks and celebrations, truly a delightful place to spend time; to see and be seen, especially as beside the gardens stood an elegant mansion house. In choosing this spot, the family were near the Pulteney Bridge area that they favoured and the wide-open boulevards and roads that they found so attractive. When their three-year lease ended in October 1804, the family moved to the previously considered but eventually ruled out Green Park Gardens. On her arrival in the city, Jane had had the opportunity to visit one of the houses there. She had been particularly happy with the size of the rooms and the potential for a little dressing room on the third floor, as they had been used to at home. As she described in detail her walk through the house to her sister, it was clear to see that she was imagining them living there and that in her mind's eye she could picture how suitable it would be for their needs and delights. There was only one disadvantage: her keen eyes noticed patches of damp in the 'offices', the kitchens and workrooms of the house, most likely housed down in the basement.[3] The property was set down by the canal in an area known for flooding and was not an ideal situation, but at that time this had not changed her overall view of the house itself as being quite suitable and desirable.

During her time in Bath, some two or three years into her life there, Jane had begun to write a new novel. Posthumously entitled *The Watsons* by her nephew JEAL, this story began to tell the tale of Emma Watson, a young woman in her prime, once on the verge of wealth and security as the preferred heiress of her uncle, but now returned to her birth family and on the brink of poverty. Emma Watson's father was ill and we learn from family record that, in Jane's imagination, he was about to die, leaving Emma an orphan, just as had happened to Jane's father. In fact, real life began to mirror her writing. George's own health began to decline. Now in his early seventies, his general signs of ageing, such as walking with a cane, had also of late been accompanied by periodic bouts of weakness.[4] Subject to episodes of shivering and fever, he had been experiencing pressure-filled tension headaches. A local doctor, Dr Bowen, had successfully treated him on these occasions in the past with a technique known as 'cupping'.[5] This was a way of drawing out blood or other toxins in order to relieve a patient from internal inflammation, or from the poison of a bite or boil from taking hold. First, an incision was made by scratching or cutting the skin, and then the cupping glass would be placed over the top of the opening to collect the escaping blood and infection using suction.

On the Saturday morning of 19 January 1805, George was again taken ill. Everything began in the same way and so Dr Bowen attempted the same treatment. Sadly though, this time it seemed unable to alleviate George's symptoms. Overnight with rest and sleep, he seemed refreshed and restored and was able to get up out of bed on the Sunday morning. The family's normal routines took over and they were relieved as George joined them for breakfast. The doctor called in on his patient at one o'clock and was happily convinced that he had recovered well. A day of rest stretched happily ahead. George was able to move gently around with the help of his cane and even indulged in a little reading. However, as the afternoon wore on and turned to evening, the symptoms returned with a vengeance. The morning had only been a lull. George was attacked once again by a redoubling of his previous symptoms, just as would happen to the heartbroken Marianne (*Sense and Sensibility*). He seemed to be more restless and in greater distress due to the return of a high fever. Dr Bowen attended him for a third time at ten o'clock that night and grew grave. The scene, reminiscent of the snapshot of worry caught in the exchanges between Elinor and Dr Harris in regard to Marianne's precarious state (*Sense and Sensibility*), caused the Austen women's fears to rise.[6] Upon his return at nine o'clock the next morning, Dr Bowen confirmed himself in favour of more expert help and a Dr Gibbs was called for. Alas, it was all too late. George's symptoms were, unlike Marianne's, irreversible, and in the doctor's view there was no more to be done. The end of George's life seemed near; the family's prayers for his merciful release were answered and it proved to be so. By twenty past ten that Monday morning, 21 January, just forty-eight hours after being taken ill, the Reverend George Austen, rector, farmer, teacher, brother, husband, uncle, father and grandfather had died. With such a swift and unexpected death, George had been insensible to the nature of his condition, and he was, as Jane wrote, 'spared all the pain of separation' as they in turn were spared the pain of seeing him suffer.[7]

Jane wrote to her brother Frank on board HMS *Leopard* with the genteel yet stoic manner becoming of a Christian young lady of her time. Overall, she and her sister and mother were relieved and consoled that George had not suffered terribly at the end and that his release from his illness had been peaceful and calm. This was a message that she hoped to convey and endeavoured in her careful choice of words to comfort her grieving brother and soften the impact of such shocking and unexpected news. It pained her to be the communicator of such sad tidings and by letter at that, thinking of him so far away and all alone in his grief. She wrote of the ending of her father's 'virtuous and happy life' with tender respect and touching empathy for Frank, kindly imprinting for him the image of their father's 'benevolent smile' in his mind's eye.[8] Her complete assurance of their shared grief in receiving such sad news out of the blue revealed their shared love for their father and the strong bond of unity and respect that he inspired amongst them all. She felt his death most strongly but chose her words carefully in order to not overdramatise the situation or exasperate her brother with the use of excessive emotions on the page. In these times it was deemed more honourable and dutiful to regather one's strength quickly and to process a death with dignity, decorum and forbearance. This resilience leant heavily on the siblings' shared Christian faith instilled and embedded in their family culture by their father himself. In his death, they relied upon and sought to uphold in his honour the hope of resurrection to eternal life, which he had taught them all to depend upon with grace.

Henry and James immediately travelled to Bath to comfort their mother and sisters and to take care of funeral arrangements. Set for the Saturday, George was buried next to his father-in-law in the crypt at Walcot Church. Perhaps in her later revisions of *Northanger Abbey*, Jane directed Mr Thorpe's horse and carriage on a drive past this very church as a nod to paying her respects to, and including, her dear father in the narrative. A memorial stone has since been moved outside into the church gardens. Henry too took up his pen to write to his brother Frank. He left off from expressing his feelings in any depth, aware that his words would fail him in capturing 'the best of fathers' on the page. The brothers' thoughts were now directed to the living.[9] With an immediacy which would have made their father proud, they quickly strove to be seen the one amongst the other to take their place as the protectors and providers of their mother and sisters. James and Jane Leigh-Perrot showed support for the family, George's excellence as a man evoking loving words and compassionate feelings of attachment even from their difficult aunt. Newly widowed Cassandra felt that her brother enjoyed having her close by and so her immediate plans were to stay in Bath.[10] There were still three months of rent paid upon their lodgings so there would be time enough to take stock and plan their next move.

The young men quickly totted up their mother's income and made their own assessment of their predicted wealth. George had made a will back in 1770 which simply left everything due to him to his wife. Her property and income would now be combined with Cassandra's inheritance from Tom Fowle. With the promise of a donation of £50 each from James, Frank and Henry, and an expected £100 from Edward, the Austen sons congratulated and reassured themselves that their mother would be happily settled with £450 per annum. With practical reassurance that the three ladies would not need such a very large accommodation and that they might now live quite commodiously with reduced outlay in the shape of just one female servant, they considered matters duly dealt with.[11] Such words might possibly call to mind for some readers a slight echo of those once uttered by Mrs Fanny Dashwood (*Sense and Sensibility*).[12] Henry was quick to reassure Frank that his offer of £100 had quite touched their mother and that, in that moment, she had showered them all in grateful praise declaring them to be the best of children. Yet some seeds of doubt had also been sown. Henry had pointed out that he would only be able to commit to this annual gift so long as he was employed as he currently was and due attention had been paid to the fluctuating finances of their sailor brothers.[13] Just over a week after their father's death, with the young men suitably satisfied that they had done their duty, they rode off back to their own lives and Jane, her mother and her sister were left alone.

As well as being concerned for her mother and how her health would stand up under the strain of such a shock and loss, Jane had had her own grief heightened by the death of one of her beloved friends, Madam Lefroy, only one month before her father's. On Jane's twenty-ninth birthday, 16 December 1804, her friend had been involved in a fatal riding accident. James had, in fact, been one of the last people and definitely the last Austen family member to meet her. He was curate at Overton village and met with her as she was preparing to ride back up the steep hill towards home. Whilst on the road back, the horse was spooked and when her groomsman attempted to catch hold of the reins, the horse bolted, resulting in Madam Lefroy falling from its back to her death. Jane was distraught at losing such a close friend. Now in losing her father, she had lost another kindred spirit. Her best friend Martha's mother, Mrs Lloyd, was also in very ill health and she too died within just another three short months. Jane fretted for her sister who had returned to Ibthorpe with Martha and Mary to help care for Mrs Lloyd and had had to face death once again so soon after witnessing it with their own father.[14]

In the same week of Mrs Lloyd's death, Jane moved with her mother into Gay Street. In August, as the summer season came to an end in Bath, they ventured out to spend some time at Godmersham Park and Goodnestone Farm with Edward and his relatives. Then they were off on holiday once more with Martha, Edward, Henry and their wives to Worthing. They saw out the year there before returning to Bath, only to move once again at the end of January 1806, this time to the once-loathed Trim Street in the centre of the city. The home did not at all turn out to the women's liking and, when addressing a letter to her daughter-in-law Mary back at Steventon in April, it was with real feeling that Mrs Austen wrote 'Trim Street still' at the top of her page.[15] Mrs Austen had started the year with a balance of £68, her stocks and shares were still paying out, but George's pension and tithes had no longer been available to her for the past year. With George's final dividend payment made over to Henry, on 17 April he closed George's Hoare's Bank account on her behalf.[16] George had not left behind great debts but nor was there an inheritance or independent fortune left to his children, in particular his daughters. His stocks and shares, including his South Sea Annuities, continued but their worth was dwindling. He had no further property to pass on as dear Mr Bingley (*Pride and Prejudice*) had received and there was no 'money to come into' as Emma had expected for Mr Martin (*Emma*).[17] George had taken care with his money, but he had not set aside dowries or laid up any fortune for 'the girls' in the event of his death.[18] Unlike Mrs and Miss Tilney (*Northanger Abbey*), neither was there any money set aside for wedding clothes that they could dip into for other needs, nor a beautiful pearl necklace heirloom that they could sell.[19] When the Musgrove daughters (*Persuasion*) had married, their brother had reflected that it was enough to put strain on any man's finances.[20] He, however, had considered it their birthright to have certain expectations of their father in regard to his particular provision for them specifically. Neither Jane nor Cassandra had imminent plans to marry, but if they had there was no bounty that could be relied upon. In the meantime, there was no funding set aside that they could use for their immediate upkeep. Whilst he was alive, George had endeavoured to ensure that as a family, they had lived within their means but each year's income and outgoings had been fairly unpredictable, and even in the good times they had mostly lived hand to mouth. The only exceptions made to their expenditure, even in times of wealth, were for furniture and books. George had invested in the education of all his children, giving them a leg up in life to help them 'better shift' for themselves, just as his grandmother had worked so hard to do for her sons.[21] For the women, however, there was no way of making their own money open to them. They were not wealthy heiresses such as Miss Lambe (*Sanditon*) and neither had they been empowered by their father's financial arrangements, their own education or society's vision to make their own way forward in life. In some ways it was as Jane would one day voice, that it was better for a woman to conceal her intelligence, and that a less intellectual woman could more easily make a way for herself in being able to apply herself less stressfully to the expectations of a dutiful wife.[22] As a result of George's financial decisions and his ability or not to save, the only recourse open to Jane and Cassandra was to fall upon the benevolence of their brothers, who graduating from the education afforded them by their father and society might yet make their own way in the world. As Emma Watson had not long ago been ruminating in the safety of Jane's imagination, so now Jane and Cassandra in real life must have felt the true meaning for themselves. That under the current financial circumstances in which they found themselves following their father's death, in not expecting to be 'individually lucky' themselves, they now had only one hope remaining that the 'luck of one member of a family' might be 'luck to all'.[23] Maybe at this point Jane did cast one thoughtful eye back over the Manydown Bigg-Wither proposal issued those few years ago.

Now that George was gone, the three women simply could not afford a whole house for themselves out on the leafy green outskirts, but their current accommodation was also increasingly intolerable to them. The women were therefore delighted and relieved when Frank hatched a plan of escape for them all. He was engaged to Mary Gibson of Ramsgate and the pair duly married in July. Frank was conscious of being called back to sea for, just as in the period when his father died, he was on active service. The new Mrs Mary Austen, now pregnant, needed companions. So he suggested that they all take a house together in the port city of Southampton. Jane and Cassandra, totally excited at the anticipation of such a plan, had agreed a scheme of their own to bring orphaned Martha with them. Since George had died, Jane had halted writing *The Watsons*. All the wind had gone from her creative sails with his loss, and it was with a true feeling of escape that she rejoiced that summer at leaving all the pain and discomfort of Bath behind for the fishy-scented scenery of the south coast.

With the move made, Jane's instincts began to return to the height of their powers. Things definitely started to look up for the women, thanks to the generous forward thinking of Frank. Mrs Austen rejoiced in her new little garden and as she was still able to invest in stocks and shares, by the end of the year she also celebrated the £30 profit she had turned.[24] Things were tight but affordable and if there was anything George and Cassandra had taught their girls to do, it was to make the best of what they had and to use their powers to improve their own situations as far as possible. They sought to grow their own food and flowers, and they coped when the basement flooded just as it had done in the old days back in Steventon. The green shoots of their shared past began to show through once again, encouraging them onward in their new lives. In Southampton the home was crowded and personalities did sometimes clash, but there was space enough made for family to visit, trips to the theatre and dancing, and the happy opportunity to stand up by the sea wall and enjoy the expanse of the waters lapping below. With this fresh view in sight, could they make a way through for themselves? With the comforting Austen culture of habits such as resourcefulness, Christian faith and duty embedded by their father, was there a way to help themselves prosper again? Something in the wind stirred in Jane's heart. There just might be.

Chapter Fourteen

A New Hope

Now that the Austen women were a home unit, vouching for themselves on a day-to-day basis and making their own way as best they could, their imaginations were deployed in securing for themselves the best situation available to them. Living together on the small income that they had and under the restrictions and restraints now known to them, Jane's scheming began to take flight and expand in her mind's eye. Times had changed for them all since George's death and life at Southampton had not always been very easy, but through necessity they had become resourceful and resilient. Edward's dear wife Elizabeth had died in October 1808, shortly after the birth of her eleventh child, and his eldest boys had been taken care of in their grief firstly by James and Mary at Steventon, and subsequently by Jane and Martha at Southampton whilst Cassandra stayed on at Godmersham to support the grieving family. The house had become quite crowded. Frank and his wife Mary were expecting their second child, and the couple began to think of settling her closer to some of her own relatives. Edward now kindly stepped forward and offered his mother the choice of one of his properties, either in Kent or at Chawton, a village near Alton, in their beloved Hampshire, somewhere he himself had been frequenting more and more. They chose Hampshire, perhaps not unsurprisingly, and with the move imminent, Jane's confidence and ambition for her writing began to resurface. George had always been interested in and championed Jane's writing and now her beloved brother Henry stepped up and into his shoes. George's family were rallying to the rescue of his widow and girls.

Come the spring of 1809, *Susan*, which Jane had sold to Crosby some six years earlier, was *still* yet to be published. So, Jane took a leaf out of her father's book and wrote to enquire as to why this was still so. She signed herself Mrs Ashton Dennis MAD and did not hold back in her questions or advice. She politely but pointedly suggested, with her father's frankness, that if they had lost their copy, she could and would produce another for them. In the end, she was unsuccessful in engaging their commitment to publish the work.[1] Unfortunately, they wasted little time in replying in the negative, just like the rebuff from Cadell all those years ago. This time the publisher did, in fact, put pen to paper. But in a spirit reminiscent of Stephen Austen, they maintained that they held the right to choose if, and when, to publish but that she should be sure they would protect their rights over the book if she undertook to have it published elsewhere.[2] For the time being, Jane was halted in her ambitions but her hunger for publication had returned and a resolve to follow her ambitions had entered her heart.

The move into Chawton cottage with her mother, sister and, thanks to Jane's schemes and persuasions, her best friend Martha, took place in the summer of 1809, not long before Mary and Frank welcomed a son. The women quickly established their own routines, with Jane taking care of the breakfast and then being absolved of all other chores by her sister and Martha. Jane began upon a ferocious period of productivity. The fires lit within back at the 'cradle of her genius' in her father's rectory rose up and out of her as the atmosphere about her returned to the once-familiar daily routine of intelligent conversation, the rituals of walking in the open countryside and reading around the fireside.[3] The women could now evolve back into their original Austen family culture that her father had set the tone for and established in the first twenty-five years of her life. Now alone in the security of the company of her nearest and dearest, Jane could indulge herself freely in her own literary moments, mulling over plot points and character traits as she roamed the routes about the cottage. She could once again write uninterrupted on the cherished writing slope her father had given her all those years ago, nudged back into a need for privacy by the useful notification of a little creaking door if anyone should dare to venture into the room where she wrote.

Their new Chawton home was a catalyst for her effusions of fancy, as George had named them, to flow. Just as Marianne (*Sense and Sensibility*) was unable to stem the tide of her effusions of misery over Mr Willoughby, or Kitty and Lydia (*Pride and Prejudice*) to cease their raptures over the militia, so Jane's thoughts were occupied with her imagination in a way beyond previous measure.[4] All that she had lived through, all that she had experienced, was flowing free. Chawton and the ambience there were like the releasing of a cork from a bottle, and her words and ideas could now not but express themselves. Her effusions, of course, amounted to so much more than those put together in their book by Emma Woodhouse and Harriet Smith and named as such by Mr Elton (*Emma*).[5] Jane herself found the courage to continue writing, a belief sown in her by her father. She would not allow herself to belittle her novels, a format both she and her father had really enjoyed, either in her heart or on the page. She allowed herself to believe in the validity of her work emphasising her point of view quite clearly amidst Catherine Morland and Isabella Thorpe's (*Northanger Abbey*) over-enthusiastic raptures about their enchantment by Gothic novels. She addressed herself as narrator directly to her reader and swore that as a matter of principle as far as she was concerned, she would have nothing to do with critiquing her 'effusions of fancy'.[6] Encouraged by the credibility given to her writing by her father's belief and by the united front she felt at Chawton, she would be brave enough to be herself and believe in her art even professionally. As she reworked *Sense and Sensibility*, *Pride and Prejudice* and *Susan*, new ideas and characters also began to present themselves to her.

By this time, Henry was more than just a banking agent and had established himself with different partnerships as a banker himself. He had various business interests in this line in London, Kent, Alton and, following on from these, in other Hampshire towns. His homes with his wife Eliza provided respite for Jane and she enjoyed staying in Sloane Square, Henrietta Street, and later, Hans Place with him, feeling that his confidence and support for her writing gave her the right atmosphere in which to relax into the flow of her creativity. Just as her father had provided previously, Henry was full of enthusiasm for Jane's talents and read all her revised manuscripts, giving his opinions on her characters and their plot lines as the family had done by the fireside at Steventon. His interest spurred her on and her talents emboldened them both, so much so that he began to act as her literary agent, following in the footsteps of her proud and determined father.

Within a year, Henry had secured her a contract for *Sense and Sensibility* with Egerton, a military publisher in London. Most of the risk was on Jane's part as the book was to be published on commission and, in theory, she would be liable for covering her own costs. This was very much a test of the waters, a debut venture to see how the public might receive her work. Risk or no risk, however, it was thrilling. George would have been elated and he must have been in Jane's thoughts as she held the confirmation in her hand. Henry was attentive and helpful in every aspect, checking in regularly with proceedings and even hurrying the printer. His business-like but kind, persistent meddling was reminiscent of George's wholehearted yet unsubtle enquiries. He made sure that he 'networked' with the publisher too, inviting Mr Egerton to one of their extravagant parties at their home in Sloane Street.

Hot on the heels of the success of *Sense and Sensibility*, Jane completed her revision of *Pride and Prejudice* which was also sold to Egerton, in November 1813. This time her work was to be published at his expense. Just as Jane had discussed all her reading with her father, she now spoke openly of her books as her own children.[7] She delighted in having her own author copies sent out to her brothers, particularly taking care that none should be left out but provided with a copy as simultaneously as possible. She was still shy, excitedly remarking that the advertisement for *Pride and Prejudice* was in their local paper, but at delighted pains to keep her identity even from her closest neighbours.[8] Jane was overjoyed with her income, but still very conscious of not inconveniencing her brother Henry. She was very aware of the precarious nature of women making 'demands' on their menfolk and ultra-conscious of this because, just six months earlier, poor Henry had suffered greatly in the death of his wife, their cousin Eliza.[9]

Nevertheless, the belief in her writing first kindled at Steventon by her father was now fully embedded in her psyche. Her dream of publication was now a reality twice over. Jane began keeping notes on people's opinions of her books and her characters, and found such fun in collecting their thoughts on this one or that. She was tickled when people contradicted each other in their likes and dislikes, and was especially delighted when they thought they saw themselves in or recognised a character as definitely Mr or Miss X. These musings are so reminiscent of the ruminations she and her father had over their own reading. A seed of enjoyment in conversing about a book was sown all those years ago in George's Steventon study and how she loved to see the same happening with her own beloved creations. She must have missed having George's opinion in the midst of them all and would have really enjoyed the family's recognition of in-jokes, particularly any at his expense. The atmosphere at Chawton recaptured the spirit of the old parsonage in so many ways that she was now ready to write something new. George, however, was never far from her thoughts, either in real life when a mention of a family member succeeding in their scholarly endeavours brought him warmly to mind, or even in fiction.[10]

A succession of manuscripts quickly followed. The first *Mansfield Park*, published by Egerton in 1814, had a particular focus on ordination and the clergy in Jane's view. Jane took great delight in earning money and providing for herself just as her father had. In using her education and talents, she was prospering herself in a way that he had always encouraged and lived by his own example. As it had always been with her father's positive support, so it was other people's praise for her work that lifted her delightful vanity and ego the most. Her innocent yet ambitious enjoyment and happiness in her success had been the motivation for George's promotions all those years ago. The freedom to dare to believe in herself and her works stemmed from a courage fostered in her by her father's words and example since the beginning. A second edition of *Mansfield Park*, along with *Emma*, was published by John Murray, a loveable London 'rogue' of a negotiator according to Jane, who, due to Henry suffering a long-term illness, had had a lot more to do with her than Egerton had.[11] He shared the family's love of literature and she and Henry enjoyed his friendly supply of reading material amongst their communications. The sweeteners of her father's library tradition were becoming the very way to reassure her in the present.[12] Her latest novel *Emma* was due to debut in

1815 and she employed her father's determination and clarity in chivvying her publisher along in regard to the printing delay. With the encouragement of the enthusiastic James Stanier Clarke for a dedication to be included to the Prince Regent, Jane, although a little loathed to be placed in such a situation, was also in the hope that a little bit of name-dropping would go a long way in helping her cause.[13] With a heroine Jane believed no one would much like other than herself, the storyline touchingly focused amongst other more famous plots on the father-daughter relationship of the protagonist. In the acceptance of praise from others, she referred to herself as a 'Writer of Fancy', her father's happy words bouncing back at her off the page, this time in her own hand.[14]

It was the writing of *Persuasion* in 1816 that brought back reminiscences of life in Bath and the sentimental seaside nostalgia of their family trips to Lyme Regis. In January 1817 she had begun *Sanditon*, a story set at a coastal health resort, a new contender on the scene with hopes of being a pretender to the tourist trade crown. Jane's genius fitted her ambition not just to mimic life but to create her own versions of it, and therefore nothing was lifted exactly directly. Her brother Frank later in life did recognise, however, that certain elements of real people's character or personality do shine through in her work.[15] In *Sanditon* the location, the seaside, became almost a protagonist itself and the coastline and Cobb in *Persuasion* are detailed and outlined with the roving eye of a relaxed visitor. Many have blamed Jane's perceived lack of productivity and writing during the early years at Bath on George's poor timing and the devastating distraction of his seemingly flighty decision to move her there. However, if George had never moved the family to Bath for his retirement, never fixed on taking them on their holiday adventures, this longing, this love for the seaside might never have taken such a hold on Jane's imagination. Jane preferred to write from what she knew. Her dedication to the seaside cause reveals the depth of feeling that she associated with her own experiences there. The interruptions to her life in Steventon actually created, perhaps, some of her happiest memories. Times when she and her sister, and, on occasion, with her brothers, were in the company of their mother, their father in nature and free from all the responsibilities and duties to their wider community. This was a time when family and the coastal countryside took precedence and when creative juices could flow. Back at Chawton, Jane let her imagination roam far away and allowed it to mix with all that this felicity had imprinted upon her mind. As she became unwell herself, it is perhaps understandable that her psyche chose to focus on health and wellbeing. Harking back to her seaside trips may well have been a conscious act of comfort, recreating scenes and backdrops of a place where she felt at her happiest and healthiest in an atmosphere of hope. A place, of course, where her father was present too.

Reading, and more importantly conversations about, literature also remained a pleasure for Jane, even if her neighbours were not at all in the same league as her father had been. At their Chawton home they continued to read regularly, swapped books with local friends and were members of the Alton book club. Jane enjoyed reading a wide range of materials just as her father had encouraged her to do. They included octavos or pamphlet books, essays, poetry, novels and a range of subjects including military history, travel in Europe and abolition of the slave trade. Indeed, the success of her book club inspired others who heard of it to set up one in their own local community. Jane, always looking for the joke, found great fun in competing with the Steventon and Manydown book societies, taking the emulation of Chawton's as the greatest of compliments.[16]

Chawton too offered wonderful walks with the winter weather not wrecking the roads as much as it had done in Steventon. The freedom of spending the majority of her time as she wished that she had once been afforded by her father's provision in the past now accompanied her as purchased by her own pen, her brother Edward and thus George's fatherly sacrifice.

Jane paid forward the investment of time and interest that George had made in her all those years ago in their shared moments. She was a great regaler of stories to her own nieces and nephews and was adored by them for the creativity and care that she showered on them. She was great fun for them and took equal delight in their company. Her young family believed in her as a trustworthy and kind mentor. They could talk to her about anything and confide in her with their innermost secrets, safe in the knowledge that she would keep their confidences.[17] Fanny, Edward's eldest daughter, even sought her advice in regard to faith and romance. Jane was a good listener and always gave honest advice from the heart, showing empathy and gentle patience – qualities reminiscent of the atmosphere George engendered in the quiet spaces he carved out for her in their Steventon home. As her nieces and nephews grew, both Anna and James Edward and even their youngest sibling, Caroline, sought out their aunt for advice on their own writing.[18] She praised and respectfully critiqued their work, taking great interest in each character as an individual just as she did her own and just as her father had done. She laughed heartily in her approval of young Caroline sending up the father of one of her home-made heroines and encouraged her to go further still in ensuring the comedic effects of comeuppance for such a parent.[19] Delighted in their choice of subject, Jane had an hilarious trick or two up her own sleeve to add as a suggestion. She was also able to give more serious advice on the conduct of their protagonists and on the etiquette and practicalities involved in their interactions. In particular, however, her greatest wisdom and advice for her budding author relations was to exhort them to read and read long and broadly.[20] She wished that she herself had spent much more time in reading and that she had resisted for longer the urge to put her own pen to paper. Just as her father had passed on *Elegant Extracts* to Frank, now Jane passed on a copy of the prose to Anna. Perhaps knowing Anna's personality, prone as it was to exuberant self-expression as a youngster, she felt this a safer and more apt anthology than the poetry version of the same. As a result of all her years spent with her nose in a book, she was very well placed to direct their steps towards worthy examples and texts. In Anne Elliot's (*Persuasion*) nurturing of Captain Benwick's reading habits, she was able to offer a healing compress, a prescription of reading materials that might tend his heart back to life after the death of his beloved. Mindful of the power of poetry to stir up passions and sentiments, she recommended a generous dose of uplifting and inspirational prose to him just as Jane may well have chosen to do for her niece Anna.[21] Having been given the free run of her father's books, from the educational and moral to the ridiculously sublime, Jane was now in a position to pass on the fruits of their literary tours, tastes and labours to the next generation. Her wisdom was well received and James Austen's two elder children went on after her death to attempt endings of her unfinished works as well as their own novels.

George's legacy as a hard-working, sensible, scholarly role model, who promoted a purposeful life for all of his children, showed up in many different ways as unique as the personalities of his children.

James went on to have a meaningful, principled and enduring career as curate of the churches of various local villages, and then as rector of Steventon following his father's death. A memorial stone erected in St Nicholas' Church by his wife and children testified that he had been well liked and respected in the village, even if the parish registers show he took a very different approach to administrative duties than his father had. Births, marriages and deaths were separated out from one another in a way that may have reflected the more modern practice of the time, but each page was no longer signed at the bottom in a careful hand and his handwriting and entries were tellingly much sloppier in appearance than before, leading one to have less confidence in the diligence of their author. James was a poet and artist who also enjoyed excursions and travel which he used to inspire his writing. He and Mary took care to support his mother and sisters where they could. They supplied the Chawton Austens with pork and produce from the Steventon area, as did their relatives at Kintbury. James, however, was to be taken all too soon. He died in 1819.

The family continued to provide for George junior, cared for at Monk Sherborne. When their mother died in 1827, all her and George's remaining shares in the South Sea Annuities were sold. The money was divided amongst

Cassandra, Henry, Frank, Charles and Edward. The latter devolved all of his share to George, approximately £457 for his use.[22] When George died in 1838 aged 72, the family caring for him registered him in the parish records as a 'gentleman'. His body was laid to rest at All Saints' Church, Monk Sherborne, the village where he had resided most of his life, yet his memory was poignantly and forever entwined with his namesake's status, that established for the family by his father George.

Edward proved himself a great businessman, well suited to his calling in life. He became a highly respected squire of his estates with a reputation for applying himself with a sense of due diligence and duty. This alone would have been enough to gratify any parent, especially one who had made his own way in the farming world too. George and Edward had enjoyed a close relationship bonding over their common interest. It was Edward's continued care for his mother and sisters, as well as the welcome he extended to his other siblings, which was George's enduring legacy. Family was family and as such was more important than anything, even when, in 1812, Edward's name was changed officially from Austen to Knight.

Henry's health took a bad turn in the autumn of 1815 and Jane went to care for him in London. Her anxiety for him only increased the following year when his business as a banker eventually failed and ended in bankruptcy. After resisting a calling throughout all his years at St John's and beyond, Henry finally opted to take holy orders too. He became curate of Chawton serving alongside the Reverend John Rawstorn Papillon, an old Tunbridge Kent connection of his father's; Henry eventually married John's niece Eleanor in 1820. He went on to have a distinguished yet varied career as a clergyman and, in a flashback to his father's career, Henry too became a master at a grammar school for four years. In this combination of clerical and educational work, he reflected the scholarly traits he shared with his father and revived the traditions of learning instilled by him in the Steventon schoolroom. Henry would even return to Kent, spending the last year of his life in nearby Tunbridge Wells in a circle that took just a little piece of George back 'home'.

Cassandra, who in time would nurse her sister Jane until the end of her life, later returned home to Chawton to care for their mother alongside their friend Martha. There the women continued life together under one roof until, following the death of Mrs Cassandra Austen in January 1827 and eleven years after Jane's death, Martha married their brother Frank – nearly thirty years after Jane had first tried to scheme their attachment, it finally came to be.[23] Cassandra lived out the remainder of her days in the village with her dogs, interspersed with visits to Frank and Martha and her other brothers. Following in her father's footsteps, she too invested in stocks and bonds and showed quite a flair for financial speculation. In 1833 she was awarded a windfall of £5,000 from her aunt Mrs Leigh-Perrot which she invested, ensuring that she lived the rest of her life as a woman of independent means.[24]

Charles and Frank continued their naval careers finding remarkable success. Frank rose to become Admiral of the Fleet and Charles to the rank of Rear-Admiral. Like his father before him, Frank also intervened on behalf of his own children with letters to influential members of the Admiralty.[25] He himself held great sway in his sons' careers, more even than his own father had had, but he approached his letters of recommendation with an equal measure of pride and commitment. He took the memorandum that his own father had written him wherever he went, on every voyage and placement throughout his whole life. The papers show signs of fire damage and considerable wear and tear, a testament to the durability of the love each of them had for one another. Frank had married Martha Lloyd five years after the death of his first wife, Mary, who died, just like Edward's Eliza had, following the birth of her eleventh child. Later in life Frank enjoyed posts abroad and extended periods at his and Martha's home, Portsdown Lodge near Portsmouth. In his later days he became a diligent warden of Wymering Church and famously preferred the old language of his father's Bible and sermons right to the end of his life.

When Jane died in College Street, Winchester, in July 1817, where she had been taken in the hope of Dr Lyford finding a cure, she was only two doors down from Burdon's Bookshop where her father and brothers had accounts and which had supplied her with reading material for many years. Being buried inside the cathedral was testimony in itself to her father's honourable reputation and service, and it was as his daughter that her memorial stone in the nave chiefly recorded her.

Charles followed in his father's footsteps in adopting the custom of teaching his own daughters at home in their early childhood. He too had a lifelong love of reading and was a subscriber to local libraries, enjoying a visit there to exchange a book when on leave from his naval duties. In his diaries we see his own neat penmanship and preference for keeping precise notes. His own training came to bear when he kept a note of weather conditions each day. He was also a great evaluator of sermons, judging their merit and weighing them up as worthy or unworthy of praise, even when listening to his own brother or friend preach. The example of his father's preaching was ever before him.[26]

Like any father and daughter relationship, Jane felt their differences including the forty-four-year age gap. She continued to read with her family by the fireside and they all loved nothing better than to give their views upon the subject matter and the author's prowess, just as we all like to give ours today. She enjoyed particular novels, poetry and sermons and took against others. She used her reading to know herself better, and to inform as well as to entertain herself. One part of the legacy of her father introducing her to reading was that she continued to read widely on all subjects, taking in the sacred and secular. Nothing was a coincidence when it came to Jane's writing. Nothing slipped in unobserved by her. All names, for example, if traceable to a real person have a resonance. They pointed to stories and characters in the current consciousness of both Jane and her immediate readership. They proved points that Jane was intending to include as she was developing and maturing her own independent opinions in adulthood. She increasingly learnt more about the world through her study of history and travel books, and she understood and defended the cause of slave trade abolitionists. Her brother Henry later asserted that she very rarely, if ever, changed her opinions. In truth, being like her father, a person of principle who chose her point of view based upon her own values, even when into her thirties Jane was not actually averse to changing her mind at all in regard to books, and on a second or third reading she could even entirely reverse her previous positive regard for a piece or its writer.[27] However, she did still continue to enjoy a well-crafted Gothic novel or a parody thereof and later examples such as *The Heroine* by Eton Stannard Barret would have been a definite candidate for George's reading list. Jane even had a preference for the format in which she read. Just like we might opt for a paperback over a hardback or an e-reader over a paper copy nowadays, so Jane came to admire the octavo over the bigger quarto-size book and teased her friends for having them lying about on their coffee tables.[28] Through her reading, Jane was fit to converse on all and any topic; just like her Catharine from her *Juvenilia*, she could have held her own when talking about modern history or the more popular consumer staples of novels, but how she must have missed having her father to talk to.[29]

Because of her father's social standing at Steventon, Jane had been lucky to attend not just the assembly rooms in Basingstoke or Newbury but the private balls held by the local dignitaries and squires such as those at Ashe Park, Oakley Hall and Hurstbourne Park. In later adult life she revelled in the changing of the guard and that her role as chaperone now involved a great deal more sitting by the fire sipping wine than having to get up and dance all night.[30] With George's permission given to the Knights to adopt Edward and their own ventures into Bath, he had opened up opportunities for her to experience a totally different set of people, and the sort of lifestyle and homes she had only been able to glimpse on entry to her mother's family's world in Adlestrop. This all filtered through into her enjoyment of life, as living at the seaside had also done, and led to further close observation of the people in these settings. Those powerful experiences were then mixed with her genius and brought us so many scenes in her novels that stand out in our memories all these years on. What a pity that due to her grief she could not continue her writing of *The Watsons* or that because of her ill health we were never to read a full account of the adventures for Miss Charlotte Heywood (*Sanditon*).

When Jane spoke of her father following his death, it was always in love and respect. The question remains, though, as she grew and matured in her understanding and outlook on life, did she feel let down by him and his lack of provision for her and Cassandra? His actions, or lack of in this regard, truly had an effect upon their lives. In educating his sons, he had provided ways and means for them to take care of the Austen women; however, he was leaving the power of setting the limits of this provision to them and relying, though it has to be said with due confidence, very heavily on their own feelings and definitions of duty and honour and their interpretation of what his expectations of them might be. Many of the fathers in Jane's novels fall short of perfect care and example to their daughters. Mr Dashwood senior (*Sense and Sensibility*) dies having failed to secure his daughters a reasonable inheritance; Mr Darcy senior (*Pride and Prejudice*) fails in his education of his son, Mr Bennet from the same novel has no thought on how the present behaviour of himself, his wife or his youngest daughters might negatively impact the lives of the others until it is too late. Mr Price and Sir Thomas Bertram (*Mansfield Park*) both underestimate their role and levels of responsibility in the lives of their young girls; General Tilney (*Northanger Abbey*) impinges constantly upon the happiness of his children; and, likewise, Sir Walter Elliot (*Persuasion*) displays an equal penchant for selfishness in valuing no one above and beyond himself. In the *Juvenilia* too, there are countless hapless fathers who go through life oblivious to the influence they might have upon their powerless and vulnerable dependants.

Mr Weston (*Emma*) almost seemed to give his only son up easily, *and yet* he did so with a high degree of self-sacrifice. His love for his child, and example of how a father might honour his child's needs above his own, was shown as something quite remarkable, even if Frank does appear to abuse the bounty of this opportunity.[31] Mr Dashwood had brought up two happy and well-read daughters, capable of building a life with what they did possess: charm and good manners to endear them in society. Mr Darcy senior was all in all a good man, beloved by his staff and with a reputation for being generous to the poor, and Mr Darcy junior had all the good traits of a perfect brother to his fatherless sister. Mr Bennet supported his daughters to express their own opinions and personalities, and he showed a warmth and appreciation for the company and wisdom of his two eldest. Sir Thomas Bertram is at least contrite and willing to learn and can recognise the error of his ways before it is completely too late. Mr Price and General Tilney are ultimately outwitted and side-lined by their own more gracious and cultured offspring.

However much Jane might have ruminated and even lamented her own situation, I think that she would also have acknowledged that her father gave her the keys to her own kingdom. He shared his own story with his children and asserted his belief in the power of education and one's duty to lead a purposeful and useful life with the talents that he believed God had provided them with. In doing so, he was giving Jane and his other children a map that they might follow for themselves. In sharing his own example of resourcefulness and commitment to hard work, his liberal-minded regard to Jane's reading and his equipping of his daughters as well as his sons to develop their minds, he was sowing seeds that ultimately enabled Jane to reap her own harvest. Albeit a harvest that was limited by the soil in which she found herself rooted, that is in the social class and society of her times.

An image of Jane and her talent cocooned away in the heart of a quiet and lowly parsonage, protected and closeted from the rest of the world was perhaps first allowed to take hold following the biography of the author by her brother Henry, included in the posthumous publication of *Persuasion* and *Northanger Abbey* together in late 1817/early 1818. Although a very respectful and 'proper' communication of a worthy and modest young lady, this was not the atmosphere or culture fostered by her father, the rector. His household was a lively one, where freedom of speech and an open attitude towards reading matter prevailed. Amateur dramatics were encouraged and enjoyed with Jane watching the somewhat 'bawdy' and risqué storylines and even taking part whilst still a child. There was no isolating her from the theatrical proceedings due to deference to any sense of necessary decorum.

No one can forget the first novel they read and loved and the nostalgia that rereading it can bring years later. For Jane, stumbling on *Sir Charles Grandison* in her father's study, the memory of that love of reading, even though much might be going on over one's head, became associated with the atmosphere of home. The acceptance of literature as a tool for educating oneself created a bond of trust between Jane and George that empowered her to follow her own instincts. The culture that George created emanated from that little library and led to a lifetime of exploration and experimentation in her reading materials. Jane continued to scour every type of text from novel to travel guide, from extract, elegant or otherwise, to newspaper article, all the while secure in the approval of her father. He affirmed her choices when she was very young, cementing a trust in herself to make her own decisions. He then fostered that feeling of permission inside her which ultimately encouraged her to give free rein to her observations, wit, intelligence and imagination through her published writing.

From his earliest memories of grief and abandonment as an orphan, George held a longing to see not only himself but his nearest and most dear, his close family, survive and thrive. He was driven by a determination to see them cared and provided for, and living out their lives in safety and security. Consolidating that certainty took many years and George suffered setbacks, brought on by his lack of control as a child and young pupil and then as a poorer young man setting out on life's path. It is true that George had more support than most, considering he had the help of his financially and sympathetic rich Uncle Francis. Yet he had to live with some harsh realities and make choices about how and when to spend his money and how to generate it when he had insufficient funds. His greatest fear, that of seeing his own family destitute, was perhaps only matched by a greater sacrifice than George could have imagined having to make, that of having to let his own child go and be adopted by another family. George did mostly achieve his goal, although his wife and daughters still faced a degree of straightened circumstances after his death which he would have lamented. Perhaps this is partly what Jane was alluding to when she wrote what a blessing it was that he was unaware as he lay ill that he would so soon be separated from his wife and daughters 'so beloved, so fondly cherished' by himself.[32]

George had struggled but he had gained a greater gift than simply proving to himself, his stepmother and his family that he could make it through – he had won a partner in life and the love and respect of his eight children. He learnt through their admiration and affection that he and his sisters could do more than simply survive by their courage and the power of their own personalities. He came to understand that through the strong bonds of family and community they could reach beyond the levels of pure subsistence to enjoy authentically purposeful and happy lives. Like Mr Bennet, George found that he could derive the chief of his own pleasures from his love of 'the country and books'.[33] His life was simple yet busy. He proved himself hard-working but through his education and training at St John's he also discovered a higher calling. In living a life of duty before his God, he could raise the meaning of his own life in this world by caring for a broader range of people than just himself, Philadelphia and Leonora. He expanded his heart and motivations to endeavour to nurture his local community and future generations too. George achieved the antithesis of being rejected and separated from family as a young child. Instead of the pain of loneliness and loss that he had once felt, he was able to put down roots and settle himself at the centre of a community to minister and to be ministered to, to be blessed and to be a blessing. In working so hard amongst this network of people carrying out a number of different roles for nearly forty years, time sped by almost without him noticing, however. With it went the opportunity of doing more in terms of saving for his girls' future. Time had passed but in securing for all his children a loving, close and caring family, he had done more than mere money could ever do. His wife, Jane and her siblings would never be alone as long as they cherished each other. The obsessive self-reliance of his youth, a necessary armour in a dangerous world, was actually healed by the mutually-minded love of his wife and children. His legacy of love and nurture, of living out his values, had embedded that culture for them all. His children's willingness to motivate themselves and improve their talents is the greatest tribute to his personal influence.

The young 6-year-old boy, who had been rejected in essence by his great-grandfather's cruel will and then again by the coldness of his stepmother's decision, had managed to elevate his own station in life. His success at school, university and in his professional life was an incredible achievement. His emotional resilience and determination honoured that of his grandparents, particularly his grandmother Elizabeth Weller. His story is a remarkable one. George went from orphan to the father of eminent clergymen, admiral and vice-admiral of the Royal Navy, the landed gentry, a woman able to live very comfortably by her own means and a world-famous author.

However, the most beautiful and poignant part of George's story is that the love of his family and the allies who gathered around him proved that there was more happiness available for him in life than he had ever imagined. Through his Uncle Francis and later his wife Cassandra, he realised that in all he was willing to do for himself, his siblings, his Tunbridge family, his wife, his children and his community, they would in turn help him by sharing their own harvest. His final healing was that he was part of a family where it was safe to see each other's flaws, to laugh at himself and the others and be laughed at in turn. He learnt that not everyone leaves and that there were those who were willing to have his back as he had theirs. George found that he could belong. His greatest fear never materialised; he was not left destitute, abandoned and alone, and he escaped the confines of his worry and anxiety completely. Moreover, George lived on in his children's minds, memories and actions. They still heard his voice and responded to it even when separated from him by death.

George's influence as 'a profound scholar' who poured his enthusiasm and, as Henry would later put it, his 'exquisite taste in every species of literature' into sowing the same such appreciation at such a young age into Jane was what her beloved brother credited as her own later motivation for becoming an author. It was that same good 'taste', nurtured in its greater part by her father, that combined with her 'inclination' to write which had also been cherished and encouraged in turn by George.[34] Jane broke through the myth of who she was 'supposed to be' according to her gender and, to a certain extent, her class, in the eyes of society and perhaps even her own parents' initial wishes. She overcame a great deal of the barriers and obstacles that these expectations provided. She found a way of capitalising upon the education and entrepreneurial spirit which her father gave her and forged her own path. Surging forwards on the childhood wave of support from her father, atypical of the time, she found a way to explore what he saw as her God-given talents to the full. His belief and encouragement in her early beginnings galvanised Jane later in life to finally break free from the marriage objective.

Jane's heroines all experienced a tussle of their own when it came to their fathers' positions of power within their families, and the paternal personalities, characters, actions and behaviours loomed large in the everyday encounters of their lives. It was their connection, or lack of it, with their fathers that helped them to learn more about themselves and the world about them, to gain self-awareness. Jane experienced these feelings too, and her associations with her father, just like theirs, were a significant part of the grit in the oyster that fashioned her and her creations as they embarked upon their journey as a heroine or hero. We see echoes of George in her as a person and in her work, and just like a character's concurrence or deviance from their father's world view enabled them to decide what they believed and wanted themselves, so it was for Jane. Her relationship with her father correlated with that experienced by the people of her own invention regarding how they too all endeavoured to stand on their own two feet, as much as was possible in their current circumstances. In short, this relationship was as key in each 'darling child's' own personal development as it was for Jane herself, and particularly so for the women she invented. Through the twists and turns of the decisions made for, and by, her female characters, Jane drew particular attention to the privilege and power that fathers exerted at this time over her fictional and real women such as herself.

Jane wrote of the marriage ending as the only exit out of poverty and towards any expression of self in life for most women. Jane had been able to step out of this route, but she still struggled under the realities of her father's decisions and eighteenth- and nineteenth-century society. She had to take on both the constraints and the opportunities offered by the publishing world, but she did it. She became a published author and had begun, before her young life was cut short so early, to fulfil her creative and economic dreams, her goals and aims of securing a financial future for herself and her loved ones. The very same aspirations which drove George himself.

Through Jane's books, we too get to partake in the joy of reading, in escaping, being entertained and educated. George's library has opened a door for all of us into a world that we so enjoy returning to again and again. We get to glimpse a little of George Austen in the fragmented wall of mirrors of Jane's imagination. In this way she echoes his influence and makes it available to us today. We too get to learn that education, with a little determination, is ours for the taking. George believed and taught those he loved that education was a tool for one's own salvation, that each one of us holds the key and we can, and must, create and direct our own futures by developing our talents. He believed that no one could do this for anyone else, that only the individual could take control and improve themselves and that each one of us has a right and also a duty to do so. We learn from George and Jane's relationship that it is never too late to make the most of what we have for ourselves and the greater good of others, both near and far, both known and unknown to us.

Now that we have turned the kaleidoscope of George's life and let the patterns settle, we have a clearer image, a treasure map that leads us to the values and ideals that he lived his life by. We have traced his experiences and now have a clearer picture of his unique fingerprints upon Jane's life and her understanding. George believed in education as a principle and truth; it was in his DNA, passed down from his father and Uncle Francis' generation having crystallised in the hearts and minds of John and Elizabeth Austen as a way out of poverty, a way of travelling from the darkness to the light. The compelling story of his grandmother's sacrifice was seared into the family's memory. They had lived it and absorbed the power of her legacy, turning their own lives into a living example of the parable of the talents from the gospel of Matthew. A tale of only three servants, nevertheless it echoed their experience. The servants in the story were entrusted with their master's possessions whilst he was away. All three set to work stewarding their treasure in order to honour him. The first two increased their bounty but the third hid his through fear and only sought to preserve what he started with. This story exemplifies the attitude towards growth and entrepreneurship as imbued and embedded in the family culture by Elizabeth Weller. She planted a generation in the good soil of education. George believed in the inspiration that this could provide and that, when matched with our own honour, perseverance, creativity and hard work, it would be the catalyst to enable one to thrive.

However, this effort was not made purely for self-gain or selfish motives. The biggest legacy that George passed on to his daughter was the same as that which he laid out front and centre to Frank in his memorandum – his orientation around his Christian faith. In Jane's surviving prayers, written for the family's evening moment of reflection, we see illuminated Jane's heartfelt commitment to God and her fellow man. Her prayers echo the tone and content of the family's beloved Book of Common Prayer and are simply crafted to invoke quiet and sincere private reflection and worship. Jane absorbed George's respect and devotion to God as her first duty and viewed her heavenly father with love and reverent tender regard. Her prayers reveal a woman who had received the messages of Anglican Christianity deep into her heart. Although it was a way of life modelled by her brothers and other family clergy in adulthood, Jane's faith was tempered and tuned in childhood by her father. When Henry's wife Elizabeth died and two of his sons were sent into her care for a while, she made sure to offer them the comfort of her family's faith and traditions, combining their days with outdoor play, games, and readings and guidance from the Bible.[35] In the personal prayers which she composed, her earnest and sincere requests for forgiveness, and her heartfelt search for spiritual growth, combined with a stream of gratitude for all that she had received in terms of earthly comfort, reflect George's teaching and his influence. Her expressions of faith revealed a strong sense of community and prioritised care and kindness towards others. This modest and unselfish expression of her faith was just as she had been encouraged and taught to think by her father. Her requests and petitions all centred on the happiness and protection of others, including her extended family, the sick, the orphaned and widowed. Underpinning each oration was the firm hope of resurrection, that one day the family might all be reunited in heaven and share once more the strong bonds of love and service which bound them all on earth.

As we read Jane's works, we see her father's seeds of faith, hope and charity mixed together with the message that the opportunity to grow, to improve and to serve, both spiritually and practically, is clearly set before us. We catch hold of the encouragement that we too could and should follow our arrows, use our talents and curate our environments to enhance them whenever and wherever we can, not just for ourselves but for the good of all. George's example and his call to fulfil ourselves is as inspirational to us today as it was for Jane nearly 250 years ago.

Jane's memorial stone laid at the site of her grave in the nave at Winchester Cathedral begins with a simple sentence naming her as the 'youngest daughter of the late Reverend George Austen, formerly Rector of Steventon in this county.' For all her beloved genius, her generosity of spirit and her profound depth of connection to her family, friends and community, Jane was and is remembered first, foremost and forever as her Daddy's girl.

Notes

Introduction
1. Based upon the opening line, Austen, J., (1818). *Northanger Abbey*. Volume I, Chapter I.
2. Campbell, J., (2008). *The Hero With A Thousand Faces*. Third Edition. Novato, California: New World Library, p.211.
3. Austen, F-W., (1852–6). 'Letters to Eliza Susan Quincy'. 23M93/63/1. Hampshire Record Office.
4. Austen, J., (c.1790–1793). *Volume the Second*. Contents page.
5. Lefroy manuscript in Le Faye, D., (2004). *A Family Record*. Second Edition. Cambridge: Cambridge University Press, p.4.
6. Austen, J., (1813). *Pride and Prejudice*. Chapter XLIII.
7. Letter 107. Jane Austen to Anna Austen, Chawton, (9–18 September 1814) in Le Faye, D., (2011). *Jane Austen's Letters*. Fourth Edition. Oxford: Oxford University Press, p.287.
8. Letter 143. Jane Austen to Caroline Austen, Chawton, (15 July 1816) in Le Faye, D., (2011). *Jane Austen's Letters*. Fourth Edition. Oxford: Oxford University Press, p.331.

Chapter One: In the Beginning
1. https://premium.weatherweb.net/weather-in-history-1700-to-1749
2. (1940). *Pedigree of Austen*. London: Printed privately by Spottiswoode, Ballantyne and Co. Ltd, pp. 11–12.
3. Shaw, W.A., and Slingsby, F.H. (eds), (1962). 'Declared Accounts: Navy', in *Calendar of Treasury Books, Volume 32, 1718*. London, pp. clii–clxx. *British History Online* http://www.british-history.ac.uk/cal-treasury-books/vol32/clii-clxx [accessed 12 February 2023].
4. Austen, J., (1814). *Mansfield Park*. Volume III, Chapter VII.
5. https://en.wikipedia.org/wiki/Barber_surgeon
6. Austen, J., (c.1790–1793). *Jack and Alice* in *Volume the Third*.
7. Austen, J., (1817). *Sanditon*. Chapter I.
8. Letter 104. Jane Austen to Anna Austen, Chawton, (10–18 August 1814) in Le Faye, D., (2011). *Jane Austen's Letters*. Fourth Edition. Oxford: Oxford University Press, p.280.
9. Austen, J., (1803/4). *The Watsons*.
10. Austen, J., (1814). *Mansfield Park*. Volume I, Chapter II.
11. Austen, J., (1816). *Emma*. Volume II, Chapter IX and Austen, J., (1814). *Mansfield Park*. Volume III, Chapter VII.
12. Reminiscent of a conversation between Elizabeth Bennet and Mr Darcy in Austen, J., (1813). *Pride and Prejudice*. Chapter XXXII.
13. (1940). *Pedigree of Austen*. London: Printed privately by Spottiswoode, Ballantyne and Co. Ltd, pp. 11–12.
14. Austen, J., (1813). *Pride and Prejudice*. Chapter XXXIII.

15. Austen Weller, E., (1706/7). *Memorandums* in Austen Leigh, R.A., (1942). *Austen Papers 1704–1856*. Privately published, London, p.4

16. Austen, J., (1813). *Pride and Prejudice*. Chapter XVI.

17. Spence, J., (2001). *A Century of Wills from Jane Austen's Family 1705–1806*. Second Edition. Paddington, NSW Australia: Jane Austen Society of Australia, p.4.

18. For more information on her biography, see Austen Weller, E., (1706/7). *Memorandums* in Austen Leigh, R.A., (1942). *Austen Papers 1704–1856*. Privately published London, pp.1–19.

19. Austen Weller, E., (1706/7). *Memorandums* in Austen Leigh, R.A., (1942). *Austen Papers 1704–1856*. Privately published London, pp.12/13.

20. (1940). *Pedigree of Austen*. London: Printed privately by Spottiswoode, Ballantyne and Co. Ltd, p.5.

21. Spence, J., (2001). *A Century of Wills from Jane Austen's Family 1705–1806*. Second Edition. Paddington, NSW Australia: Jane Austen Society of Australia, p.15.

22. Spence, J., (2001). *A Century of Wills from Jane Austen's Family 1705–1806*. Second Edition. Paddington, NSW Australia: Jane Austen Society of Australia, p.15.

23. Austen, J., (c.1790–1793). *Catharine, or the Bower* in *Volume the Third*.

24. Austen, J., (1814). *Mansfield Park*. Volume II, Chapter III.

25. Austen, J., (1814). *Mansfield Park*. Volume I, Chapter II.

26. According to an Austen family unpublished manuscript as confirmed by Le Faye, D., (1998) 'Leonora Austen'. pp.55–57 in *The Jane Austen Society report for 1998*. Winchester: Sarsen Press for The Jane Austen Society, p.55.

27. Spence, J., (2001). *A Century of Wills from Jane Austen's Family 1705–1806*. Second Edition. Paddington, NSW Australia: JAS of Australia, p.21.

28. Austen, J., (1813). *Pride and Prejudice*. Chapter VII.

29. Macky, J., (1714). *Journey through England*. Quoted by Willes, M., (2022). *In The Shadow Of St. Paul's Cathedral*. New Haven and London: Yale University Press, p.173.

30. Austen, J., (c.1790–1793). *A collection of letters* in *Volume the Second*.

31. Austen, J., (1811). *Sense and Sensibility*. Volume I, Chapter XVII.

32. Deazley, R., (2004). *The Origin of the Right to Copy*. Oxford: Hart, 2004. pp. 79–80

33. Cawthorn, M.J., (2017). *James Cawthorn, George Austen and The Curious Case of the Schoolboy Who Was Killed*. Kibworth Beauchamp: Matador, p.11.

34. Land registry records assert Stephen Austen lived in Castle Baynard 1738–41 as cited by Cawthorn, M.J., (2017). *James Cawthorn, George Austen and The Curious Case of the Schoolboy Who Was Killed*. Kibworth Beauchamp: Matador, p.189.

35. Willes, M., (2022). *In The Shadow Of St. Paul's Cathedral*. New Haven and London: Yale University Press, p.178.

36. Tonbridge School records as cited by Cawthorn, M.J., (2017) *James Cawthorn, George Austen and The Curious Case of the Schoolboy Who Was Killed*. Kibworth Beauchamp: Matador, p.11.

37. Willes, M., (2022) *In The Shadow Of St. Paul's Cathedral*. New Haven and London: Yale University Press, p.210.

38. Le Faye, D., (1998). 'Leonora Austen'. p.55–57 in *The Jane Austen Society report for 1998*. Winchester: Sarsen Press for The Jane Austen Society, p.55.

39. A rumination similar to that undertaken by Sir Thomas Bertram in Austen, J., (1814). *Mansfield Park*. Volume I, Chapter I.

Chapter Two: Schooldays
1. Austen, J., (1816). *Emma.* Volume II, Chapter IV.
2. Austen, J., (1816). *Emma.* Volume II, Chapter IV.
3. Letter from Henry Austen to James-Edward Austen Leigh in Austen Leigh, R.A., (1942). *Austen Papers 1704–1856.* Privately published, London, p.16.
4. Austen. J., (1813). *Pride and Prejudice.* Chapter VII.
5. Austen, J., (1811). *Sense and Sensibility.* Volume II, Chapter IX.
6. Austen, J., (1803/4). *The Watsons.*
7. Austen, J., (1816). *Emma.* Volume III, Chapter XVII.
8. Austen, J., (1793–4). *Lady Susan, Letter One, Lady Susan Vernon to Mr Vernon.*
9. Austen, J., (1816). *Emma.* Volume I, Chapter III.
10. Rivington, S., (1869). *The History of Tonbridge School from its Foundation in 1553 to The Present Day.* London, Oxford and Cambridge: Rivingtons, p.48.
11. Somervell, D.C., (1947). *A History of Tonbridge School.* London: Faber and Faber, p.17.
12. Lefroy manuscript in Le Faye, D., (2004). *A Family Record.* Second Edition. Cambridge: Cambridge University Press, p.4.
13. Austen, J., (1803/4). *The Watsons.*
14. Rivington, S., (1869). *The History of Tonbridge School from its Foundation in 1553 to The Present Day.* London, Oxford and Cambridge: Rivingtons, p.53.
15. The Skinners' Company: Cawthorn. J., letter read at the committee of leases, 1 Nov 1757, court book no. 11, 1752–1761. CLC/L/SE/B/001/MS30708/011, Guildhall Library, London.
16. Austen, J., (1816). *Emma.* Volume I, Chapter III.
17. The Skinners' Company, court book no. 11, 1752–1761. CLC/L/SE/B/001/MS30708/011, Guildhall Library, London.
18. The Skinners' Company, minutes of the committee of leases, 1 Nov 1757, court book no. 11, 1752–1761. CLC/L/SE/B/001/MS30708/011, Guildhall Library, London.
19. The Skinners' Company, minutes of the committee of leases, 1 Nov 1757, court book no. 11, 1752–1761. CLC/L/SE/B/001/MS30708/011, Guildhall Library, London.
20. Somervell, D.C., (1947). *A History of Tonbridge School.* London: Faber and Faber, p.15; The Skinners' Company, minutes of the court of assistants, 6 January 1759, court book no. 11, 1752–1761. CLC/L/SE/B/001/MS30708/011, Guildhall Library, London.
21. Austen, J., (1816). *Emma.* Volume I, Chapter III.
22. Rivington, S., (1869). *The History of Tonbridge School from its Foundation in 1553 to The Present Day.* London, Oxford and Cambridge: Rivingtons, p.65.
23. Austen, J., (1816). *Emma.* Volume I, Chapter VIII.
24. Austen, J., (1803/4). *The Watsons.*
25. Letter 86. Jane Austen to Francis Austen, Chawton, (3–6 July 1813) in Le Faye, D., (2011). *Jane Austen's Letters.* Fourth Edition. Oxford: Oxford University Press, p.223.
26. Letter 146. Jane Austen to James Edward Austen, Chawton, (16–17 July 1816) in Le Faye, D., (2011). *Jane Austen's Letters.* Fourth Edition. Oxford: Oxford University Press, p.336.
27. Rivington, S., (1869). *The History of Tonbridge School from its Foundation in 1553 to The Present Day.* London, Oxford and Cambridge: Rivingtons, p.55.
28. Southam, B., (2000). 'George Austen: Pupil, Usher and Proctor.' pp.6–11 in *The Jane Austen Society, Report for 2000.* Winchester: Sarsen Press for The Jane Austen Society, p.6.
29. Southam, B., (2000). 'George Austen: Pupil, Usher and Proctor.' pp.6–11 in *The Jane Austen Society, Report for 2000.* Winchester: Sarsen Press for The Jane Austen Society, p.7.

30. Southam, B., (2000). 'George Austen: Pupil, Usher and Proctor.' pp.6–11 in *The Jane Austen Society, Report for 2000*. Winchester: Sarsen Press for The Jane Austen Society, p.8.

31. Cawthorn, M.J., (2017). *James Cawthorn, George Austen and The Curious Case of the Schoolboy Who Was Killed*. Kibworth Beauchamp: Matador, p.6.

32. Austen, J., (1816). *Emma*. Volume II, Chapter VII.

33. Cawthorn, M.J., (2017). *James Cawthorn, George Austen and The Curious Case of the Schoolboy Who Was Killed*. Kibworth Beauchamp: Matador, p.8.

34. Rivington, S., (1869). *The History of Tonbridge School from its Foundation in 1553 to The Present Day*. London, Oxford and Cambridge: Rivingtons, p.117.

35. Somervell, D.C., (1947). *A History of Tonbridge School*. London: Faber and Faber, p.29.

36. Austen, J., (1818). *Northanger Abbey*. Volume I, Chapter VI.

37. Somervell, D.C., (1947). *A History of Tonbridge School*. London: Faber and Faber, p.30.

38. Rivington, S., (1869). *The History of Tonbridge School from its Foundation in 1553 to The Present Day*. London, Oxford and Cambridge: Rivingtons, p.119; Somervell, D.C., (1947). *A History of Tonbridge School*. London: Faber and Faber, p.29.

39. Rivington, S., (1869). *The History of Tonbridge School from its Foundation in 1553 to The Present Day*. London, Oxford and Cambridge: Rivingtons, p.68.

40. The Skinners' Company, minutes of the court for leases, 12 June 1744, court book no. 9, 1733–1748. CLC/L/SE/B/001/MS30708/009, p.463. Guildhall Library, London.

41. Rivington, S., (1869). *The History of Tonbridge School from its Foundation in 1553 to The Present Day*. London, Oxford and Cambridge: Rivingtons, p.117.

42. Rivington, S., (1869). *The History of Tonbridge School from its Foundation in 1553 to The Present Day*. London, Oxford and Cambridge: Rivingtons, p.120.

43. Austen, J., (1814). *Mansfield Park*. Volume III, Chapter III.

44. Austen, J., (1811). *Sense and Sensibility*. Volume I, Chapter XVII.

45. Letter 132 (D). Jane Austen to James Stanier Clarke, (11 December 1815) in Le Faye, D., (2011). *Jane Austen's Letters*. Fourth Edition. Oxford: Oxford University Press, p.319.

46. The Skinners' Company, minutes of the court of assistants, 25 Feb 1752, court book no. 11, 1752–1761. CLC/L/SE/B/001/MS30708/011, Guildhall Library, London.

47. Rivington, S., (1869). *The History of Tonbridge School from its Foundation in 1553 to The Present Day*. London, Oxford and Cambridge: Rivingtons, p.114.

48. The Skinners' Company, minutes of the court for leases, 12 June 1744, court book no. 9, 1733–1748. CLC/L/SE/B/001/MS30708/009, Guildhall Library, London.

49. Weller family correspondence. U1000/18. Kent Archives Office, Maidstone.

50. Somervell, D.C., (1947). *A History of Tonbridge School*. London: Faber and Faber, p.30.

51. The Skinners' Company, minutes of the court of assistants, 21 June 1748, court book no. 9, 1733–1748. CLC/L/SE/B/001/MS30708/009, Guildhall Library, London.

52. Cawthorn, M.J., (2017). *James Cawthorn, George Austen and The Curious Case of the Schoolboy Who Was Killed*. Kibworth Beauchamp: Matador, p.50.

53. Rivington, S., (1869). *The History of Tonbridge School from its Foundation in 1553 to The Present Day*. London, Oxford and Cambridge: Rivingtons, p.21.

54. Southam, B., (2000). 'George Austen: Pupil, Usher, and Proctor.' pp.6–11 in *The Jane Austen Society Report for 2000*. Winchester: Sarsen Press for The Jane Austen Society, pp.7–8.

55. Austen, J., (c.1790–1793). *History of England*, 'Edward VI' in *Volume the Second*.

56. Letter 67. Jane Austen to Cassandra, (30 January 1809) in Le Faye, D., (2011). *Jane Austen's Letters*. Fourth Edition. Oxford: Oxford University Press, p.180.

57. Vick, R., (1999). 'The Hancocks.' *The Jane Austen Society Report for 1999*. Winchester: Sarsen Press for The Jane Austen Society, pp.19–23.
58. Austen, J., (1811). *Sense and Sensibility*. Volume II, Chapter XIV.
59. Letter 142. Jane Austen to James-Edward Austen, Chawton, (9 July 1816) in Le Faye, D., (2011). *Jane Austen's Letters*. Fourth Edition. Oxford: Oxford University Press, p.330.
60. Austen Weller, E., (1706/7). *Memorandums* in Austen Leigh, R.A., (1942). *Austen Papers 1704–1856*. Privately published, London, pp.1–16.
61. Austen, J., (1814). *Mansfield Park*. Volume I, Chapter XI.

Chapter Three: Student Life

1. Austen, J., (1814). *Mansfield Park*. Volume I, Chapter II.
2. St John's College, Buttery Book entry, 26 June 1747. ACC V.E.97. St John's College, Oxford.
3. Letter 154. Jane Austen to Caroline Austen, Chawton, (14 March 1817) in Le Faye, D., (2011). *Jane Austen's Letters*. Fourth Edition. Oxford: Oxford University Press, p.349.
4. Costin, W.C., (1958). *The History of St. John's College Oxford 1598–1860*. Oxford: Oxford University Press. p.38.
5. Costin, W.C., (1958). *The History of St. John's College Oxford 1598–1860*. Oxford: Oxford University Press. p.109 and 195.
6. Austen, J., (1811). *Sense and Sensibility*. Volume I, Chapter XIX.
7. St John's College, Register 1730–1794, 30 November 1751, p.243 and 30 November 1758. ADM 1.A.7, p.325. St John's College, Oxford.
8. St. John's College, Register 1730–1794, 1 April 1752. ADM 1.A.7, p.245. St John's College, Oxford.
9. Letter 78. Jane Austen to Cassandra, Chawton, (24 January 1813) in Le Faye, D., (2011). *Jane Austen's Letters*. Fourth Edition. Oxford: Oxford University Press, p.207.
10. Austen Leigh, R.A., (1942). Letter from Henry Thomas Austen to Warren Hastings, 5 June 1802 in *Austen Papers 1704–1856*. Privately published, London, p.177.
11. The Skinners' Company, minutes of the court of assistants, 19 October 1753, court book no. 11, 1752–1761. CLC/L/SE/B/001/MS30708/011, Guildhall Library, London.
12. Rivington, S., (1869). *The History of Tonbridge School from its Foundation in 1553 to The Present Day*. London, Oxford and Cambridge: Rivingtons, p.21.
13. Somervell, D.C., (1947). *A History of Tonbridge School*. London: Faber and Faber, p.26.
14. Austen, J., (c.1787–1793). *Edgar and Emma, a tale*, in *Volume the First*.
15. See the original statutes in Rivington, S., (1869). *The History of Tonbridge School from its Foundation in 1553 to The Present Day*. London, Oxford and Cambridge: Rivingtons, p.48.
16. See the original statutes in Rivington, S., (1869). *The History of Tonbridge School from its Foundation in 1553 to The Present Day*. London, Oxford and Cambridge: Rivingtons, p.49.
17. Rivington, S., (1869). *The History of Tonbridge School from its Foundation in 1553 to The Present Day*. London, Oxford and Cambridge: Rivingtons, p.50.
18. Austen, J., (1814). *Mansfield Park*. Volume I, Chapter IX.
19. Rivington, S., (1869), *The History of Tonbridge School from its Foundation in 1553 to The Present Day*. London, Oxford and Cambridge: Rivingtons, p.50.
20. Rivington, S., (1869), *The History of Tonbridge School from its Foundation in 1553 to The Present Day*. London, Oxford and Cambridge: Rivingtons, p.53.

21. The Skinners' Company, minutes of the court of assistants, 17 June 1756, court book no. 11, 1752–1761, CLC/L/SE/B/001/MS30708/011, Guildhall Library, London.

22. Southam, B., (2000). 'George Austen: Pupil, Usher, and Proctor.' pp.6–11 in *The Jane Austen Society, Report for 2000*. Winchester: Sarsen Press for The Jane Austen Society, pp.8–9.

23. The Skinners' Company, minutes of the court of assistants, 20 January 1756, court book no. 11, 1752–1761, CLC/L/SE/B/001/MS30708/011, Guildhall Library, London.

24. The Skinners' Company, minutes of the committee of leases, 28 July 1756, court book no. 11, 1752–1761, CLC/L/SE/B/001/MS30708/011, Guildhall Library, London.

25. The Skinners' Company, minutes of the court of assistants, 27 October 1756, court book no. 11, 1752–1761, CLC/L/SE/B/001/MS30708/011, Guildhall Library, London.

26. Cawthorn, M.J., (2017). *James Cawthorn, George Austen and The Curious Case of the Schoolboy Who Was Killed.* Kibworth Beauchamp: Matador, p.81.

27. The Skinners' Company, minutes of the court of assistants, 11 May 1757, court book no. 11, 1752–1761, CLC/L/SE/B/001/MS30708/011, Guildhall Library, London.

28. The Skinners' Company, minutes of the court of assistants, 25 May 1758, court book no. 11, 1752–1761, CLC/L/SE/B/001/MS30708/011, Guildhall Library, London.

29. The Skinners' Company, accounts book, payments ledger, 1745–1787. CLC/L/SE/D/009/MS30729/002 and CLC/L/SE/D/009/MS30729/003, Guildhall Library, London.

Chapter Four: University Life

1. Costin, W.C., (1958). *The History of St. John's College Oxford 1598–1860.* Oxford: Oxford University Press. p.70.

2. Costin, W.C., (1958). *The History of St. John's College Oxford 1598–1860.* Oxford: Oxford University Press. p.187.

3. St John's College, Register 1730–1794, 7 February 1758. ADM 1.A.7, p.314. St John's College, Oxford.

4. St John's College, Register 1730–1794. ADM 1.A.7, p.211. St John's College, Oxford.

5. Costin, W.C., (1958). *The History of St. John's College Oxford 1598–1860.* Oxford: Oxford University Press. p.215.

6. St John's College, Register 1730–1794, 30 November 1758. ADM 1.A.7, p.325. St John's College, Oxford.

7. Sillery, V., (ed.), (1990). *St. John's College Biographical Register 1660–1775.* Oxford: privately printed. p.58.

8. Lefroy manuscript in Le Faye, D., (2004). *A Family Record.* Second Edition. Cambridge: Cambridge University Press, p.4.

9. Austen, J., (1814). *Mansfield Park.* Volume I, Chapter IX.

10. Austen, J., (1818). *Northanger Abbey.* Volume I, Chapter IX.

11. Austen, G. and Wright, W., (1759). '*An answer to the objections made in convocation to the representation of the conduct of the proctors…with respect to the two explanatory statutes proposed by the vice-chancellor.*' ESTC T220246. Wellcome Collection.

12. Austen, G. and Wright, W., (1759). 'An answer to the objections made in convocation to the representation of the conduct of the proctors…with respect to the two explanatory statutes proposed by the vice-chancellor.' ESTC T220246. Wellcome Collection.

13. Sutherland, L.S., (1986). 'The Laudian Statutes in the Eighteenth Century' in L.S. Sutherland, and L.G. Mitchell (eds.), *The History of the University of Oxford, Volume V: The Eighteenth Century.* Oxford: Oxford University Press, pp.201–2.

14. Sutherland, L.S., (1986). 'The Laudian Statutes in the Eighteenth Century' in L.S. Sutherland, and L.G. Mitchell (eds.), *The History of the University of Oxford, Volume V: The Eighteenth Century*. Oxford: Oxford University Press, p.201.

15. St John's College, Register 1730–1794, 30 November 1759. ADM 1.A.7, p.336. St John's College, Oxford.

16. St John's College, Register 1730–1794, 22 October 1761. ADM 1.A.7, p.351. St John's College, Oxford.

17. Archdeaconry of Winchester, Induction Mandate, November 1761. 21M65/E2/844/1. Hampshire Record Office.

18. Archdeaconry of Winchester, Induction Mandate, 11 November 1761. 35M48/6/687. Hampshire Record Office.

19. St John's College, testimonial for the post at Steventon. 21M65/E2/844/2. Hampshire Record Office.

20. The Skinners' Company, minutes of the court for leases, 12 June 1744, court book no. 9, 1733–1748. CLC/L/SE/B/001/MS30708/009, pp.463–4. Guildhall Library, London.

21. Costin, W.C., (1958). *The History of St. John's College Oxford 1598–1860*. Oxford: Oxford University Press. p.177.

22. Costin, W.C., (1958). *The History of St. John's College Oxford 1598–1860*. Oxford: Oxford University Press. p.191.

23. Costin, W.C., (1958). *The History of St. John's College Oxford 1598–1860*. Oxford: Oxford University Press. p.175.

24. Costin, W.C., (1958). *The History of St. John's College Oxford 1598–1860*. Oxford: Oxford University Press. p.210.

25. Austen, J., (1813). *Pride and Prejudice*. A view on Mr Collins' want of education (Chapter XV) and a distinction regarding a certain quality of education made by Mr Darcy (Chapter XXXV).

26. Doolittle, I.G., (1986). 'College Administration' in L.S. Sutherland, and L.G. Mitchell (eds.), *The History of the University of Oxford, Volume V: The Eighteenth Century*. Oxford: Oxford University Press, p.254.

27. St John's College, Computus Annuus for 1757–8 which records the cautions. ACC I.A.111, p.60. St John's College, Oxford.

28. Looser, D., 'Breaking the Silence: The Austen Family's Complex Entanglements with Slavery,' *Times Literary Supplement*, 21 May 2021, pp. 2–3. https://www.the-tls.co.uk/articles/jane-austen-family-slavery-essay-devoney-looser/

29. Oliver, Vere Langford., (1896). *The History of the Island of Antigua*. Volume II. London: Mitchell and Hughes; repr. London: Forgotten Books, 2015, p.296.

30. https://www.ucl.ac.uk/lbs/estates/ Centre for the Study of the Legacies of British Slavery, UCL.

31. https://www.ucl.ac.uk/lbs/person/view/2146639657 and https://www.ucl.ac.uk/lbs/estates/ Centre for the Study of the Legacies of British Slavery, UCL.

32. https://www.ucl.ac.uk/lbs/claim/view/1109 and https://www.ucl.ac.uk/lbs/estates/ Centre for the Study of the Legacies of British Slavery, UCL.

33. White, G.D.V., (2006). *Jane Austen In The Context Of Abolition*. Basingstoke: Palgrave, Macmillan. Preface p.IX.

34. Austen, J., (1816). *Emma*. Volume II, Chapter XVII.

35. https://www.ucl.ac.uk/lbs/person/view/2146639585 Centre for the Study of the Legacies of British Slavery, UCL.

36. Austen, J., (1814). *Mansfield Park*. Volume II, Chapter III.

37. Austen, J., (1814). *Mansfield Park.* Volume III, Chapter I.
38. https://www.ucl.ac.uk Centre for the Study of the Legacies of British Slavery, UCL.
39. Letter 33. Jane Austen to Cassandra, Steventon, (25 January 1801) in Le Faye, D., (2011). *Jane Austen's Letters.* Fourth Edition. Oxford: Oxford University Press, p.81.
40. https://www.ucl.ac.uk Centre for the Study of the Legacies of British Slavery, UCL.
41. https://www.ucl.ac.uk Centre for the Study of the Legacies of British Slavery, UCL.
42. Austen, J., (1818). *Persuasion.* Volume II, Chapter XII.
43. Le Faye, D., (2004). *Jane Austen: A Family Record.* Second Edition. Cambridge: Cambridge University Press. p.11.

Chapter Five: Our Steventon Home
1. Ward, W. R., (ed.), (1995). *Parson and Parish in Eighteenth Century Hampshire: Replies to Bishop's Visitations,* entry 396, Steventon. Hampshire Record Series Vol XIII. Winchester: Hampshire County Council. p.127.
2. Morrin, J., (2016). *The Victoria History of Hampshire: Steventon.* London: University of London and Victoria County History. p.21.
3. Morrin, J., (2016). *The Victoria History of Hampshire: Steventon.* London: University of London and Victoria County History. p.78.
4. Steventon Parish Register. CMB 1737–1812. 71M82 PR2. Hampshire Record Office.
5. Letter from Edward Randalls to Thomas Knight, Chawton, (26 Feb 1764). 18M61/Box/C/16. Hampshire Record Office.
6. Morrin, J., (2016). *The Victoria History of Hampshire: Steventon.* London: University of London and Victoria County History. p.90.
7. Austen, J., (1811). *Sense and Sensibility.* Volume III, Chapter II.
8. Austen, J., (1813). *Pride and Prejudice.* Chapter XXX.
9. Austen, J., (1811). *Sense and Sensibility.* Volume III, Chapter III.
10. Austen. J., (1813). *Pride and Prejudice.* Chapter XVI.
11. Austen, J., (1811). *Sense and Sensibility.* Volume III, Chapter V.
12. Austen, J., (1814). *Mansfield Park.* Volume I, Chapter III.
13. Austen, J., (1813). *Pride and Prejudice.* Chapter XV.
14. Austen, J., (1814). *Mansfield Park.* Volume I, Chapter XI.
15. Austen-Leigh, J.E., (reissued 2008). *A Memoir of Jane Austen and Other Family Recollections,* ed. Sutherland, K. Oxford: Oxford University Press. p.13.
16. Letter from JEAL to Anna Lefroy, Steventon, (8 July 1869). Appendix in Austen-Leigh, J.E., (reissued 2008). *A Memoir of Jane Austen and Other Family Recollections,* ed. Sutherland, K. Oxford: Oxford University Press. p.189.
17. Austen, J., (1811). *Sense and Sensibility.* Volume III, Chapter XIV; Austen, J., (1818). *Northanger Abbey.* Volume II, Chapter XI.
18. Letter 150(C). Jane Austen to Alethea Bigg, Chawton, (24 Jan 1817) in Le Faye, D., (2011). *Jane Austen's Letters.* Fourth Edition. Oxford: Oxford University Press, p.341.
19. Austen, J., (1811). *Sense and Sensibility.* Volume III, Chapter V.
20. Austen, J., (1811). *Sense and Sensibility.* Volume I, Chapter XIX.
21. Austen, J., (1818). *Persuasion.* Volume I, Chapter IX.
22. Austen, J., (1814). *Mansfield Park.* Volume I, Chapter III.
23. Austen, J., (1814). *Mansfield Park.* Volume I, Chapter VIII.
24. Austen Leigh, R.A., (1942). *Austen Papers 1704–1856.* Privately published, London, p.43–4.
25. Austen Leigh, R.A., (1942). *Austen Papers 1704–1856.* Privately published, London, p.43–4.

26. George Austen's Hoare's Bank Account, customer ledgers L7, folio 302; 11, folio 293; and 16, folio 419. C. Hoare & Co. Archive.

27. Austen, J., (1818). *Northanger Abbey*. Volume II, Chapter XI.

28. Austen, J., (1816). *Emma*. Volume I, Chapter X. Regarding the Steventon Parsonage: Morrin, J., (2016). *The Victoria History of Hampshire: Steventon*. London: University of London and Victoria County History. p.80.

29. Hubback manuscript in Le Faye, D., (2004). *Jane Austen: A Family Record*. Second Edition. Cambridge: Cambridge University Press. p.20.

30. Austen-Leigh, J.E., (reissued 2008). *A Memoir of Jane Austen and Other Family Recollections*, ed. Sutherland, K. Oxford: Oxford University Press. p.23.

31. Ring, J., account books, 1785–1792. 8M62/14, pp.192–269. Hampshire Record Office.

32. *Dictionary of English Furniture Makers, 1660–1840*. British History Online (accessed via bifmo.history.ac.uk).

33. Ring, J., account books, 1785–1792. 8M62/14, p.269. Hampshire Record Office.

34. Ring, J., account books, 1792–1800, entry 7 Nov 1792. 8M62/15. Hampshire Record Office.

35. Ring, J., account books, 1785–1792 (8M62/14) and 1792–1800 (8M62/15). Hampshire Record Office.

36. Letter 23. Jane Austen to Cassandra, Steventon, (25–27 October 1800) in Le Faye, D., (2011). *Jane Austen's Letters*. Fourth Edition. Oxford: Oxford University Press, p.52.

37. Letter 25. Jane Austen to Cassandra, Steventon, (8 November 1800) in Le Faye, D., (2011). *Jane Austen's Letters*. Fourth Edition. Oxford: Oxford University Press, p.57.

38. Austen, J., (1816). *Emma*. Volume III, Chapter V.

39. Austen, J., (1803/4). *The Watsons*.

40. Ring, J., account books, 1792–1800. 8M62/15, Folio 103. Hampshire Record Office.

41. Lefroy, A., (reprinted 1977). 'Anna Lefroy's description of Steventon Rectory in the Rev. George Austen's time.' *Collected reports of the Jane Austen Society 1966–1975*. Folkestone: Wm Dawson and Sons Ltd for The Jane Austen Society. pp.245–248.

42. Austen, J., (1814). *Mansfield Park*. Volume I, Chapter XVI.

43. Letter 13. Jane Austen to Cassandra, Steventon, (1–2 December 1798) in Le Faye, D., (2011). *Jane Austen's Letters*. Fourth Edition. Oxford: Oxford University Press, p.25.

44. Austen, J., (1816). *Emma*. Volume III, Chapter IV.

45. Lefroy, A., (reprinted 1977). 'Anna Lefroy's description of Steventon Rectory in the Rev. George Austen's time.' *Collected reports of the Jane Austen Society 1966–1975*. Folkestone: Wm Dawson and Sons Ltd for The Jane Austen Society. p.245.

46. Austen, J., (1818). *Persuasion*. Volume I, Chapter V.

47. Lefroy, A., (reprinted 1977). 'Anna Lefroy's description of Steventon Rectory in the Rev. George Austen's time.' *Collected reports of the Jane Austen Society 1966–1975*. Folkestone: Wm Dawson and Sons Ltd for The Jane Austen Society. p.246.

48. Austen, J., (1817). *Sanditon*. Chapter IV.

49. Austen, J., (1816). *Emma*. Volume III, Chapter VI.

50. Austen, J., (1818). *Northanger Abbey*. Volume I, Chapter I.

51. Letter 23. Jane Austen to Cassandra, Steventon, (25–27 October 1800) in Le Faye, D., (2011). *Jane Austen's Letters*. Fourth Edition. Oxford: Oxford University Press, p.53.

52. Austen, J., (c.1787–1793). '*Frederic and Elfrida*', in *Volume the First*.

53. Austen, J., (1816). *Emma*. Volume I, Chapter X.

54. Austen, J., (1814). *Mansfield Park*. Volume II, Chapter IV.

55. Letter 27. Jane Austen To Cassandra, Steventon, (20–21 November 1800) in Le Faye, D., (2011). *Jane Austen's Letters*. Fourth Edition. Oxford: Oxford University Press, p.65.

56. Lefroy, A., (reprinted 1977). 'Anna Lefroy's description of Steventon Rectory in the Rev. George Austen's time.' *Collected reports of the Jane Austen Society 1966–1975*. Folkestone: Wm Dawson and Sons Ltd for The Jane Austen Society. p.246; poem by Cassandra Austen Senior mentioned in Le Faye, D., (2004). *A Family Record*. Second Edition. Cambridge: Cambridge University Press, p.72.

Chapter Six: Community Cleric at Large
1. Letter from George Austen to his sister-in-law Susannah Walter, Bolton Street, (2 May 1770) in *Austen Papers 1704–1856*. Privately published, London, p.22.
2. Letter from George Austen to his sister-in-law Susannah Walter, Steventon, (8 July 1770) in *Austen Papers 1704–1856*. Privately published, London, p.24.
3. Letter from Tysoe Saul Hancock to his wife Philadelphia, India, (9 August 1773) in *Austen Papers 1704–1856*. Privately published, London, p.72.
4. Letter from George Austen to his sister-in-law Susannah Walter, Steventon, (17 December 1775) in Austen Leigh, R.A., (1942). *Austen Papers 1704–1856*. Privately published, London, p.32.
5. https://premium.weatherweb.net/weather-in-history-1750-to-1799.
6. Spence, J., (2001). *A Century of Wills from Jane Austen's Family 1705–1806*. Second Edition. Paddington, NSW Australia: Jane Austen Society of Australia, p.42.
7. Letter from Elizabeth Hancock to Philadelphia Walter, Paris, (16 May 1780) in Austen Leigh, R.A., (1942). *Austen Papers 1704–1856*. Privately published London, pp.1–19.
8. Letter from J. Woodman to Warren Hastings, London, (7 August 1781) in Austen Leigh, R.A., (1942). *Austen Papers 1704–1856*. Privately published, London, p.98.
9. Austen, J., (1814). *Mansfield Park*. Volume III, Chapter XVII.
10. Letters from Revds. Bradley, Morris and Stockwell, (18 March 1773). 21M65/ E2/224/2, 3, 4 and 5. Hampshire Record Office.
11. Induction Mandate to Deane Rectory, (1 April 1773). 35M48/6/796. Hampshire Record Office.
12. Austen, J., (1818). *Persuasion*. Volume I, Chapter III.
13. Steventon Parish Register. CMB 1737–1812. 71M82/PR3. Hampshire Record Office.
14. Austen, J., (c.1787–1793). *The Three Sisters* in *Volume the First*.
15. Austen, J., (c.1790–1793). *Catharine, or the Bower* in *Volume the Third*.
16. Selwyn, D., (2001). 'Some Sermons of Mr Austen' in *The Jane Austen Society Report for 2001*. Winchester: Sarsen Press for The Jane Austen Society, pp.35–36.
17. Austen-Leigh, E., (1937). *Jane Austen and Steventon*. London: Spottiswoode, Ballantyne and Co. Ltd., pp.2–3.
18. Tucker, G. H., (1983). *A Goodly Heritage, A History Of Jane Austen's Family*. Manchester: Carcanet New Press and Mid Northumberland Arts Group, p.30.
19. Austen, J., (1814). *Mansfield Park*. Volume I, Chapter IX.
20. Letter 150(C). Jane Austen to Alethea Bigg, Chawton, (24 Jan 1817) in Le Faye, D., (2011). *Jane Austen's Letters*. Fourth Edition. Oxford: Oxford University Press, p.342.
21. Letter 109. Jane Austen to Fanny Knight, Chawton, (18–20 November 1814) in Le Faye, D., (2011). *Jane Austen's Letters*. Fourth Edition. Oxford: Oxford University Press, p.292; also Letter 90. Jane Austen to Francis Austen, Godmersham Park, (25 September 1813), p.241.
22. Kenning, M. (Revd.), (2021). *Steventon. The Cradle of Jane Austen's Genius*. Steventon PCC. p.8.
23. Austen, J., (1814). *Mansfield Park*. Volume III, Chapter III.

24. Austen, J., (1803/4). *The Watsons.*
25. Austen, J., (1818). *Persuasion.* Volume I, Chapter III.
26. Austen, J., (1814). *Mansfield Park.* Volume I, Chapter IX.
27. Letter 60. Jane Austen to Cassandra, Castle Square, (24 October 1808) in Le Faye, D., (2011). *Jane Austen's Letters.* Fourth Edition. Oxford: Oxford University Press, p.157.
28. Austen, J., (1816). *Emma.* Volume II, Chapter III; Kenning, M. (Revd.) (2021). *Steventon. The Cradle of Jane Austen's Genius.* Steventon PCC. p.8.
29. Austen, J., (1814). *Mansfield Park.* Volume III, Chapter III.
30. Austen, J., (1814). *Mansfield Park.* Volume II, Chapter VII.
31. Letter 90. Jane Austen to Francis, Godmersham Park, (25 September 1813) in Le Faye, D., (2011). *Jane Austen's Letters.* Fourth Edition. Oxford: Oxford University Press, p.241.
32. Austen, H., (1818). 'Biographical Notice Of The Author' in Austen-Leigh, J.E., (reissued 2008). *A Memoir of Jane Austen and Other Family Recollections,* ed. Sutherland, K. Oxford: Oxford University Press, p.137.
33. Austen, J., (1814). *Mansfield Park.* Volume I, Chapter IX and Volume III, Chapter IX.
34. Austen, J., (1816). *Plan of a Novel* in Austen-Leigh, J.E., (reissued 2008). *A Memoir of Jane Austen and Other Family Recollections,* ed. Sutherland, K. Oxford: Oxford University Press, pp.97–99.
35. Austen, J., (1816). *Plan of a Novel* in Austen-Leigh, J.E., (reissued 2008). *A Memoir of Jane Austen and Other Family Recollections,* ed. Sutherland, K. Oxford: Oxford University Press, p.14.
36. Osborn, H., (2021). *Our Village Ancestors.* Marlborough: Robert Hale, p.64.
37. Austen, J., (1816). *Emma.* Volume I, Chapter XII.
38. Austen, J., (1816). *Emma.* Volume III, Chapter XVI.
39. Le Faye, D., (2007). *Jane Austen's Steventon.* Chawton: The Jane Austen Society, p.42
40. Ward, W.R. (ed.), (1995). *Parson and Parish in Eighteenth-century Hampshire: Replies to Bishop's Visitations,* entry 396, Steventon. Hampshire Record Series Vol XIII. Winchester: Hampshire County Council, p222.

Chapter Seven: Farmer Austen

1. Austen-Leigh, J.E., (reissued 2008). *A Memoir of Jane Austen and Other Family Recollections,* ed. Sutherland, K. Oxford: Oxford University Press, p.15.
2. Austen. J., (1813). *Pride and Prejudice.* Chapter XVIII.
3. Austen. J., (1813). *Pride and Prejudice.* Chapter XV.
4. Austen, J., (1814). *Mansfield Park.* Volume I, Chapter IX.
5. Lefroy manuscript in Le Faye, D., (2004). *Jane Austen: A Family Record.* Second Edition. Cambridge: Cambridge University Press, p.17.
6. As documented at the Court Baron of Thomas Knight Esquire, Stevington Manor, 28 December 1767. 18M61/Box/C/16. Hampshire Record Office.
7. Austen, J., (1814). *Mansfield Park.* Volume I, Chapter IX.
8. Austen, J., (1814). *Mansfield Park.* Volume II, Chapter VII.
9. Austen, J., (1814). *Mansfield Park.* Volume II, Chapter VII.
10. Clark, R., and Dutton, G., (2005). *Farmer George, or Jane Austen and Sheep. An essay in Literary Biography.* 75A18/C4. Hampshire Record Office.
11. Austen, J., (1811). *Sense and Sensibility.* Volume I, Chapter XI.
12. Austen. J., (1813). *Pride and Prejudice.* Chapter VII.
13. Austen, J., (1814). *Mansfield Park.* Volume I, Chapter VI.

14. Austen, J., (1814). *Mansfield Park*. Volume I, Chapter VIII.

15. Brabourne, Lord E., (1884). *Letters of Jane Austen, edited with an Introduction and Critical Remarks by Edward Lord Brabourne*. Volume I. London: Richard Bentley & Son, p.151.

16. Austen, J., (1816). *Emma*. Volume I, Chapter IV.

17. Austen, J., (1816). *Emma*. Volume I, Chapter IV.

18. Austen, J., (1816). *Emma*. Volume II, Chapter XII.

19. Austen, J., (1816). *Emma*. Volume I, Chapter IV.

20. Austen, J., (1816). *Emma*. Volume I, Chapter IV.

21. Austen, J., (c.1790–1793). *Volume the Second*.

22. Austen, J., (1816). *Emma*. Volume I, Chapter XII.

23. Austen, J., (1816). *Emma*. Volume III, Chapter XVIII.

24. Letter 11. Jane Austen to Cassandra, Steventon, (17–18 November 1798); Letter 12. Jane Austen to Cassandra, Steventon, (25 November 1798); Letter 13. Jane Austen to Cassandra at Godmersham, Steventon, (1–2 December 1798) in Le Faye, D., (2011). *Jane Austen's Letters*. Fourth Edition. Oxford: Oxford University Press, pp.20, 23 and 25.

25. Letter 18. Jane Austen to Cassandra, Steventon, (21–23 January 1799) in Le Faye, D., (2011). *Jane Austen's Letters*. Fourth Edition. Oxford: Oxford University Press, p.40.

26. Letter 18. Jane Austen to Cassandra, Steventon, (21–23 January 1799) in Le Faye, D., (2011). *Jane Austen's Letters*. Fourth Edition. Oxford: Oxford University Press, p.40.

27. Letter 13. Jane Austen to Cassandra, Steventon, (1–2 December 1798) in Le Faye, D., (2011). *Jane Austen's Letters*. Fourth Edition. Oxford: Oxford University Press, p.26.

28. Letter from Cassandra Austen Senior to Susannah Walter, Steventon, (20 August 1775). 28All/B9. Hampshire Record Office.

29. Historical evidence of these fodder crops locally in Morrin, J., (2016). *The Victoria History of Hampshire: Steventon*. London: University of London and Victoria County History. pp.40, 41 and 44.

30. Letter from Cassandra Austen presumed to Susannah Austen, Steventon. 28All/B3 part. Hampshire Record Office.

31. Letter 13. Jane Austen to Cassandra, Steventon, (1–2 December 1798) in Le Faye, D., (2011). *Jane Austen's Letters*. Fourth Edition. Oxford: Oxford University Press, p.25.

32. Austen, J., (1814). *Mansfield Park*. Volume I, Chapter X.

33. Austen, J., (1814). *Mansfield Park*. Volume II, Chapter VII.

34. Austen, J., (1814). *Mansfield Park*. Volume II, Chapter VII.

35. Austen, J., (1814). *Mansfield Park*. Volume II, Chapter VII.

36. Austen, J., (1814). *Mansfield Park*. Volume II, Chapter VII.

37. Austen, J., (1816). *Emma*. Volume I, Chapter IV.

Chapter Eight: Schoolmaster Austen

1. George Austen's Hoare's bank account, customer ledger: 86, folio 91. C. Hoare & Co. Archive; Winchester Diocese, 'Presentation deed, Deane rectory', 23 March/1 April 1773. 21M65/E2/224. Hampshire Record Office.

2. Austen, J., (1816). *Emma*. Volume III, Chapter XVII.

3. Austen, J., (1816). *Emma*. Volume III, Chapter XVI.

4. Letters from Cassandra Austen Senior to Susannah Walter, Steventon, (6 June 1773) and (20 August 1775) in Austen Leigh, R.A., (1942). *Austen Papers 1704–1856*. Privately published, London, pp. 29 and 30–32.

5. Letters from Cassandra Austen Senior to Susannah Walter, Steventon, (12 Dec 1773 and 20 Aug 1775) in Austen Leigh, R.A., (1942). *Austen Papers 1704–1856*. Privately published, London, pp.30–32.
6. Austen, J., (1817). *Sanditon*. Chapter VI; Austen, J., (1816). *Emma*. Volume II, Chapter VIII.
7. Austen, J., (1818). *Northanger Abbey*. Volume I, Chapter. I.
8. Austen, J., (1811). *Sense and Sensibility*. Volume II, Chapter XIV.
9. Austen, J., (1811). *Sense and Sensibility*. Volume I, Chapter III.
10. Austen, J., (1811). *Sense and Sensibility*. Volume I, Chapter XXII.
11. Austen, J., (1811). *Sense and Sensibility*. Volume II, Chapter IX.
12. Austen, J., (1811). *Sense and Sensibility*. Volume III, Chapter X.
13. Austen. J., (1813). *Pride and Prejudice*. Chapter VIII.
14. Austen. J., (1813). *Pride and Prejudice*. Chapter XI.
15. Austen. J., (1814). *Mansfield Park*. Volume II, Chapter IX.
16. Austen. J., (1813). *Pride and Prejudice*. Chapter XV.
17. Austen, J., (1816). *Emma*. Volume I, Chapter IV.
18. Austen. J., (1813). *Pride and Prejudice*. Chapter XXIX; Austen, J., (1818). *Northanger Abbey*. Volume I, Chapter. I.
19. Austen. J., (1813). *Pride and Prejudice*. Chapter XXIX.
20. Austen, J., (1816). *Emma*. Volume II, Chapter II.
21. Austen, J., (1818). *Northanger Abbey*. Volume I, Chapter I.
22. Austen, J., (1818). *Northanger Abbey*. Volume I, Chapter I.
23. Austen, J., (1818). *Northanger Abbey*. Volume I, Chapter XIV.
24. Austen, J., (1803/4). Emma and her sister discuss this in *The Watsons*.
25. Austen, F.W., Memoir. Unpublished. Sotheby's Sale, 11 July 1996. Lot 133, extract as described by them. Part of the Le Faye, Deirdre collection at Chawton House Library, Chawton. With permission of the family.
26. George Austen's Hoare's bank account, customer ledger 16, folio 419. C. Hoare & Co. Archive.
27. Rowse, Dr A.L., (1975, reprinted 1977). 'The England of Jane Austen' pp. 251–265 in *Collected Reports of the Jane Austen Society 1966–1975*. Folkestone: Wm Dawson and Sons Ltd for The Jane Austen Society, p.257.
28. Lefroy, A., in her original memories of JA in Le Faye, D., (2004). *Jane Austen: A Family Record*. Second Edition. Cambridge: Cambridge University Press. p.46.
29. Austen-Leigh, J.E., (reissued 2008). *A Memoir of Jane Austen and Other Family Recollections*, ed. Sutherland, K. Oxford: Oxford University Press, p.18.
30. Austen, J., (1816). *Emma*. Volume III, Chapter XVII.
31. George Austen's Hoare's bank account, customer ledger 23, folio 117. C. Hoare & Co. Archive.
32. Austen, J., (1814). *Mansfield Park*. Volume III, Chapter I.
33. Austen, J., (1816). *Emma*. Volume I, Chapter III.
34. Austen, J., (1814). *Mansfield Park*. Volume I, Chapter I.
35. Austen, J., (1818). *Northanger Abbey*. Volume I, Chapter IX.
36. Austen, J., (1816). *Emma*. Volume III, Chapter VII.
37. Vick, R., (1993). Notes the items mentioned in the list of items auctioned in 'The Sale at Steventon Parsonage' in *The Jane Austen Society Report for 1993*. Winchester: Sarsen Press for the Jane Austen Society, p.14.

38. Austen, F. W., Course of Mathematics at Naval Academy Portsmouth, 1786–1788. AUS/14. National Maritime Museum Greenwich, London.

39. Vick, R., (1993). Notes the items mentioned in the list of items auctioned in 'The Sale at Steventon Parsonage' in *The Jane Austen Society Report for 1993*. Winchester: Sarsen Press for the Jane Austen Society, p.14; Letter 42. Jane Austen to Francis Austen, Green Park Buildings, Bath, (29 January 1805) in Le Faye, D., (2011). *Jane Austen's Letters*. Fourth Edition. Oxford: Oxford University Press, p.102.

40. George Austen's Hoare's bank account, customer ledger 98, folio 109. C. Hoare & Co. Archive.

Chapter Nine: The Library

1. Austen. J., (1813). *Pride and Prejudice*. Chapter III.

2. Austen, J., (1816). *Emma*. Volume III, Chapter VI.

3. Spence, J., Ed. (2005). Jane Austen's Brother Abroad: *The Grand Tour Journals Of Edward Austen*. Paddington, NSW: Jane Austen Society of Australia Press.

4. The Eighteenth-Century Short Title Catalogue as referenced in Bolton, C., (1994). Revised Edition. *A Winchester Bookshop and Bindery 1729–1994*. Winchester: P&G Wells, p.14.

5. Bolton, C., (1994). Revised Edition. *A Winchester Bookshop and Bindery 1729–1994*. Winchester: P&G Wells, p.14.

6. Bolton, C., (1994). Revised Edition. *A Winchester Bookshop and Bindery 1729–1994*. Winchester: P&G Wells, pp.11–12.

7. Vick, R., (1993). Notes the items mentioned in the list of items auctioned in 'The Sale at Steventon Parsonage', pp.13–16, *The Jane Austen Society Report for 1993*. Winchester: Sarsen Press for the Jane Austen Society, p.14.

8. Letter 10. Jane Austen to Cassandra, Steventon, (27–28 October 1798) in Le Faye, D., (2011). *Jane Austen's Letters*. Fourth Edition. Oxford: Oxford University Press, p.17.

9. Austen, J., (1814). *Mansfield Park*. Volume I, Chapter IX.

10. Ring, J., account books, 1792–1800. 8M62/15. Folio 102 and 103. Hampshire Record Office.

11. George Austen's Hoare's bank account, customer ledger 61, folio 287. C. Hoare & Co. Archive; Letter 32. Jane Austen to Cassandra, Steventon, (21–22 January 1801) in Le Faye, D., (2011). *Jane Austen's Letters*. Fourth Edition. Oxford: Oxford University Press, p.79.

12. Austen, J., (c.1790–1793). *Love and Freindship* in *Volume the Second*.

13. Austen, J., (1814). *Mansfield Park*. Volume I, Chapter II.

14. Austen, J., (1818). *Northanger Abbey*. Volume II, Chapter VIII; Austen. J., (1813). *Pride and Prejudice*. Chapter XXIX.

15. Austen, J., (1814). *Mansfield Park*. Volume I, Chapter XVI and Volume III, Chapter IX.

16. Letter 14. Jane Austen to Cassandra, Steventon, (18–19 December 1798) in Le Faye, D., (2011). *Jane Austen's Letters*. Fourth Edition. Oxford: Oxford University Press, p.28.

17. Letter 22. Jane Austen to Cassandra, Queen's Square, (19 June 1799) in Le Faye, D., (2011). *Jane Austen's Letters*. Fourth Edition. Oxford: Oxford University Press, pp.50–1.

18. Austen. J., (1813). *Pride and Prejudice*. Chapter XII.

19. Austen, J., (c.1790–1793). *Love and Freindship* in *Volume the Second*.

20. Letter 12. Jane Austen to Cassandra, Steventon, (25 November 1798) in Le Faye, D., (2011). *Jane Austen's Letters*. Fourth Edition. Oxford: Oxford University Press, p.23.

21. Letter 12. Jane Austen to Cassandra, Steventon, (25 November 1798) and Letter 14 to the same, Steventon, (18–19 December 1798) in Le Faye, D., (2011). *Jane Austen's*

Letters. Fourth Edition. Oxford: Oxford University Press, pp.23 and 28; Austen, H., (1818). 'Biographical Notice Of The Author' in Austen-Leigh, J.E., (reissued 2008). *A Memoir of Jane Austen and Other Family Recollections*, ed. Sutherland, K. Oxford: Oxford University Press, p.141.

22. Austen, J., (1814). *Mansfield Park.* Volume III, Chapter XIV.
23. Letter 25. Jane Austen to Cassandra, Steventon, (8–9 November 1800) in Le Faye, D., (2011). *Jane Austen's Letters.* Fourth Edition. Oxford: Oxford University Press, p.57.
24. Letter 14. Jane Austen to Cassandra, Steventon, (18–19 December 1798) in Le Faye, D., (2011). *Jane Austen's Letters.* Fourth Edition. Oxford: Oxford University Press, p.27.
25. Lathom, F., (1798). *The Midnight Bell.*
26. Austen, J., (1818). *Northanger Abbey.* Volume I, Chapter. XIV.
27. Austen, J., (1818). *Northanger Abbey.* Volume I, Chapter VII.
28. Austen, J., (1817). *Sanditon.* Chapters VII and VIII.
29. Letter 4. Jane Austen to Cassandra, Rowling, (1 Sep 1796) in Le Faye, D., (2011). *Jane Austen's Letters.* Fourth Edition. Oxford: Oxford University Press, p.6.
30. Letter 54. Jane Austen to Cassandra, Godmersham, (26 June 1808) in Le Faye, D., (2011). *Jane Austen's Letters.* Fourth Edition. Oxford: Oxford University Press, p.138.
31. Austen, J., (1816). *Emma.* Volume I, Chapter IV.
32. Austen, J., (1816). *Emma.* Volume I, Chapter IX.
33. Lefroy, A., in her original memories of JA in Le Faye, D., (2004). *Jane Austen: A Family Record.* Second Edition. Cambridge: Cambridge University Press. p.21.
34. Austen, J., (1814). *Mansfield Park.* Volume I, Chapter XIII.
35. Austen, J., (1814). *Mansfield Park.* Volume II, Chapter I.
36. Austen. J., (1813). *Pride and Prejudice.* Chapter VIII.
37. Austen, J., (1813). *Pride and Prejudice.* Chapter XI.
38. Austen, J., (1817). *Sanditon.* Chapter VIII.
39. Austen, J., (1816). *Emma.* Volume I, Chapter V.
40. Austen, J., (1816). *Emma.* Volume I, Chapter IX.
41. Austen, J., (c.1790–1793). *Catharine, or the Bower* in *Volume the Third.*
42. Austen, H., (1818). 'Biographical Notice Of The Author' in Austen-Leigh, J.E., (reissued 2008). *A Memoir of Jane Austen and Other Family Recollections*, ed. Sutherland, K. Oxford: Oxford University Press, p.141.
43. Austen, J., (1818). *Persuasion.* Volume I, Chapter X.
44. Austen, C., (1867). 'My Aunt Jane Austen: A Memoir' in Austen-Leigh, J.E., (reissued 2008). *A Memoir of Jane Austen and Other Family Recollections*, ed. Sutherland, K. Oxford: Oxford University Press, p.141.

Chapter Ten: George's Barn

1. As documented at the Court Baron of Thomas Knight Esquire, Stevington Manor, 28 December 1767. 18M61/Box/C/16. Hampshire Record Office.
2. Austen Leigh, R.A., (1942). *Austen Papers 1704–1856.* Privately published, London, p. XI.
3. Austen, J., (1814). *Mansfield Park.* Volume I, Chapter XIV.
4. Letter from Philadelphia Walter to James Walter, Seale, Kent, (19 September 1787) in Austen Leigh, R.A., (1942). *Austen Papers 1704–1856.* Privately published, London, p.126.
5. Austen, J., (1814). *Mansfield Park.* Volume I, Chapter XIII and XIV.

6. Le Faye, D., (2004). *Jane Austen: A Family Record.* Second Edition. Cambridge: Cambridge University Press. p.46.
7. Letter from Elizabeth De Feuillide to Philadelphia Walter, Orchard Street, (16 November 1787) in Austen Leigh, R.A., (1942). *Austen Papers 1704–1856.* Privately published, London, p.127.
8. Austen, J., (c.1787–1793). *The Generous Curate a moral Tale, setting forth the Advantages of being Generous and a Curate* in *Volume the First.*
9. Lefroy manuscript in Le Faye, D., (2004). *Jane Austen: A Family Record.* Second Edition. Cambridge: Cambridge University Press. p.43.
10. Austen Leigh, R.A., (1942). *Austen Papers 1704–1856.* Privately published, London, p.221.
11. Letter 77. Jane Austen to Martha Lloyd, Chawton, (29–30 November 1812) in Le Faye, D., (2011). *Jane Austen's Letters.* Fourth Edition. Oxford: Oxford University Press, p.205.
12. Austen, J., (1816). *Emma.* Volume II, Chapter II.
13. Austen, J., (1816). *Emma.* Volume III, Chapter XIX.
14. Austen, J., (1814). *Mansfield Park.* Volume I, Chapter II.
15. Austen, J., (1816). *Emma.* Volume I, Chapter II.
16. Austen, J., (1816). *Emma.* Volume II, Chapter XVIII.
17. Austen, J., (1816). *Emma.* Volume III, Chapter XIV.
18. Austen-Leigh, J.E., (reissued 2008). *A Memoir of Jane Austen and Other Family Recollections,* ed. Sutherland, K. Oxford: Oxford University Press, p.36.
19. Martin, Sir H., letter of recommendation, 18 December 1788, Portsmouth Dock Yard, inside 'Course of Mathematics at Naval Academy Portsmouth, 1786–1788'. AUS/14. National Maritime Museum Greenwich, London.
20. Austen, G., (1788), *Memorandums for the use of MR F W Austen on his going to the East Indies Midshipman on board His Majesty's ship Perseverance. Cap: Smith Dec 1788.* Unpublished. With permission of the family.
21. Southam, B.C., (1981). *Jane Austen's 'Sir Charles Grandison'.* Oxford: Oxford University Press, p.16.
22. Southam, B.C., (1981). *Jane Austen's 'Sir Charles Grandison'.* Oxford: Oxford University Press, pp.13 and 22.

Chapter Eleven: Jane's Effusions

1. Letter 79. Jane Austen to Cassandra, Chawton, (29 January 1813) in Le Faye, D., (2011). *Jane Austen's Letters.* Fourth Edition. Oxford: Oxford University Press, p.210.
2. George Austen's Hoare's bank account, customer ledger 47, folio 347. C. Hoare & Co. Archive.
3. Ring, J., account books, 1792–1800. 8M62/15, folio 65. Hampshire Record Office.
4. See Southam, B.C., (1964). *Jane Austen's Literary Manuscripts.* Oxford: Oxford University Press. Chapter 3.
5. Letter, Rev G. Austen to Thomas Cadell, Steventon, (1 November 1797). MS 279 Letter 1. St John's College, Oxford.
6. Letter, Rev G. Austen to Warren Hastings Steventon, (8 Nov 1794) in Austen Leigh, R.A., (1942). *Austen Papers 1704–1856.* Privately published, London, p.226.
7. Lefroy manuscript in Le Faye, D., (2004). *Jane Austen: A Family Record.* Second Edition. Cambridge: Cambridge University Press. p.4.

8. Letter from Eliza de Feuillide to Philadelphia Walter, Steventon (26 October 1792) in Austen Leigh, R.A., (1942). *Austen Papers 1704–1856*. Privately published, London, pp.120–150.

9. Letter from Eliza de Feuillide to John Woodman, Manchester Street, (12 June 1797) in Austen Leigh, R.A., (1942). *Austen Papers 1704–1856*. Privately published, London, pp.160–1.

10. Letter 10. Jane Austen to Cassandra, Steventon, (27–28 October 1798) in Le Faye, D., (2011). *Jane Austen's Letters*. Fourth Edition. Oxford: Oxford University Press, p.18.

11. Letter 11. Jane Austen to Cassandra, Steventon, (17–18 November 1798) in Le Faye, D., (2011). *Jane Austen's Letters*. Fourth Edition. Oxford: Oxford University Press, p.19.

12. Austen, J., (1811). *Sense and Sensibility*. Volume III, Chapter XI.

13. Letter 132 (D). Jane Austen to James Stanier Clarke. (11 Dec 1815) in Le Faye, D., (2011). *Jane Austen's Letters*. Fourth Edition. Oxford: Oxford University Press, p.319.

14. Austen, J., (1813). *Pride and Prejudice*. Chapter XV.

15. Austen, J., (1814). *Mansfield Park*. Volume III, Chapter VI.

16. Austen, J., (1813). *Pride and Prejudice*. Chapter XVIII.

17. Austen, J., (1814). *Mansfield Park*. Volume III, Chapter IV.

18. Austen, J., (1814). *Mansfield Park*. Volume III, Chapter I.

19. Austen, J., (1813). *Pride and Prejudice*. Chapter XXVI.

20. Austen, J., (1816). *Emma*. Volume I, Chapter XI.

21. Austen, J., (1814). *Mansfield Park*. Volume III, Chapter VII.

22. Austen, J., (1814). *Mansfield Park*. Volume III, Chapter XIV.

23. Austen, J., (1818). *Northanger Abbey*. Volume II, Chapter V.

24. Austen, J., (1814). *Mansfield Park*. Volume III, Chapter I.

25. Austen, J., (1818). *Persuasion*. Volume I, Chapter I.

26. Austen, J., (1813). *Pride and Prejudice*. Chapter XXXVII.

27. Austen, J., (1814). *Mansfield Park*. Volume I, Chapter VII; Austen, H., (1818). 'Biographical Notice Of The Author' in Austen-Leigh, J.E., (reissued 2008). *A Memoir of Jane Austen and Other Family Recollections*, ed. Sutherland, K. Oxford: Oxford University Press, p.141.

28. Austen, J., (1814). *Mansfield Park*. Volume I, Chapter VII.

29. Austen, J., (1813). *Pride and Prejudice*. Chapter LVIII.

30. Austen, J., (1793–4). *Lady Susan, Letter Twenty-Four, Mrs Vernon to Lady De Courcy*.

31. Austen, J., (1813). *Pride and Prejudice*. Chapter XLVIII.

32. Austen, J., (1816). *Emma*. Volume I, Chapter I.

33. Austen, J., (1803/4). *The Watsons*.

34. Austen, J., (1816). *Emma*. Volume I, Chapter I.

35. Austen, J., (1803/4). *The Watsons*.

36. Letter 78. Jane Austen to Cassandra, Chawton, (24 January 1811) in Le Faye, D., (2011). *Jane Austen's Letters*. Fourth Edition. Oxford: Oxford University Press, p.206.

37. Austen, J., (1816). *Emma*. Volume III, Chapter XIX.

Chapter Twelve: A New Chapter

1. Austen, J., (1818). *Persuasion*. Volume II, Chapter X.

2. Austen, J., (c.1790–1793). *Love and Freindship, Letter The First* in *Volume the Second*.

3. Austen, J., (c.1790–1793). *A Letter From A Young Lady* in *Volume the Second*.

4. Austen, J., (c.1790–1793). *Lesley Castle, Letter the First* in *Volume the Second*.

5. Austen, J., (1813). *Pride and Prejudice*. Chapter XXIII.

6. Austen. J., (1813). *Pride and Prejudice.* Chapter XXVIII.
7. Letter from Mrs Cassandra Austen to Mary Lloyd, Steventon, (30 November 1796) in Austen Leigh, R.A., (1942). *Austen Papers 1704–1856.* Privately published, London, pp.220–254.
8. Austen. J., (1813). *Pride and Prejudice.* Chapter XLI.
9. Austen. J., (1813). *Pride and Prejudice.* Chapter XLII.
10. Austen. J., (1813). *Pride and Prejudice.* Chapter XLVIII and L.
11. Austen, F.W., Memoir. Unpublished. Sotheby's Sale, 11 July 1996. Lot 133, extract as described by them. Part of the Le Faye, Deirdre collection at Chawton House Library, Chawton. With permission of the family.
12. As confirmed in letter from Eliza de Feuillide to Philadelphia Walter, Margate, (7 January 1791) in Austen Leigh, R.A., (1942). *Austen Papers 1704–1856.* Privately published, London, p.139.
13. Letter Caroline Austen to JEAL, (1 April 1869) in Austen-Leigh, J.E., (reissued 2008). *A Memoir of Jane Austen and Other Family Recollections,* ed. Sutherland, K. Oxford: Oxford University Press, Appendix p.185.
14. Austen-Leigh, J.E., (reissued 2008). *A Memoir of Jane Austen and Other Family Recollections,* ed. Sutherland, K. Oxford: Oxford University Press, p.50.
15. Austen-Leigh, W., and R.A, (1913). *Jane Austen, Her Life and Letters: A Family Record.* London: Smith, Elder and Co. p.135.
16. Austen, J., (c.1790–1793). *Lesley Castle, Letter the third* in *Volume the Second.*
17. Austen, J., (1814). *Mansfield Park.* Volume I, Chapter XI.
18. Austen, J., (1818). *Persuasion.* Volume I, Chapter IX.
19. Letter 29. Jane Austen to Cassandra, Steventon, (3–5 January 1801) in Le Faye, D., (2011). *Jane Austen's Letters.* Fourth Edition. Oxford: Oxford University Press, p.71.
20. Vick, R., (1993). Named in 'The Sale at Steventon Parsonage' in *The Jane Austen Society Report for 1993* (Winchester: Sarsen Press for the Jane Austen Society), p.13.
21. Letter 30. Jane Austen to Cassandra, Steventon, (8–9 January 1801) in Le Faye, D., (2011). *Jane Austen's Letters.* Fourth Edition. Oxford: Oxford University Press, p.72.
22. Lefroy, A., (2007). *The Letters of Mrs Lefroy: Jane Austen's Beloved Friend,* ed. H. Lefroy and G. Turner. Letter 21, (17 March 1802). Winchester: Sarsen Press/the Jane Austen Society, p.61
23. Letter 29. Jane Austen to Cassandra, Steventon, (3–5 January 1801) in Le Faye, D., (2011). *Jane Austen's Letters.* Fourth Edition. Oxford: Oxford University Press, p.69.
24. Letter 31. Jane Austen To Cassandra, Steventon, (14–16 January 1801) in Le Faye, D., (2011). *Jane Austen's Letters.* Fourth Edition. Oxford: Oxford University Press, p.76.
25. George Austen's Hoare's bank account, customer ledgers 69, folio 200 and 74, folio 357. C. Hoare & Co. Archive.
26. Austen, J., (1816). *Emma.* Volume I, Chapter I.
27. Letter 29. Jane Austen to Cassandra, Steventon, (3–5 January 1801) and Letter 35 to the same, Paragon, Bath, (5–6 May 1801) in Le Faye, D., (2011). *Jane Austen's Letters.* Fourth Edition. Oxford: Oxford University Press, pp.69–70 and 86.
28. Letter 29. Jane Austen to Cassandra, Steventon, (3–5 January 1801) in Le Faye, D., (2011). *Jane Austen's Letters.* Fourth Edition. Oxford: Oxford University Press, pp.69–70.
29. Letter 31. Jane Austen to Cassandra, Steventon, (14–16 January 1801) in Le Faye, D., (2011). *Jane Austen's Letters.* Fourth Edition. Oxford: Oxford University Press, p.76.
30. Letter 33. Jane Austen to Cassandra, Steventon, (25 January 1801) in Le Faye, D., (2011). *Jane Austen's Letters.* Fourth Edition. Oxford: Oxford University Press, p.82.

31. Letter 25. Jane Austen to Cassandra, Steventon, (8–9 November 1800) and Letter 30. Jane Austen to Cassandra, Steventon, (8–9 January 1801) in Le Faye, D., (2011). *Jane Austen's Letters*. Fourth Edition. Oxford: Oxford University Press, pp.59 and 74.

32. Austen. J., (1813). *Pride and Prejudice*. Chapter XXXIX.

33. Austen, J., (1818). *Persuasion*. Volume I, Chapter III.

34. Letter 4. Jane Austen to Cassandra, Rowling (1 September 1796) in Le Faye, D., (2011). *Jane Austen's Letters*. Fourth Edition. Oxford: Oxford University Press, p.5.

35. Letter 6. Jane Austen to Cassandra, Rowling, (15–16 September 1796) in Le Faye, D., (2011). *Jane Austen's Letters*. Fourth Edition. Oxford: Oxford University Press, p.12.

36. Letter 9. Jane Austen to Cassandra, 'The Bull and George', Dartford, (24 October 1798) in Le Faye, D., (2011). *Jane Austen's Letters*. Fourth Edition. Oxford: Oxford University Press, p.15.

37. Vick, R., (1999). 'Mr Austen's Carriage,' pp.23–25 in *The Jane Austen Society Report for 1999*. Winchester: Sarsen Press for The Jane Austen Society, p.24.

38. Le Faye, D., (1999). 'Another Book Owned By Mr Austen,' in *The Jane Austen Society Report for 1999*. Winchester: Sarsen Press for The Jane Austen Society, pp.27–8.

39. Vick, R., (1999). 'Mr Austen's Carriage,' pp.23–25 in *The Jane Austen Society Report for 1999*. Winchester: Sarsen Press for The Jane Austen Society, p.24.

40. Austen, J., (1803/4). *The Watsons*.

41. Letter 11. Jane Austen to Cassandra, Steventon, (17–18 November 1798) in Le Faye, D., (2011). *Jane Austen's Letters*. Fourth Edition. Oxford: Oxford University Press, p.20.

42. Letter from Caroline Austen to JEAL, (Wed evg. 1869) in Austen-Leigh, J.E., (reissued 2008). *A Memoir of Jane Austen and Other Family Recollections*, ed. Sutherland, K. Oxford: Oxford University Press, Appendix, p.188.

43. Austen-Leigh, J.E., (reissued 2008). *A Memoir of Jane Austen and Other Family Recollections*, ed. Sutherland, K. Oxford: Oxford University Press, p.29.

44. Austen, J., (1814). *Mansfield Park*. Volume II, Chapter III.

45. Austen, J., (1814). *Mansfield Park*. Volume III, Chapter I.

46. Austen, J., (1814). *Mansfield Park*. Volume II, Chapter III.

47. Austen. J., (1813). *Pride and Prejudice*. Chapter XX.

48. Austen, J., (1818). *Northanger Abbey*. Volume II, Chapter XVI.

49. Austen, J., (1818). *Persuasion*. Volume I, Chapter II.

50. Austen, J., (1793–4). *Lady Susan, Letter Twelve, Sir Reginald De Courcy to His Son*.

51. Austen, J., (1818). *Persuasion*. Volume I, Chapter V.

52. Worsley, L., (2017). *Jane Austen at Home: A Biography*. London: Hodder and Stoughton. p.182.

53. As confirmed six years later in Letter 68(D). Jane Austen to B. Crosby & Co, Southampton, (5 April 1809) in Le Faye, D., (2011). *Jane Austen's Letters*. Fourth Edition. Oxford: Oxford University Press, p.182.

54. Letter 43. Jane Austen to Cassandra, Gay Street, (8–11 April 1805) p.106 and letter 39. From the same to the same, Lyme Regis, (14 September 1804) in Le Faye, D., (2011). *Jane Austen's Letters*. Fourth Edition. Oxford: Oxford University Press, p.96.

55. Letter 39. Jane Austen to Cassandra, Lyme Regis, (14 September 1804) in Le Faye, D., (2011). *Jane Austen's Letters*. Fourth Edition. Oxford: Oxford University Press, p.99.

56. Letter 39. Jane Austen to Cassandra, Lyme Regis, (14 September 1804) in Le Faye, D., (2011). *Jane Austen's Letters*. Fourth Edition. Oxford: Oxford University Press, p.97–9.

57. Lefroy manuscript in Le Faye, D., (2004). *Jane Austen: A Family Record*. Second Edition. Cambridge: Cambridge University Press, p.136.

58. Lefroy manuscript (1802) in Le Faye, D., (2004). Jane Austen: *A Family Record*. Second Edition. Cambridge: Cambridge University Press, p.136.

Chapter Thirteen: A New Reality
1. George Austen's Hoare's bank account, customer ledgers 74, folio 357 and 81, folio 217. C. Hoare & Co. Archive.
2. Austen-Leigh, J.E., (reissued 2008). *A Memoir of Jane Austen and Other Family Recollections*, ed. Sutherland, K. Oxford: Oxford University Press, Appendix p.59.
3. Letter 35. Jane Austen to Cassandra, Paragon, (5–6 May 1801) in Le Faye, D., (2011). *Jane Austen's Letters*. Fourth Edition. Oxford: Oxford University Press, p.86.
4. Worsley, L., (2017). *Jane Austen at Home: A Biography*. London: Hodder and Stoughton, p.193.
5. Letter 40. Jane Austen to Francis Austen, Green Park Bgs, Bath, (21 January 1805) in Le Faye, D., (2011). *Jane Austen's Letters*. Fourth Edition. Oxford: Oxford University Press, p.100.
6. Austen, J., (1811). *Sense and Sensibility*. Volume III, Chapter VII.
7. Letter 40. Jane Austen to Francis Austen, Green Park Bgs, Bath, (21 January 1805) in Le Faye, D., (2011). *Jane Austen's Letters*. Fourth Edition. Oxford: Oxford University Press, p.100.
8. Letter 41. Jane Austen to Francis Austen, Green Park Bgs, Bath, (22 January 1805) in Le Faye, D., (2011). *Jane Austen's Letters*. Fourth Edition. Oxford: Oxford University Press, p.102.
9. Letter from Henry Austen to Francis Austen, Bath, (27 January 1805) in Austen Leigh, R.A., (1942). *Austen Papers 1704–1856*. Privately published, London, p.232.
10. Letter from Henry Austen to Francis Austen, Bath, (27 January 1805) in Austen Leigh, R.A., (1942). *Austen Papers 1704–1856*. Privately published, London, p.234.
11. Letter from Henry Austen to Francis Austen, Bath, (27 January 1805) in Austen Leigh, R.A., (1942). *Austen Papers 1704–1856*. Privately published, London, p.233.
12. Austen, J., (1811). *Sense and Sensibility*. Volume I, Chapter II.
13. Letter from Henry Austen to Francis Austen, Bath, (28 January 1805) in Austen Leigh, R.A., (1942). *Austen Papers 1704–1856*. Privately published, London, p.234–5.
14. Letter 43. Jane Austen to Cassandra, Gay St, Bath, (8–11 April 1805) in Le Faye, D., (2011). *Jane Austen's Letters*. Fourth Edition. Oxford: Oxford University Press, p.104.
15. Letter from Mrs Cassandra Austen to Mary Austen, Trim St, Bath, (10 April 1806) in Austen Leigh, R.A., (1942). *Austen Papers 1704–1856*. Privately published, London, p.237.
16. George Austen's Hoare's bank account, customer ledger 93, folio 99. C. Hoare & Co. Archive.
17. Austen, J., (1816). *Emma*. Volume I, Chapter IV.
18. Lefroy (Austen), A., (1864). 'Recollections of Aunt Jane' in Austen-Leigh, J.E., (reissued 2008). *A Memoir of Jane Austen and Other Family Recollections*, ed. Sutherland, K. Oxford: Oxford University Press, Appendix, p.157.
19. Austen, J., (1818). *Northanger Abbey*. Volume I, Chapter IX.
20. Austen, J., (1818). *Persuasion*. Volume II, Chapter X.
21. Austen Weller, E., (1706/7). *Memorandums* in Austen Leigh, R.A., (1942). *Austen Papers 1704–1856*. Privately published, London, p.13.
22. Austen, J., (1818). *Northanger Abbey*. Volume I, Chapter XIV.
23. Austen, J., (1803/4). *The Watsons*.

24. Letter 49. Jane Austen to Cassandra, Southampton, (7–8 January 1807) in Le Faye, D., (2011). *Jane Austen's Letters*. Fourth Edition. Oxford: Oxford University Press, p.121.

Chapter Fourteen: A New Hope

1. Letter 68(D). Jane Austen to B. Crosby & Co, Southampton, (5 April 1809) in Le Faye, D., (2011). *Jane Austen's Letters*. Fourth Edition. Oxford: Oxford University Press, p.182.

2. Letter 68(A). R. Crosby, London, (8 April 1809) in Le Faye, D., (2011). *Jane Austen's Letters*. Fourth Edition. Oxford: Oxford University Press, p.182–3.

3. Austen-Leigh, J.E., (reissued 2008). *A Memoir of Jane Austen and Other Family Recollections*, ed. Sutherland, K. Oxford: Oxford University Press, Appendix p.24.

4. Austen, J., (1811). *Sense and Sensibility*. Volume I, Chapter XVI and Austen. J., (1813). *Pride and Prejudice*. Chapter VII.

5. Austen, J., (1816). *Emma*. Volume I, Chapter IX.

6. Austen, J., (1818). *Northanger Abbey*. Volume I, Chapter V.

7. Letter 71. Jane Austen to Cassandra, Sloane Street, (25 April 1811) in Le Faye, D., (2011). *Jane Austen's Letters*. Fourth Edition. Oxford: Oxford University Press, p.190.

8. Letter 79. Jane Austen to Cassandra, Chawton, (29 September 1813) in Le Faye, D., (2011). *Jane Austen's Letters*. Fourth Edition. Oxford: Oxford University Press, p.210.

9. Letter 77. Jane Austen to Martha Lloyd, Chawton, (29–30 November 1812) in Le Faye, D., (2011). *Jane Austen's Letters*. Fourth Edition. Oxford: Oxford University Press, p.205.

10. Letter 78. Jane Austen to Cassandra, Chawton, (24 January 1811) in Le Faye, D., (2011). *Jane Austen's Letters*. Fourth Edition. Oxford: Oxford University Press, p.207.

11. Letter 121. Jane Austen to Cassandra, Hans Place, London, (17–18 October 1815) in Le Faye, D., (2011). *Jane Austen's Letters*. Fourth Edition. Oxford: Oxford University Press, p.303.

12. Letter 130. Jane Austen to John Murray, Hans Place, London, (11 December 1815) in Le Faye, D., (2011). *Jane Austen's Letters*. Fourth Edition. Oxford: Oxford University Press, p.317.

13. Letter 128. Jane Austen to Cassandra, Hans Place, London, (26 November 1815) in Le Faye, D., (2011). *Jane Austen's Letters*. Fourth Edition. Oxford: Oxford University Press, p.313.

14. Letter 134(D). Jane Austen to the Countess of Morley, (31 December 1815) in Le Faye, D., (2011). *Jane Austen's Letters*. Fourth Edition. Oxford: Oxford University Press, p.322.

15. Austen Leigh, R.A., (1942). *Austen Papers 1704–1856*. Privately published, London, p.303.

16. Letter 78. Jane Austen to Cassandra, Chawton, (24 January 1811) in Le Faye, D., (2011). *Jane Austen's Letters*. Fourth Edition. Oxford: Oxford University Press, p.208.

17. Lefroy, F.C., Extract from 'Family History', in Austen-Leigh, J.E., (reissued 2008). *A Memoir of Jane Austen and Other Family Recollections*, ed. Sutherland, K. Oxford: Oxford University Press, Appendix p.197.

18. Letter 104. Jane Austen to Anna Austen, Chawton, (10–18 August 1814) and Letter 143 to Caroline Austen, Steventon, (15 July 1816) in Le Faye, D., (2011). *Jane Austen's Letters*. Fourth Edition. Oxford: Oxford University Press, pp.280 and 331.

19. Letter 115. Jane Austen to Caroline Austen, (6 December 1814) and Letter 143 from the same to the same, Chawton, (15 July 1816) in Le Faye, D., (2011). *Jane Austen's Letters*. Fourth Edition. Oxford: Oxford University Press, pp. 300 and 331.

20. Austen, C., (1867). 'My Aunt Jane Austen: A Memoir', in Austen-Leigh, J.E., (reissued 2008). *A Memoir of Jane Austen and Other Family Recollections*, ed. Sutherland, K. Oxford: Oxford University Press, p.174.

21. Austen, J., (1818). *Persuasion*. Volume I, Chapter XI.

22. Austen Leigh, R.A., (1942). *Austen Papers 1704–1856*. Privately published, London, p.334.

23. Letter 15. Jane Austen to Cassandra, Steventon, (24–26 December 1798) in Le Faye, D., (2011). *Jane Austen's Letters*. Fourth Edition. Oxford: Oxford University Press, p.30.

24. Hunter, P., (2008). *Through The Years; Tales From The Hoare's Bank Archive Volume Two*. London: C. Hoare & Co., p.38.

25. Austen, F.W., Letters. 23M93. Hampshire Record Office.

26. Austen, C. J., (1817). In Austen Family Papers (AUS/101-163.) Diary 01 Jan–16 Sep 1817 Manuscript (AUS/109). National Maritime Museum Greenwich, London (on loan from a private lender).

27. Austen, H., (1818). 'Biographical Notice Of The Author' in Austen-Leigh, J.E., (reissued 2008). *A Memoir of Jane Austen and Other Family Recollections*, ed. Sutherland, K. Oxford: Oxford University Press, p.141.

28. Letter 81. Jane Austen to Cassandra, Chawton, (9 February 1811) in Le Faye, D., (2011). *Jane Austen's Letters*. Fourth Edition. Oxford: Oxford University Press, p.215.

29. Austen, J., (c.1790–1793). *Catharine, or the Bower* in *Volume the Third*.

30. Letter 96. Jane Austen to Cassandra, Godmersham Park, (6–7 November 1813) in Le Faye, D., (2011). *Jane Austen's Letters*. Fourth Edition. Oxford: Oxford University Press, p.261.

31. Austen, J., (1816). *Emma*. Volume I, Chapter II.

32. Letter 41. Jane Austen to Francis Austen, Green Pk Buildings, Bath, (22 January 1805) in Le Faye, D., (2011). *Jane Austen's Letters*. Fourth Edition. Oxford: Oxford University Press, p.102.

33. Austen. J., (1813). *Pride and Prejudice*. Chapter XLII.

34. Austen, H., (1818). 'Biographical Notice Of The Author' in Austen-Leigh, J.E., (reissued 2008). *A Memoir of Jane Austen and Other Family Recollections*, ed. Sutherland, K. Oxford: Oxford University Press, pp.137 and 140.

35. Letter 60. Jane Austen to Cassandra, Castle Square, Southampton, (24–25 October 1808) in Le Faye, D., (2011). *Jane Austen's Letters*. Fourth Edition. Oxford: Oxford University Press, p.156–158.

Bibliography

Primary sources

Archdeaconry of Winchester, 'Induction Mandate: George Austen, BD, Deane', 1 April 1773, Hampshire Record Office, 35M48/6/796

Austen, Admiral F.W., Memoir. Unpublished. Sotheby's Sale, 11 July 1996. Lot 133 extract as described by them. Part of the Le Faye, Deirdre collection at Chawton House Library, Chawton.

Austen, G. Rev., 'letter to Thomas Cadell, from Steventon', 1 November 1797, St John's College, Oxford, MS 279/1

Austen, G., 'Memorandums for the use of MR F W Austen on his going to the East Indies Midshipman on board His Majesty's ship Perseverance. Cap: Smith Dec 1788', 1788, unpublished. Part of the Le Faye, Deirdre collection at Chawton House Library, Chawton.

Austen, G. and Wright, W., 'An answer to the objections made in convocation to the representation of the conduct of the proctors ... with respect to the two explanatory statutes proposed by the vice-chancellor', 1759, Wellcome Collection, ESTC T220246

Austen, J., *Volume the First* (c.1787–1793)

Austen, J., *Volume the Second* (c.1790–1793)

Austen, J., *Volume the Third* (c.1790–1793)

Austen, J., *The Watsons* (1803/4)

Austen, J., *Sense and Sensibility* (1811)

Austen, J., *Pride and Prejudice* (1813)

Austen, J., *Mansfield Park* (1814)

Austen, J., *Emma* (1816)

Austen, J., *Sanditon* (1817)

Austen, J., *Northanger Abbey* (1818)

Austen, J., *Persuasion* (1818)

Austen J., *The Prayers of Jane Austen* (Oregon: Harvest House Publishers, 2015)

Austen-Leigh family, letters to and concerning Sir Francis Austen, 1852–6, Hampshire Record Office, 23M93/63/1

Hellier family, 'Stevington Manor Court Baron document', Dec 1767, Hampshire Record Office, 18M61/Box/C/16

C. Hoare & Co Archive, customer ledgers: 86, folio 91; 23, folio 117; 98, folio 109; 61, folio 287; 47, folio 347; 74, folio 357; 81, folio 217; and 93, folio 99

Knight, T., 'Induction Mandate to the Rectory of Steventon', Nov 1761, Hampshire Record Office, 21M65/E2/844/1

Lathom, F., *The Midnight Bell* (1798)

Lefroy, A., 'Anna Lefroy's description of Steventon Rectory in the Rev. George Austen's time' in *Collected Reports of The Jane Austen Society 1966–1975* (Folkestone: Wm Dawson and Sons Ltd for The Jane Austen Society, repr. 1977), pp.245–248

Martin, Sir H., letter of recommendation, 18 December 1788, Portsmouth Dock Yard, inside 'Course of Mathematics at Naval Academy Portsmouth, 1786–1788, National Maritime Museum, Greenwich, AUS 14

Randalls, Edward, letter to Thomas Knight, Chawton, 26 Feb 1764, Hampshire Record Office, 18M61/Box/C/16

Ring, J., account books, 1785–1792, Hampshire Record Office, 8M62/14

Ring, J., account books, 1792–1800, Hampshire Record Office, 8M62/15

St John's College, Buttery Books, 1746–7 and 1747–8, St John's College, Oxford, ACC V.E.97 and ACC V.E.98

St John's College, Computus Annuus for 1757–8, St John's College, Oxford, ACC I.A.111

St John's College, Computus Annuus for 1759, St John's College, Oxford, ACC I.A.112

St John's College, Register, 1730–1794, St John's College, Oxford, ADM 1.A.7

St John's College, Oxford, 'testimonial for the post at Steventon', Hampshire Record Office, 21M65/E2/844/2

Skinners' Company, The (Worshipful Company of Skinners), court book no. 9, 1733–1749, Guildhall Library, London, CLC/L/SE/B/001/MS30708/009

Skinners' Company, The (Worshipful Company of Skinners), payments ledger, 1745–1787, Guildhall Library, London, CLC/L/SE/D/009/MS30729/003

Skinners' Company, The (Worshipful Company of Skinners), court book no. 11, 1752–1761, Guildhall Library, London, CLC/L/SE/B/001/MS30708/011

Steventon Parish Register, CMB 1737–1812, Hampshire Record Office, 71M82 PR2

Weller family correspondence, Kent Archives Office, Maidstone, U1000/18

Winchester Diocese, 'letters to Archbishop of Canterbury, Lord High Chancellor of England and Lord Bishop of Winchester from Revds. Stockwell, Goddard and Bradley, 1773'; 'testimonials about Revd G. Austen and confirmation of the valuation and legitimate geographical proximity of Deane and Steventon', Hampshire, Record Office, 21M65/E2/224/2, 3, 4 and 5

Winchester Diocese, 'Presentation deed, Deane rectory', March/April 1773, Hampshire Record Office, 21M65/E2/224

Winchester, Bishop of, to Archdeaconry of Winchester, Induction Mandate to the Rectory of Steventon, Nov 1761, 35M48/6/687, Hampshire Record Office

Secondary sources

Andrews, K., *Wanderers: A History Of Women Walking* (London: Reaktion Books, 2020)

Austen-Leigh, E., *Jane Austen and Steventon* (London: Spottiswoode, Ballantyne and Co. Ltd, 1937)

Austen-Leigh, J.E., *A Memoir of Jane Austen and Other Family Recollections*, ed. K. Sutherland (2nd edition, Oxford: Oxford University Press, 2008)

Austen Leigh, R.A., *Austen Papers 1704–1856* (London: privately published, 1942)

Austen-Leigh, W., and R.A., *Jane Austen, Her Life and Letters: A Family Record.* (London: Smith, Elder and Co, 1913)

Barchas, J., *Matters of Fact in Jane Austen: History, Location, and Celebrity* (Baltimore: The John Hopkins University Press, 2013)

Bolton, C., *A Winchester Bookshop and Bindery 1729–1994* (Winchester: P&G Wells, revised edition, 1994)

Brabourne, Lord E., *Letters of Jane Austen, edited with an Introduction and Critical Remarks by Edward Lord Brabourne*, Volume I (London: Richard Bentley & Son, 1884)

Campbell, J., *The Hero With A Thousand Faces* (3rd edition, Novato, California: New World Library, 2008)

Cawthorne, M.J., *James Cawthorn, George Austen and The Curious Case of the Schoolboy Who Was Killed* (Kibworth Beauchamp: Matador, 2017)

Clark, R., and Dutton, G., 'Farmer George, or Jane Austen and Sheep. An essay in Literary Biography', 2005, 75A18/C4, Hampshire Record Office

Costin, W.C., (1958). *The History of St John's College Oxford 1598–1860* (Oxford: Oxford University Press, 1958)

Doolittle, I.G., 'College Administration' in L.S. Sutherland, and L.G. Mitchell (eds.), *The History of the University of Oxford, Volume V: The Eighteenth Century* (1986), pp.227–68

Kenning, M. (Rev)., *Steventon: The Cradle of Jane Austen's Genius* (Steventon PCC, 2021)

Le Faye, D., 'Leonora Austen' in *The Jane Austen Society Report for 1998* (Winchester: Sarsen Press for The Jane Austen Society, 1998), pp.55–57

Le Faye, D., 'Another Book Owned By Mr Austen' in *The Jane Austen Society Report for 1999* (Winchester: Sarsen Press for The Jane Austen Society, 1999), pp.27–8

Le Faye, D., *Jane Austen: A Family Record* (2nd edition, Cambridge: Cambridge University Press, 2004)

Le Faye, D., *Jane Austen's Steventon* (Chawton: The Jane Austen Society, 2007)

Le Faye, D., *Jane Austen's Letters* (4th edition, Oxford: Oxford University Press, 2011)

Lefroy, A., *The Letters of Mrs Lefroy: Jane Austen's Beloved Friend*, ed. H. Lefroy and G. Turner (Winchester: Sarsen Press/the Jane Austen Society, 2007)

Looser, D., 'Breaking the Silence: The Austen Family's Complex Entanglements with Slavery,' *TLS*, 21 May 2021, pp. 2–3. https://www.the-tls.co.uk/articles/jane-austen-family-slavery-essay-devoney-looser/

Morrin, J., *The Victoria History of Hampshire: Steventon* (London: University of London and Victoria County History, 2016)

Oliver, Vere Langford, *The History of the Island of Antigua*, Volume II (London: Mitchell and Hughes (1896); repr. London: Forgotten Books, 2015)

Rivington, S., *The History of Tonbridge School from its Foundation in 1553 to The Present Day* (London, Oxford, and Cambridge: Rivingtons, 1869)

Selwyn, D., 'Some Sermons of Mr Austen' in *The Jane Austen Society Report for 2001* (2001), pp.35–36

Sillery, V., (ed.), *St John's College Biographical Register 1660–1775* (Oxford: privately printed, 1990)

Somervell, D.C., *A History of Tonbridge School* (London: Faber and Faber, 1947)

Southam, B.C., *Jane Austen's Literary Manuscripts* (Oxford: Oxford University Press, 1964), chapter 3

Southam, B.C., *Jane Austen's 'Sir Charles Grandison'* (Oxford: Oxford University Press, 1981)

Southam, B., 'George Austen: Pupil, Usher, and Proctor' in *The Jane Austen Society, Report for 2000* (Winchester: Sarsen Press for The Jane Austen Society, 2000) pp.6–11

Spence, J., *A Century of Wills from Jane Austen's Family 1705–1806* (2nd edition, Paddington, NSW Australia: JAS of Australia, 2001)

Sutherland, L.S., 'The Laudian Statutes in the Eighteenth Century' in L.S. Sutherland, and L.G. Mitchell (eds.), *The History of the University of Oxford, Volume V: The Eighteenth Century.* (Oxford: Oxford University Press, 1986), pp.191–204

Vick, R., 'The Sale at Steventon Parsonage' in *The Jane Austen Society Report for 1993* (Winchester: Sarsen Press for The Jane Austen Society, 1993), pp.13–16

Vick, R., 'Deane Parsonage' in *The Jane Austen Society Report for 1994* (Winchester: Sarsen Press for The Jane Austen Society, 1994), p.13

Vick, R., 'The Hancocks' in *The Jane Austen Society Report for 1999* (Winchester: Sarsen Press for The Jane Austen Society, 1999), pp.19–23

Vick, R., 'Mr Austen's Carriage' in *The Jane Austen Society Report for 1999* (Winchester: Sarsen Press for The Jane Austen Society, 1999), pp.23–6

Ward, W.R. (ed.), *Parson and Parish in Eighteenth Century Hampshire: Replies to Bishop's Visitations*, Hampshire Record Series XIII (Winchester: Hampshire County Council, 1995)

Willes, M., *In The Shadow Of St Paul's Cathedral* (New Haven and London: Yale University Press, 2022)

Worsley, L., *Jane Austen at Home: A Biography* (London: Hodder and Stoughton, 2017)

Other books read

Austen, *Pedigree of Austen of Horsmonden, Broadford, Grovehurst, Kippington, Capel Manor Etc.* (London: privately printed by Spottiswoode, Ballantyne and Co. Ltd, 1940)

Collins, I., *Jane Austen, The Parson's Daughter* (London: Bloomsbury Academic, repr. 2013)

Creigh Cass, J., 'In Defence of George Austen' in *Persuasions* (JASNA), 16(1994), 55–62

Felgate, M., and Applin, B., *Going Down Church Street to the Felgate Bookshop* (Basingstoke: Fisher Miller Publishing for the Basingstoke Archaeological & Historical Society, 1998)

Ford. B. (ed.), *The Cambridge Cultural History of Britain: Volume 5, Eighteenth-Century Britain* (Cambridge: Cambridge University Press, 1992)

Ford. B. (ed.), *The Cambridge Cultural History of Britain: Volume 6, The Romantic Age In Britain* (Cambridge: Cambridge University Press, 1992)

Hawkridge, A., *Hampshire Papers: Jane Austen and Hampshire* (Winchester: Hampshire County Council, 2001)

Hoare's Bank., 'South Sea Company Stock Certificate 1720' in *Through The Years, Tales from the Hoare's Bank Archive*, Volume 1 (London: C. Hoare and Co., 2012), p.9

Holbert Tucker, G., *A Goodly Heritage* (Manchester: Carcanet New Press, 1983)

Hoole, G.P., *A Tonbridge Miscellany*. (Canterbury: Fordwich Typesetting, and The Canterbury Printers Ltd., n.d.)

Hunter, P., 'Chapter 16: Jane Austen's Bank Account, 1816–7' in *Through The Years, Tales from the Hoare's Bank Archive. Volume II* (London: C. Hoare and Co., 2018), 38-9

Kenning, M., 'Jane Austen's Novels – Regulated And Checked By Religion?', unpublished lecture (2012)

Kenning, M., 'A clergyman is nothing – a present-day clergyman delivers a riposte to Mary Crawford', unpublished lecture given to the Jane Austen Society Conference at Creation House, Northamptonshire (2014)

Lane, M., *Jane Austen's Family Through Five Generations* (London: Robert Hale Ltd, 1992)

Lane, M., *Jane Austen and Lyme Regis* (Chawton: The Jane Austen Society, 2013)

Nicolson, N., *Godmersham Park, Kent – before, during, and since Jane Austen's day* (Chawton: The Jane Austen Society, repr. 2003)

Nixon, C.L., 'The Legal Guardian and Ward: Discovering the Orphan's "Best Interests" in *Mansfield Park* and Mrs Fitzherbert's Notorious Adoption Case' in D. Warren and L. Peters (ed.), *Rereading Orphanhood: Texts, Inheritance, Kin* (Edinburgh: Edinburgh University Press, 2020), pp.10–32.

Osborn, H., *Our Village Ancestors: A Genealogist's Guide to Understanding the English Rural Past* (Wiltshire: Robert Hale, 2021)

Perry, R., 'Austen and Empire: A Thinking Woman's Guide to British Imperialism', *Persuasions* (JASNA), 16(1994), pp.95–106

Ross. J., *Jane Austen And Her World* (London: National Portrait Gallery Publications, 2017)

Sutherland, E., 'Tithes and the Rural Clergyman in Jane Austen's England', *Persuasions* (JASNA), 16(1994), pp.48–54

Waldron Smithers, D., *Jane Austen in Kent* (Kent: Hurtwood Publications Ltd, 1981)

White, G.D.V., *Jane Austen in the Context of Abolition: A Fling at the Slave Trade* (Basingstoke: Palgrave Macmillan, 2006)

White, P., *Quarter Sessions Records in the Hampshire Record Office* (Winchester: Hampshire County Council, 1991)

Wilson, M., *Jane Austen's Family and Tonbridge* (Chawton: The Jane Austen Society, 2001)

Index